# " NORTHUMBERLAND "

## CAPACITIES OF INSULATED CARGO HOLDS.

| | Grain Cub Ft | Tons @40 Cf | Bale Cub F | Tons @40Cf |
|---|---|---|---|---|
| Nº 2 Tween Deck | 27270 | 682 | 25042 | 648 |
| Nº 3 Hold | 33970 | 849 | 71572 | 1789 |
| Nº 3 Tween Deck | 36860 | 921 | 35208 | 880 |
| Nº 3 Hold | 75430 | 1886 | 73000 | 1825 |
| Nº 4 Tween Deck | 21550 | 539 | 20447 | 511 |
| Nº 4 Hold | 43630 | 1091 | 42014 | 1060 |
| Nº 5 Tween Deck  Ford | 12280 | 301 | 11543 | 288 |
| Centre | 17450 | 436 | 16674 | 416 |
| Aft | 9150 | 229 | 8518 | 215 |
| Nº 5 Hold | 56350 | 1410 | 54284 | 1357 |
| Nº 6 Tween Deck | 29810 | 745 | 28338 | 708 |
| Shelter Tween Stern | 7330 | 183 | 6732 | 168 |
| | 411,480 | 10,287 | 394,282 | 9,855 |

## CAPACITIES OF UNINSULATED CARGO HOLDS.

| | Grain Cub Ft | Tons @40Cf | Bale Cub F | Tons @40Cf |
|---|---|---|---|---|
| Forecastle Tween Deck | 21657 | 541 | 20178 | 504 |
| Nº 1 Tween Deck | 27665 | 692 | 25738 | 643 |
| Lower | 14849 | 371 | 13528 | 338 |
| Nº 1 Hold | 20182 | 505 | 18845 | 471 |
| Nº 6 | 35885 | 897 | 33419 | 835 |
| Shelter Tween Ford | 88186 | 2205 | 81751 | 2044 |
| Aft | 59682 | 1492 | 56112 | 1403 |
| Bridge Tween Forward | 8188 | 205 | 7790 | 195 |
| Hatch Trunk Nº1 Shelter | 4509 | 112 | 4362 | 109 |
| Nº 3 | 5432 | 136 | 5349 | 134 |
| Nº 4 | 3296 | 82 | 3231 | 81 |
| Nº 5 | 5165 | 29 | 5080 | 127 |
| Nº 4 Bridge | 3895 | 97 | 3829 | 96 |
| Main Tween alongside Casings | 10944 | 274 | 9950 | 249 |
| Shelter | 27481 | 687 | 26598 | 665 |
| Bridge | 31380 | 786 | 29772 | 744 |
| Bridge Ford Trunk Hatch | 2195 | 65 | 2195 | 55 |
| Aft | 2195 | 55 | 2195 | 55 |
| Special lock up Aft including Trunk | 3646 | 91 | 3259 | 82 |
| | 376442 | 9411 | 353181 | 8830 |

## WATER BALLAST TANKS

| | Tons @ 35 Cf |
|---|---|
| Nº 1 D B Tank | 67 0 |
| 2 | 265 0 |
| 3 | 337 0 |
| 4 | 246 0 |
| 5 | 270 8 |
| Overflow | 49 2 |
| Nº 6 D B. | 199 0 |
| 7 | 197 0 |
| Total Double Btm | 1631 0 |
| Fore Peak | 104 0 |
| | 1735 0 |

## FRESH WATER TANKS

| | Tons @ 36 Cf |
|---|---|
| Nº 8 D B. Tank | 110 8 |
| Aft Peak | 108 7 |
| Main Tween Deck Tank Port | 258 2 |
| Stard | 258 2 |
| | 735 9 |

## INSULATED STORE ROOMS

| | Grain Cub Ft | Tons @40Cf | Bale Cub Ft | Tons @40Cf |
|---|---|---|---|---|
| Provision Chamber Aft Port | 2310 | 58 | 2131 | 53 |
| Stard | 1290 | 31 | 1171 | 29 |
| Centre | 810 | 19 | 767 | 19 |
| | 4410 | 110 | 4069 | 101 |

## UNINSULATED STORE ROOMS

| | Grain Cub Ft | Tons @40Cf | Bale Cub Ft | Tons @40Cf |
|---|---|---|---|---|
| Stewards Store Bridge Tween | 3395 | 85 | 3283 | 82 |
| Fore Peak  Upper | 650 | 16 | 520 | 13 |
| Shelter | 3121 | 78 | 2918 | 73 |
| Tween | 2611 | 65 | 2182 | 55 |
| Lower | 1929 | 48 | 1576 | 39 |
| Deck Store Main Mast | 666 | 17 | 601 | 15 |
| Paint Locker | 490 | 12 | 451 | 11 |
| Lamp Room | 400 | 10 | 382 | 10 |
| Engine Store Engine Room | 835 | 22 | 817 | 20 |
| Electric Store | 331 | 8 | 321 | 8 |
| Refrig | 904 | 23 | 844 | 21 |
| CO2 | 518 | 13 | 518 | 13 |
| | 124 | 6 | 224 | 6 |
| | 16134 | 402 | 14643 | 366 |

## OIL FUEL CAPACITIES

| | Tons @ 39.5 Cf |
|---|---|
| Nº 1 Tank Double Bottom | 61 5 |
| Nº 2 " " P & S | 244 0 |
| Nº 3 " " | 310 6 |
| Nº 4 " " | 227 0 |
| Nº 5 " " | 349 6 |
| Nº 6 " " | 182 6 |
| Nº 7 " " | 181 7 |
| Total Double Bottom | 1457 0 |
| Deep Tank Centre | 528 2 |
| Port Wing | 341 0 |
| Stard | 341 0 |
| Shelter Tween Deck Tank Centre | 79 4 |
| Port Wing | 112 5 |
| Stard | 112 5 |
| Total Oil Fuel | 2971 6 tons |
| D B. Overflow Tank | 45 3 tons |

98 % of Full Capacity

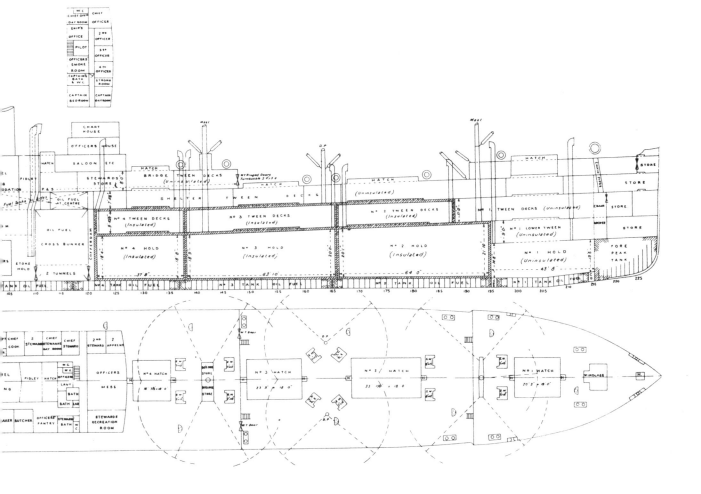

R.M.S. RANGITANE (71) (Captain A.W. McKellar) leaving Auckland, 1938  (From the painting by Captain R.E. Baker, courtesy of Mr. David McKellar of Auckland, son of the late Captain A.W. McKellar)

# CROSSED FLAGS

## THE HISTORIES OF THE NEW ZEALAND SHIPPING COMPANY LIMITED AND THE FEDERAL STEAM NAVIGATION COMPANY LIMITED AND THEIR SUBSIDIARIES

BY

## W. A. LAXON

with

## I. J. FARQUHAR and N. J. KIRBY

based on the draft by the late

## F. W. PERRY

World Ship Society
England

**Endpapers:** Front: Capacity plan of NORTHUMBERLAND, 1916 (F.21)
Back: Capacity plan of HINAKURA, 1949 (88)

Introductory page illustration: The Crossed Flags, Maritime Building, Napier

––––––––––––

Published by the World Ship Society, P.O. Box 706, Gravesend, DA12 5UB.

Printed by William Gibbons & Sons Ltd., Willenhall, West Midlands WV13 3XT

ISBN 0 905617 87 8

# CONTENTS

## DEDICATION

To the memory of all NZS Group staff, past and present, ashore and afloat, who made the Group what it was and its achievements possible.

# FOREWORD

This history is very much a team effort. The preliminary research and draft was done by the late Fred Perry. After Fred's untimely death in June 1993, the task was taken over by Bill Laxon in conjunction with Nigel Kirby, who had already been in preliminary touch with Fred, and Ian Farquhar. With this new triumvirate, the focus of the book shifted almost inevitably from England to New Zealand.

Not surprisingly, Fred's draft reflected very much the English sources that were readily available to him but had little of the flavour of the New Zealand origins and continued influence on the Company's development. In preliminary discussions with Michael Crowdy, Founder of the World Ship Society, and Barry Parsons of the New Zealand Shipping Company Association, it was agreed that the emphasis of the book should change, and the pattern was set at the first face to face meeting for the purpose between Nigel, Ian and Bill. Appropriately this was held in the Company's original home port of Lyttelton in November 1994.

Among a number of decisions made was that the book should be recast on the lines of the World Ship Society's highly successful P&O history of 1989, that is the ship histories should be broken into sections by a linking narrative. As this did not exist, Bill undertook the writing of the narrative and the re-writing and expansion of the material on the individual ships, but its collection and checking has been the work of all four. Of the other policy decisions taken, probably the most important was that the book should be confined to subsidiaries of NZS/Federal, thus eliminating what were essentially joint ventures like Australind, MANZ and Crusader where NZS/Federal had neither financial control nor ultimate command of policy. This freed space for expansion of coverage of Group companies and ships.

It was also decided that in contrast to previously published works on the Group, which tended to portray the ships in British waters, the illustrations emphasis here would be on views in New Zealand or Australia unless there was no alternative. Another decision was that because space limitations restricted the length of the narrative, it would concentrate on the companies, their crews and staff in their normal commercial activities. While service in time of war tends to make much more compelling reading, it was generally the antithesis of what the Group was established for and, in any event, has been dealt with in detail elsewhere. Those readers requiring wider coverage are referred to ''Merchant Adventurers'' for the First World War and ''Ordeal by Sea'' for the Second World War.

The lengthy research needed for a book of this kind has brought some material to light for the first time and has resulted in the exploding of some old myths such as the origins of the WAIMEA. Every care has been taken to eliminate error, and the untiring efforts of Nigel and Ian on this aspect cannot be too highly praised. With Fred no longer able to add his further contribution, the final decisions on conflicting information, inclusion or exclusion, and overall emphasis have had to be taken by Bill who accepts responsibility for such errors and omissions as (inevitably) remain.

In writing a history such as this, the contributions of many hands must be acknowledged. For the New Zealand trio, outstanding among them have been Stephen Rabson, the P&O Group Information Manager, Michael Crowdy, Barry Parsons and the members of the New Zealand Shipping Company Association, Warwick Dunsford and the members of the DURHAM Association, John Cotton of Plymouth who had been exchanging information with Nigel and Barry for some 10 years, Arnold Kludas of Hamburg, Bard Kolltveit of the Norsk Sjofartsmuseum, Oslo, the Bergens Sjofartsmuseum, Bergen, David Burrell of Cumnock, Rowan Hackman of Petersfield, Peter Newall of Blandford Forum, John Bartlett of London, Rodney Agutter of Coventry, Bill Schell of Holbrook, Ma., Frank Clapp of Victoria, B.C., Gareth Butler of Stockton, Tony Atkinson of Falmouth, Florent van Otterdijk of Antwerp, Ron Parsons of Adelaide, Tom Stevens of Melbourne, Warwick Foote and George Dickins of Brisbane, Mike Pryce of Wellington, Colin Amodeo of Christchurch, Graham Ferguson of Greymouth and Rob McKinney of Timaru. Those who are known to us to have assisted Fred at an earlier stage include Philip Salisbury, Alan Tennent and Kerry Hodges and the staff of the institutions listed in the Bibliography. To these must be added the staffs of the Auckland Institute & Museum, the Auckland Public Library, the Hocken Library, Dunedin, the New Zealand National Maritime Museum, Auckland, and the Wellington Maritime Museum. Those who have supplied photographs are acknowledged beneath the relevant illustration. The basic foundation for the book however has been and remains the NZS Group's own records in the National Maritime Museum, housed at Woolwich, and in New Zealand.

There have been a number of books written about the NZS Group and its ships over the years, the most important of which are included in the Bibliography. We would like to pay particular tribute though, in respect of the sailing ships, to Henry Brett's ''White Wings'' and Alan Bott's ''The Sailing Ships of the New Zealand Shipping Company'', and, for general company developments, to Sydney Waters' ''Clipper Ship to Motor Liner'' and ''Ordeal by Sea''. Without their efforts, much valuable material would have been lost. We hope that with the benefit of a slightly greater distance in time from the events recorded, this book can take its place alongside them as a fitting tribute to the achievements of a Group which played such a pivotal part in the development of New Zealand and Australia for nearly 100 years.

# FLEET LIST NOTES

1. The official number is that allocated to a ship on first registry. For the ships dealt with in this book, a common numbering system applied throughout the British Empire and Commonwealth and pertained to the ship throughout its life under the British flag notwithstanding intervening periods under other registries.

2. Tonnages given are those on first acquisition by a Group company. There were frequent minor changes during service, but only those reflecting a major alteration are recorded. Some later ships had a dual tonnage, depending on the draft to which the ship was loaded, and whether the shelter deck was open or closed.

3. Dimensions are the registered figures given in feet and tenths of a foot, and in the order of length, beam and depth. Overall length and draft are also given where available.

4. For steam reciprocating engines, the abbreviations ''C'', ''T'' and ''Q'' indicate compound, triple and quadruple expansion machinery, the figure following giving the number of cylinders. For steam turbine engines, the number of expansions of the steam is given and the method of gearing to the shaft(s). For diesel engines, 2 S.C. indicates a 2 stroke cycle engine and S.A. or D.A. indicates single acting or double acting. Horsepower is shown as ihp for reciprocating engines, shp for turbines and bhp for diesels where available in preference to nhp which is a theoretical figure related to engine dimensions. The speed is service speed unless otherwise shown.

5. Unless shown as ''iron'' or ''wood'', all ships were built of steel.

6. Passenger numbers are generally as at completion. These varied enormously during a ship's life and only major later changes are recorded.

7. Unless otherwise noted all Federal and Avenue ships were registered at London, as were NZS ships from 1946 onwards. From 1890 to 1945 NZS ships were registered at Plymouth unless otherwise shown.

8. Place name spellings are given as at the time of the incident recorded.

9. Refrigerated space: Where a number of carcasses is referred to, it is based on the approximate mix of mutton and lamb at the time. The earlier vessels carried a high proportion of mutton (which occupied a greater space), the later vessels a mixture of mutton and lamb, and after World War II there was a much higher percentage of lamb (which occupied a lesser space).

10. ''End of service'' dates quoted are generally dates of sale. These can be quite different from dates of delivery.

The Fleet List data has been corrected to July 1997.

# PICTURE SOURCE ACKNOWLEDGEMENTS:

| | |
|---|---|
| ATL | Alexander Turnbull Library, Wellington |
| DNB | D.N. Brigham Collection, Auckland |
| IJF | I.J. Farquhar Collection, Dunedin |
| JYF | J.Y. Freeman, Sydney |
| NJK | N.J. Kirby Collection, Lyttelton |
| WAL | W. A. Laxon Collection, Auckland |
| NMM | National Maritime Museum, Greenwich, London |
| MP | Marine Photos, Auckland |
| NZA | The New Zealand Shipping Company Association, Auckland |
| P&O | P&O S.N. Co., London |
| RCP | R.C. Pulley (Auckland Maritime Society) |
| VHY | V.H. Young/L. A. Sawyer Collection |

# THE NEW ZEALAND SHIPPING COMPANY LTD

## Chapter 1: The Company Ethos

The New Zealand Shipping Company remains unique in being the only deep sea liner operation founded in the heyday of Britain's 19th century imperial expansion in one of the then colonies rather than in the mother country. Throughout its career it was an entity established under New Zealand law with its registered office in Christchurch, even though its financial and operational control had moved to London after its first 15 years.

For this reason, although in Britain it remained, albeit highly respected, but one of the many second rank liner companies, in New Zealand it wove itself into the national life in a manner difficult to understand from the other side of the world. In part this was due to local pride that its founders had been from amongst their own, and people identified with it as a local company despite that having long since ceased to be the reality. But it went much deeper than that. Until the advent of efficient long distance aircraft in the 1960's, travel by sea was the only means of communication. For a nation like New Zealand, isolated by 1,200 miles from its nearest neighbour, and on the other side of the world from Europe, the means of bridging those gaps assumed far greater importance than in many other countries. The coming and going of liners with the delivery of mails and goods were matters of daily general concern, and few people did not have contact in some way or another with passengers who had recently completed such a journey. The presence of a substantial office building and wool store in all major towns, with the local manager one of the community leaders, emphasised the place of the Company in the general scheme of things.

The founders of the New Zealand Shipping Company were very conscious of this dependence on the sea for transport and trade and were determined that their new fleet should meet public expectations. The highest standards were laid down for the accommodation of emigrants on the outward voyage, not only in dietary scale as best the limitations of a 3 to 4 month voyage would allow, but also by the provision of a doctor and for the training of apprentices under supervision. The bestowal of the description "clipper" on the Company's early sailing ships was an acknowledgement both of their generally good passage times and of the meticulous standards to which they were run.

The crew assembled on the stemhead of the WAIPA (12) at Port Chalmers showing the Company badge and motto                                                                 (ATL/NZA)

In the Company's early years the passenger trade was dominated by the outward voyage with relatively few passengers carried on the return journey. After steam took over and New Zealand returned to more prosperous conditions on the back of the burgeoning frozen meat industry in the mid-1890's, the northbound trade assumed increasing importance as established settlers began to make voyages to the countries where they or their parents had been born. The attractions of a world encircling voyage with calls at east coast South American ports in one direction and the Atlantic Isles and Cape Town in the other, began to feature in Company promotions both in New Zealand and on United Kingdom railway stations. There was considerable pride in the ever increasing size and improved accommodation of the Company's ships, and there were few times in any of the major New Zealand ports when there was not at least one yellow funnel visible at the wharves.

It is perhaps the years from the 1920's to the 1960's which are best remembered as the heyday of the Company's operations. Sailing day of one of the passenger ships from Auckland or Wellington was a major event not only for those travelling, but for the friends and relations. With few exceptions, promptly on the stroke of midday the ship with a sea of paper streamers linking those on board with those on shore would start moving away from the wharf. The musical sequence over the ship's public address system never varied. It began with ''Anchors Aweigh'', followed by ''A Life on the Ocean Wave'' and then as the vessel turned to head for the open sea ''Now is the Hour''. No one could be left in any doubt that sailing day was an OCCASION.

RUAHINE (91) — sailing day 1953                     (VHY/NZA)

It was some of the little details that singled out the New Zealand Shipping Company as a concern with a character of its own. The passenger ships, notably the 1929 RANGIs, carried their names in big brass letters at bow and stern, and at the latter was the distinguishing port of Plymouth—carried by no other ships in the Australasian trades. Long after other lines abandoned it, the New Zealand Shipping Company retained a mainmast in its fleet with a signal gaff from which the ensign flew on departure. The ''steam cornet'', flown above the houseflag because the funnel of the early steamers was often obscured by the sails, was a unique feature retained long after the need to distinguish the steam fleet from the sailing ships had gone, until regrettably dropped in the 1960's. Another New Zealand Shipping feature was the large square box painted at the waterline amidships containing the Plimsoll mark which broke the white riband separating the black hull from the red boot-topping. An attractive light green colour to the underside of the deck heads in the outside passenger decks was a restful feature against the glare during the passage through the tropics.

RANGITIKI (69) floodlit at Wellington

*(WAL)*

Because the first wireless installations were provided to existing ships after they were built, New Zealand Shipping installed the radio room at the after end of the boat deck. Unlike other companies which soon placed the radio equipment adjacent to the bridge, New Zealand Shipping retained the radio quarters in the same position through to the 1960's. One could never mistake being in the officers' accommodation in post-war years where cretonne covers were a standard feature of all easy chairs.

As one of the two major passenger carriers in the New Zealand service, NZS attracted more than its fair share of notable passengers. One of the earliest occasions was the RUAHINE taking the Premier, Richard Seddon, and the New Zealand contingent to Queen Victoria's Diamond Jubilee celebrations in London in 1897. NZS was also chosen when the first All Black rugby team to tour Britain sailed in the second RIMUTAKA in 1905. Another occasion, though somewhat shrouded in wartime secrecy, was when the third RIMUTAKA took the Duke of Gloucester and his family to Australia in 1944 on his taking up the post of Governor General of that country. This royal connection was repeated when the Duchess launched the RANGITANE in 1949. Before the coming of air transport, most Governors General of New Zealand arrived and sailed in NZS vessels, the last arrivals being Lord Cobham in the RANGITIKI in 1957 and Sir Bernard Fergusson in the RANGITANE in 1962, both with their respective families. One such occasion even provoked a newspaper cartoon when Lord Freyberg, generally known as "Tiny", who had already made a coastal journey in the RANGITOTO on her maiden voyage, sailed in the RANGITANE at the conclusion of his term, and the ship was depicted pulling away from the wharf with the name on the bows relettered as RANGITINY.

"RANGITINY" The Minhinnick cartoon on Lord Freyberg's departure *(WAL)*

11

Maritime Building, Wellington, floodlit for the coronation of King George VI    *(Wellington Maritime Museum)*

The Company was woven into the life of New Zealand in so many ways that now tend to be forgotten. After its own offices were re-established, a "Maritime Building" as they were invariably known, became a major landmark in each port. Company ships played a leading part in local events such as acting as flagship at the annual Auckland Anniversary regattas on a number of occasions. As "overseas experience" became more and more popular with

WAIMATE (31) as regatta flagship at Auckland, 1908
*(WAL)*

young New Zealanders, the passenger ships served as an introduction to the wider world for many, an experience that lingered long in memory. In the days when ships tended to be on the New Zealand coast for anything between a month and 6 weeks each voyage, strong links developed between crews and those ashore, sometimes based on voyages as passengers but often through the local Seafarers' clubs and sporting events between ship's and local teams. The large number of marriages of officers and crew who met their future wives either on the passenger ships or at shore social functions did much to further cement the bonds.

Nor were these social occasions confined to the New Zealand end. In London shortly after the First World War the Company was among the first to acquire a sporting ground for the use of its staff under the aegis of the "Maori Club". At first this was briefly at East Finchley in association with the Atlantic Transport Line, but in 1923 it moved to its own property at Worcester Park where the Maori Club grounds remain to this day the principal sports ground for the P&O Group as a whole. For many years it was here that New Zealand cricket teams on a U.K. tour had their warm up practices and first unofficial matches following a voyage in an NZS ship.

Above all, NZS was looked on with affection—apart from those involved in the annual freight rate negotiations, who tended to have a rather different view of all shipping companies. Its place in the scheme of things can best be summed up in the fact that in New Zealand it was known simply as "The Shipping Company". There was no need to ask for any more specific description.

PIAKO (15) under full sail.

*From the painting by Jack Spurling*

TONGARIRO (42) sailing from Cape Town outward bound for New Zealand.
*From the painting by Charles Dixon*

DURHAM (F.41) off Oriental Bay, Wellington, 1950

*From the gouache by Captain R. E. Baker*

PAPAROA (83) at Wellington

*Cliff Parsons Collection*

HAURAKI (93) at Auckland dressed overall for Anniversary Day

*WAL*

RUAHINE sailing from Auckland

*WAL*

MATAURA (104) entering Otago heads

*IJF*

WILD CURLEW (F.92) at Lyttelton

*NJK*

# THE NEW ZEALAND SHIPPING COMPANY LTD
## Chronology

*1 July 1872*   The New Zealand Freight Company Ltd was registered in Auckland, the first meeting having been held on 3 May. Dr J. Logan Campbell was elected Chairman, finance being provided by the Bank of New Zealand. Similar freight associations were formed in other provinces.

*20 November 1872*   A meeting in Christchurch resolved to form ''a colonial shipping company'' to carry emigrants and cargo between London and New Zealand. The authorised capital was £100,000 in £10 shares of which 3,300 were taken up paid to 10/- per share. 1,000 shares were taken by the New Zealand Loan & Mercantile Agency Company Ltd, an associate of the Bank of New Zealand.

*24 December 1872*   First meeting of the provisional directors at Christchurch.

*6 January 1873*   The New Zealand Shipping Company Ltd was registered in Christchurch. C.W. Turner was sent to England on 23 January 1873 to make arrangements there and to tender for an emigrant contract.

*24 January 1873*   First general meeting of NZS and election of directors. J.L. Coster of the Bank of New Zealand was elected Chairman.

*3 March 1873*   First New Zealand Freight Company sailing from London by the HYLTON CASTLE (562g, 1865) which arrived at Auckland on 25 June 1873.

*June 1873*   Otago Freight Association of Dunedin absorbed into NZS.

*2 June 1873*   The PUNJAUB (883g, 1862) sailed from London on the first charter sailing for NZS, arriving at Lyttelton on 20 September 1873.

*20 June 1873*   A shareholders meeting authorised the formation of a Board of Advice in London and local boards in major New Zealand ports. The paid up capital was increased by a further £2 per share being called up.

*21 July 1873*   The authorised capital was increased to £250,000. The New Zealand Freight Company Ltd was absorbed. The first contract to carry emigrants to New Zealand was announced.

*12 September 1873*   The HINDOSTAN, the first ship owned by NZS, left London and arrived at Auckland on 28 December 1873.

*1 November 1873*   The first shipbuilding orders for two ships from J. Blumer & Company were announced.

*24 January 1874*   At the first AGM of NZS it was reported that 37 ships had been despatched from London and 6 from New Zealand with 6 more loading. The paid up capital was increased to £5 per share.

*19 May 1874*   First meeting of the London Board of Advice. The Chair changed from meeting to meeting but was usually taken by Falconer Larkworthy, London manager of the Bank of New Zealand until he resigned from the board in August 1884. O.R. Strickland was appointed London manager in October 1874.

*January 1875*   At the second AGM in Christchurch it was announced that the company had lost £14,360 since its formation, but that agreements had been reached with Shaw Savill & Company and with the Albion Line for ''uniform scales of freightage''.

*26 January 1875*   The London board authorised the issue of badges of rank to officers.

*10 August 1875*   The London board recommended a fleet colour scheme—black hulls with white painted ports, white masts, yards and boats - which was duly implemented.

*1876*   The directors decided to take 3 to 5 apprentices on each ship.

*1877*   A 5 year contract for the carriage of immigrants was made with the New Zealand Government. The average cabin fare from England to New Zealand was £52-10-0 and the immigrant fare £15.

*5 February 1879*   The steamer STAD HAARLEM (2,729g, 1875) left London for Port Chalmers, Lyttelton and Wellington under joint charter to NZS and Shaw Savill as a result of New Zealand Government pressure for a steam link with Britain. The result was a loss but there were two further similar charters in 1880.

*12 July 1881*   The London board received estimates for fitting dry air refrigerating machinery in a vessel and in September a set was ordered for the MATAURA. Four of the sailing ships were so equipped. These early machines were made by the Haslam Foundry & Engineering Company Ltd and cargoes were carried, in part, on a royalty basis.

*December 1881*   An office was opened in Liverpool.

*1882*   The New Zealand Government offered subsidies totalling £30,000 per year to NZS and Shaw Savill for a steam service to Britain. On 13 June 1882 NZS agreed to negotiate, and opened its service in January 1883 with chartered vessels. The first sailing for NZS was made by the BRITISH KING (3,559g, 1881) which embarked passengers at Plymouth and sailed on 29 January 1883, arriving at Wellington on 19 March 1883. Each of the companies was required to provide a monthly sailing from Britain, 45 days out via the Cape of Good Hope and 42 days back via Cape Horn.

*23 May 1882*   A meeting at Christchurch increased the authorised capital to £1,000,000 to meet the cost of the new steam fleet. Less than 60,000 shares were actually issued.

*November 1882*   The first 3 steamers were ordered from John Elder & Company of Govan. Sir William Pearce, the senior partner of the builders, joined the London board from 11 December 1883.

*December 1884*   After publication of the annual report, an anonymous broadsheet entitled ''Other People's Money'' criticised NZS's financial management claiming that provision for depreciation was inadequate while large amounts were outstanding on loans. The major crisis for the company was however delayed for 18 months.

*11 February 1886*   J.L. Coster addressed the London board to emphasise that it was to function solely as a board of advice.

*31 May 1886*   A letter addressed to the London board from a London shareholder, J. Halls, was reprinted in the influential British shipping journal ''Fairplay'' and received great publicity. It pointed out that, although dividends were good, there was little provision for depreciation and that the Company's debts totalled £677,000. The £10 shares, which had been paid to £7 from June, were quoted on the Stock Exchange at only 10/-. It subsequently emerged that the sailing vessels were mortgaged to the New Zealand Loan & Mercantile Agency Company to secure £300,000, the TONGARIRO was pledged to the Bank of New Zealand for £67,500 and the AORANGI, RUAPEHU and RIMUTAKA to Sir William Pearce against a debt of £260,000. In the case of liquidation a further £2 a share would need to be called up to clear outstanding debts.

*21 July 1886* A London shareholders meeting resolved that the control of the Company should be transferred to London and appointed a committee including Sir William Pearce, Sir John Gorst and J.B. Westray with T. Johnson in the chair. The board in New Zealand was slow to respond, but sent its solicitor, Leonard Harper, to London to negotiate.

*1886* G.D. Tyser & Company were appointed the Company's London freight brokers.

*29 June 1887* Using his delegated powers, Leonard Harper provisionally handed over control to the London board before sailing for New Zealand in July to arrange the necessary changes in the Articles of Association. By this time the quoted price of NZS shares had fallen to 5/-.

*November 1887* The Bank of New Zealand, a major creditor, was severely criticised for promoting the sale of NZS shares from August 1883.

*28 December 1887* and *19 January 1888* Meetings at Christchurch confirmed that the London board would become the controlling board with effect from 13 February 1888. The registry of the ships was changed from Lyttelton to London in consequence.

*25 January 1888* The London board made a further call of £1 per share with the option to pay a further £2 to make the shares fully paid.

*18 December 1888* The first annual report of the London board recommended that no dividend be paid. Sir William Pearce, the Company's largest creditor, died. E.S. Dawes eventually purchased the Pearce interests in the Company from the executor, Richard Barnwell, and also acquired the debt owing to the Bank of New Zealand.

*7 December 1889* First NZS North American sailing when the chartered barque LURLINE (801g, 1877) sailed from Auckland for New York. There had been occasional southbound sailings, commencing with the chartered A. T. STALLKNECHT (540n, 1875) from New York on 15 December 1881.

*December 1889* The mail contract expired and was not renewed on a permanent basis.

*1890* The OTARAMA was purchased as the Company's first cargo steamer and, as with all the ships acquired over the next few years, the initial ownership of the vessel was held in trust until the full purchase price was paid. Many of the ships were heavily mortgaged until after the First World War.

*25 June* and *16 July 1890* Extraordinary general meetings recommended reducing the paid up value of each share from £10 to £8 and the New Zealand board agreed on 16 September. A meeting of the London board on 15 October approved the resumption of dividend payments.

*15 October 1890* G.D. Tyser & Company were replaced as NZS freight, passenger and insurance brokers by J.B. Westray & Company.

*12 December 1891* The RUAHINE was delivered as the first of a new generation of economically powered passenger ships.

*18 November 1892* "Fairplay" reported: "The New Zealand Shipping Company has adopted the form of accounts in vogue with the famous British India Line; a form which, while it assuredly neither states or implies anything that is untrue, most certainly does not state many things which less conscientious concerns think necessary to reveal. But there is a difference. The mystery of the British India accounts is tempered to the fortunate shareholders by the excellence and symmetry of the dividends." (It should be remembered that E.S. Dawes was a close associate of British India's Sir William Mackinnon.)

*1896* NZS gave partial backing to the reconstruction of the Canadian Australian Royal Mail Steamship Company Ltd (C A) under the management of James Huddart. The line had provided a service from Sydney to Brisbane, Honolulu and Victoria, B.C. under contract to the New South Wales and Canadian Governments from 1893, receiving £25,000 p.a. from the former and £10,000 p.a. from the latter. In 1896 the New Zealand Government added £20,000 p.a. for Wellington to be substituted for Brisbane and an extra call at Suva.

*December 1897* NZS, as chief creditor, applied for the winding up of the C A.

*24 January 1898* The C A was placed in the hands of receivers by court order and in February NZS was appointed managers of the line by the receivers.

*December 1898* The first New Zealand Marine Superintendent, Captain John Bone, then commodore and master of the RUAHINE, was appointed. He was based in Christchurch until 1919, and in Wellington until his retirement in 1924.

*April 1899* The C A's New Zealand contract expired and was replaced by one with the Queensland Government at £7,500 p.a. and the call at Brisbane was reinstated.

*16 August 1899* The assets of C A were purchased by NZS for £142,200.

*22 September 1899* It was reported that the Company's last 4 sailing ships had been sold.

*December 1900* The New Zealand Government invited tenders for a 6-weekly service to South Africa for 6 years. NZS, Shaw Savill & Albion Company, Turnbull Martin & Company and G.D. Tyser & Company offered a service of 5 ships each from the first two companies and 3 ships each from the last two. In February 1901 NZS, Shaw Savill and Tyser suggested an experimental service without subsidy with the New Zealand-South Africa leg running on to London. They began a joint service but profitability was poor and after 6 sailings, the 7th was cancelled. In February 1902 the New Zealand Government made a second call for tenders and NZS, Union Steam Ship Company of New Zealand and Shaw Savill offered a joint 3 ship service for £27,000 p.a. The contract was awarded to the Australian shipowner, H.C. Sleigh, but never got under way. (For the third tender, see Federal chronology)

*1 February 1901* Union Steam Ship Company of New Zealand Ltd bought the WARRIMOO and half the NZS interest in the C A Line for £60,000. The Union Company became managers of C A and purchased the remaining NZS interest piecemeal through to 1910.

*21 May 1910* The RAKAIA sailed from Montreal to open a new joint monthly service with Shaw Savill under contract to the Canadian Government from east coast Canadian ports to Australia and New Zealand.

*24 April 1911* The Board agreed that wireless telegraphy should be fitted in the REMUERA, ROTORUA, RUAHINE, TURAKINA and RUAPEHU.

*24 December 1911* The Company purchased the EVERTON GRANGE (7,144g, 1903) from Houlder Bros & Company Ltd with an understanding for the purchase of the Houlder Australasian business. That deal was concluded on 25 April 1912 for £300,000 including a further 3 ships. The service continued as the Federal-Shire Line.

*30 December 1911* NZS purchased a majority of the shares in the Federal Steam Navigation Company Ltd through the allotment of 27,818 unissued shares valued at £20 each for 43,116 of the £10 Federal shares. The first approaches had been made in January 1911 and the deal was approved in principle by the NZS board on 5 May. The announcement to shareholders was made on 3 January 1912.

*July 1912* The four ex-Houlder ships were sold to the Union Steam Ship Company together with the rights in the Federal-Shire Line. For financial reasons, the legal transfer of the 3 surviving ships was not effected until 1915.

PAPAROA (37) in the Thames with extra deck while on B.I. charter c.1912

*(Michael Jones)*

*2 October 1913* It was announced that the nominal value of NZS ordinary shares would be increased from £8 to £10 fully paid plus a bonus issue of one £10 preference share for every 4 ordinary shares.

*1914-1918* The First World War. 5 NZS ships were lost out of 21 owned in 1914.

*April 1915* All insulated space in ships in the Australian and New Zealand trades was requisitioned by the War Office.

*30 May 1916* The OTAKI was the first NZS ship to transit the Panama Canal, bound Wellington to London.

*29 June 1916* The NZS board agreed on the sale of the Company to The Peninsular and Oriental Steam Navigation Company through the exchange of each £10 ordinary share for £10 of P&O deferred stock. NZS shares were valued at £21 and P&O stock at £32. At that time NZS issued capital stood at £906,720. The formal agreement was concluded on 7 September, but the actual purchaser of the shares was the British India Steam Navigation Company Ltd which paid P&O for the issue of its deferred stock.

*July 1916* The Panama route was adopted as the main one in both directions, the first passenger transit being by REMUERA, bound Wellington to London, on 15 July 1916.

*1919* The principal office of the Company in New Zealand was transferred from Christchurch to Wellington and all offices were combined with those of the Union Steam Ship Company of New Zealand Ltd.

*January 1920* Southampton became the main NZS passenger port in England until replaced by London in November 1932. The move had been projected in 1914, but was delayed by the First World War.

*August 1924* Curacao was adopted as the Company bunkering port for oil burners.

*1925* Large new passenger liners were projected, but orders for RANGITIKI, RANGITATA and RANGITANE were not placed with John Brown & Company Ltd at Clydebank until 16 August 1927, the first ship being delivered in January 1929.

*1928* A service recommenced between east coast North American ports and Australia and New Zealand but NZS withdrew after 3 months of intense competition, particularly from Canadian National Steamships.

TEKOA (65) arriving at Lyttelton in 1935 with a snow covered Mt Herbert in the background *(NJK)*

RANGITANE (71) in the Panama Canal *(James L. Shaw)*

138 Leadenhall Street, London, in the 1950's *(D.F. Raines/NZA)*

*29 May 1933* P&O transferred to NZS 127,000 £1 shares in the Aberdeen & Commonwealth Line Ltd which had been formed by P&O, Orient, Shaw Savill and Furness Withy to acquire the Aberdeen and Commonwealth operation from the Royal Mail Steam Packet liquidators. NZS interest was passive with Shaw Savill managing the company. The NZS/P&O/Orient holding was sold to Shaw Savill for £3-10-0 per share on 21 December 1953.

*6 August 1936* Montreal, Australia and New Zealand Line Ltd (MANZ) was formed jointly by NZS, Ellerman & Bucknall and Port Line to trade between the places named in the title. The proposal was first reported to the NZS board on 5 May 1936 and it took up 160 £1 shares. MANZ was essentially an operating company and the ships contributed by NZS were managed by Trinder Anderson & Co. until NZS withdrew from MANZ in February 1966. MANZ itself was wound up on 26 April 1971.

*1939-1945* The Second World War. 8 NZS ships out of the 33 in the combined fleet were lost.

*5 August 1949* The first postwar passenger ship, RANGITOTO, was delivered. Typical fares were £94 in a 2 berth cabin and £64 in a 6 berth cabin.

*29 August 1954* The subsidiary company Avenue Shipping Company Ltd was formed to provide supplementary services with Trinder Anderson & Company as its managers. It was absorbed by the P&O Group in 1972.

*22 November 1957* Crusader Shipping Company Ltd was formed jointly with Shaw Savill, Port Line and Blue Star to provide services from New Zealand to Japan and later to the west coast of North America, the north Pacific coast of South America and the Caribbean. NZS took up 5,000 £1 shares and the company was managed by Shaw Savill. In 1972 the services were split between three of the four companies, Port Line withdrawing.

*December 1962* The NZS head office at 138 Leadenhall Street, London was sold to P&O for demolition to enable construction of the new P&O Building.

*2 September 1965* P&O announced that in conjunction with Blue Funnel, Furness Withy and British & Commonwealth, Overseas Containers Ltd would be formed to introduce container operations in the four groups' existing liner trades.

*1 January 1966* All NZS ships except HORORATA adopted the Federal funnel colours. This was done progressively with some ships actually changing before this date.

*1966* A joint committee of NZS, Shaw Savill, Port and Blue Star was set up to investigate the future of the New Zealand trade. The resulting Molyneux Report was in favour of containerisation and, after discussion with the New Zealand producer boards responsible for the export of meat, dairy produce and fruit, it was announced in December 1969 that four large container ships would be ordered, 2 each by Overseas Containers Ltd (NZS/Shaw Savill) and by Associated Container Transportation Ltd (Port/Blue Star).

*28 December 1966* All NZS owned and operated ships except the TAUPO and TEKOA were transferred into nominal Federal ownership, with those two and the TONGARIRO following in June 1969.

*December 1967* The closing of the passenger service was announced and the last sailing was by the RANGITOTO from Auckland on 14 June 1969. The fares were £388 for a single cabin and £238 in a 6 berth cabin.

*May 1971* The projected New Zealand container project was cancelled due to escalating costs. Construction was well advanced on only one of the four ships ordered which emerged in 1973 as the REMUERA, later REMUERA BAY.

*1 August 1971* The Bay of Islands tourist launch operator, A.E. Fuller & Sons Ltd, was purchased. The company was sold to its management in December 1985.

*1 October 1971* Management of the remaining ships, owned by Federal but until now managed by NZS, passed to the P&O General Cargo Division. The New Zealand Shipping Company Ltd was renamed P&O (NZ) Ltd. The brackets were removed and New Zealand spelt in full in December 1989. The shareholding had been transferred to P&O Australia Ltd in January 1987.

# CHAIRMEN OF THE BOARDS OF THE NEW ZEALAND SHIPPING COMPANY LTD

J.L. Coster                    (WAL)

W. Reeves        (Canterbury Museum; Ref: 15298)

| In New Zealand: | | In England: | |
|---|---|---|---|
| 1872 | J.L. Coster | 1888 | Sir John Gorst |
| 1874 | W. Reeves | 1894 | Sir Edwyn S. Dawes |
| 1875 | J.L. Coster | 1904 | W.C. Dawes |
| 1886 | H.P. Murray-Aynsley | 1919 | A. Hughes |
| 12.1887 | The chair rotated among the directors | 1928 | C.J. Cowan |
| | | 1944 | T.F. Tallents |
| 1889 | L. Harper (resigned 1893 when he became bankrupt) | 1947 | H.W.S. Whitehouse |
| | | 1952 | Sir Frederic Harmer |
| 1893 | H.P. Murray-Aynsley | 1966 | C.A.W. Dawes |
| 1917 | A.E.G. Rhodes | 1970 | H.T. Beazley |
| 1922 | J. Anderson | | |
| 1923 | G. Gould | | |
| 1941 | Sir Robert A. Anderson | | |
| 1942 | C.M. Turrell | | |
| 1944 | J. Deans | | |
| 1963 | D.W.J. Gould | | |

H.P. Murray-Aynsley
(Canterbury Museum; Ref: 1667)

Sir John Gorst                    (P&O)

Sir Edwyn Dawes                    (P&O)

W.C. Dawes                         (P&O)

A. Hughes                          (P&O)

C. J. Cowan                        (P&O)

T. F. Tallents                     (P&O)

H.W.S. Whitehouse                  (P&O)

Sir Frederic Harmer                (P&O)

C.A.W. Dawes                       (P&O)

H. T. Beazley                      (P&O)

# Chapter 2: From Colonial Clipper to the Advent of Steam

From the beginning of official European settlement in New Zealand following the signing of the Treaty of Waitangi in 1840, shipping services between Britain and New Zealand tended to be on a single ship/voyage basis with emigrants and their needs carried on the outward voyage. The vessels then left in ballast to load elsewhere in the absence of any volume of return cargo. Willis Gann & Co. of London had specialised as brokers for the New Zealand trade, but the first fully organised service did not begin until 1856 when P. Henderson & Co. sent their first ship to Otago, following earlier spasmodic charters, a service which subsequently adopted the trade name of Albion Line until it was incorporated as such in 1864. Another major enterprise was founded in 1858 when two employees of Willis Gann set up in business as Shaw Savill & Co. and soon came to dominate the trade to ports of the country north of Otago.

The next major impetus in the New Zealand trade came as the country settled down at the end of the Land Wars in 1869 and embarked on a major expansion programme of public works, emigration, transport and supporting infrastructure under the premiership of Julius Vogel in 1870. The pressures brought about by this upsurge of activity focused attention on the existing shipping services from Britain. Although Shaw Savill and the Albion Line were theoretically in competition for the trade, the reality was rather different. The former's sailings were from London with the majority of destinations in the North Island and the north of the South Island whereas the latter's were from Glasgow to Otago and southern South Island ports. It was a mutually satisfactory arrangement for the two lines with little to encourage them to more active competition.

In the sturdily robust atmosphere of the early 1870's, as the first settlers became established and sought to flex their muscles to secure their own destiny, the attitude of the two existing companies was unacceptable, and efforts to launch a locally controlled service "broke out" during 1872 independently in each of the main cities. First off the ground was Auckland with the convening of a meeting on May 3rd. There was standing room only at the Chamber of Commerce, and most of the leading members of the Auckland business community were present. A resolution was carried unanimously that "the Auckland Freight Company" should be established, and by the next meeting two weeks later a prospectus had been drawn up for a company with a capital of £10,000 to operate on a co-operative basis and to charter rather than own ships in recognition of the limited funds available. More significantly, the possibility of extending the new concern to other parts of the country was adopted, and delegations were organised to visit Napier, Wellington, Christchurch and Dunedin to encourage similar participation. Despite the combined Albion/Shaw Savill presence in Dunedin, that city produced the most immediate response with the formation of the Otago Freight Association, followed in the capital city by the Wellington Freight Association.

In Christchurch events followed a more separate course with the local promoters finally producing a prospectus dated 20th November 1872 for "the New Zealand Shipping Company Ltd" whose capital of £100,000 was reserved as to one half for Canterbury and the other half for the remainder of the country. The company was formally registered on 6th January 1873, and that month C.W. Turner was despatched to London by the provisional directors to open an office there and negotiate an emigrant contract.

Meanwhile, after some unnecessary delays with the attornies appointed in London (it was alleged that they had been suborned by Shaw Savill), the Auckland company had been in fact the first to get under way when it was registered as the New Zealand Freight Company Ltd on 1st July 1872 with a capital of £25,000. Its initial charter, the HYLTON CASTLE, left London on 3rd March 1873 and reached Auckland on 25th June.

That same month the Wellington and Dunedin Freight Associations elected to throw in their lots with the Christchurch company but it was not until July that the Auckland promoters did likewise, by which time their second charter was already at sea and the third vessel loading in London. Part of the terms of merger was the election of three local directors and the appointment of an agent in Auckland. Thus from the 4 individual enterprises was the New Zealand Shipping Company selected as the vehicle of colonial shipping aspirations; its registered office remained at Hereford Street in Christchurch during the whole of its 98 years existence under that name.

The first NZS despatch was the chartered PUNJAUB on 2nd June 1873, but the greater financial resources given by it now being a country wide concern enabled it to early embark on actual ownership. The first 4 ships were purchased second hand, but the founding directors were determined on nothing but the best model of ships built to their own specification. By the end of that year the first building orders had been placed in a major programme which finally totalled 12 ships spread over 3 yards from the Wear, the Tyne and the Clyde. Despite their differing builders, they were a remarkably homogeneous group which soon developed an excellent reputation for the standards of their emigrant accommodation and the regularity of their passages, the average time at sea being 90 days though many voyages were better. To meet the requirements of the emigration contract, all ships carried a doctor and were obliged to comply with the minimum areas per migrant and dietary scale as laid down. Initially migrants boarded the ships in London, but after the collision off Portland between the WAITARA and the HURUNUI in 1883 with loss of passenger lives, migrants were generally taken on board at Plymouth where there was a large emigrant depot to house pending migrants and which avoided the passage down the crowded English Channel. Because of this close association with Plymouth which continued into the days of steam, the Company's ships were registered at that port from 1890 to 1945.

Within 4 years of its formation the Company had grown to a fleet of 17, all iron ships or barques, sailing southwards via the Cape of Good Hope and northwards via Cape Horn. But change was in the air. Under pressure from the New Zealand Government which wanted the reliability and regularity of direct steam communication, the Company joined with its rivals, Shaw Savill, to charter the Dutch steamer STAD HAARLEM for a round voyage. It was financially unrewarding but the outcome was inevitable and in 1882 the two companies each individually arranged for the commencement of a regular subsidised steam service the following year. Although the sailing fleet was profitable, the building of the 5 steamers necessary to maintain the new service was beyond the Company's resources. Notwithstanding that an increase in capital to £1,000,000 was authorised, the subsequent issue was heavily undersubscribed, many people in New Zealand not believing a steam service to be financially viable even with a subsidy. It was only the intervention of Sir William Pearce who took up a substantial shareholding in return for the 5 new ships being built at his Govan yard that enabled the project to proceed.

In the meantime an equally momentous change was in the offing when the Albion Line's DUNEDIN demonstrated in 1882 that meat could be successfully frozen and shipped to Britain from New Zealand. NZS was not slow in

MATAURA (2) — the funnel is for the refrigerating machinery boiler

*(ATL/WAL)*

following the lead with the MATAURA receiving the fleet's first refrigerating machinery in November 1881 and subsequently lifting the first shipment from Auckland in May 1883 after an initial shipment from Port Chalmers in 1882. All the new steamers were also given insulated cargo space and refrigerating plant.

To meet the requirements of the steam contract, chartered tonnage had to be employed pending the arrival of the new ships. Some of this was satisfactory, some less so, but two rebounded in the directors' faces. These were the White Star ships IONIC and DORIC which, after being launched into the trade with considerable publicity and

IONIC at Wellington flying the NZS houseflag at the main while on charter, and the White Star flag of her owners at the mizzen          *(WAL)*

expense as Company charters, were suddenly found after their initial voyages to have been allocated to a new joint service between White Star and the recently combined Shaw Savill & Albion Company, an arrangement which lasted until the withdrawal of White Star in 1934. A contemporary verse summed up the situation

## THE LOST TRIUMPH

Coster heaved a heavy sigh.
Poor man, he felt so in the blues
When casting round his rolling eye
It fell upon the shipping news.

He took it up: "What's this I see,
The TRIUMPH stranded on a rock?
Oh, to that rival company
This will be something like a shock".

"Come hither quick, my Strickland bold,
Likewise my little office boy;
Those other men they are so sold
That really I could jump for joy".

"Do either of you know a man
To write the TRIUMPH's epitaph?"
Says office boy: "Please, sir, I can,
As well as any on your staff".

A rara avis was this child
Though Coster surely did not know it;
His verses they were very mild,
He proved a prophet, not a poet.

He wrote about the TRIUMPH's fate
In lines he meant to be ironic,
And loudly did the praises state
Of DORIC and the swift IONIC.

Now Coster had it printed soon
And then to all the shippers sent it.
But on that very afternoon
Most grievously did he repent it.

Those ships he praised so lustily
Whose rapid trips are daily seen
By that most rival company
That very day had chartered been.

Now dire confusion holds him tight,
He fancied he had been so clever,
He thought himself triumphant quite
But found that he was lost for ever.

*References: The TRIUMPH was a steamer chartered by Shaw Savill & Albion which stranded in the Hauraki Gulf on 29.11.1883. Coster was the NZS Chairman. Strickland was the NZS London manager.*

AORANGI (20) in dock at her original home port of Lyttelton                                    *(IJF)*

The Company's existing sea staff had no experience of steam so assistance had to be sought elsewhere. Captain Thos Underwood, lately commander of the Union Steam Ship Company of New Zealand's crack liner ROTOMAHANA, was engaged as Marine Superintendent while masters such as W. C. Crutchley from the "Cape" Union Steam Ship Company and E. A. Hallett, formerly of the Royal Yachts and who succeeded Underwood as Marine Superintendent in 1887, were recruited for the new steamers. The arrival of each new ship in New Zealand waters was a time of rejoicing with banquets and fullsome speech making at each port of call. As the largest ships owned by a colonial shipping company, they were objects of admiration and pride, but the outward facade was brittle and the euphoria was to be short-lived.

## Ships 1 to 23: WAITARA—RIMUTAKA

No. 271

**PASSENGERS' CONTRACT TICKET.**

1.—A Contract Ticket in this form must be given to every Passenger engaging a passage from the United Kingdom to any place out of Europe, and not being within the Mediterranean Sea.
2.—The Victualling Scale for the voyage must be printed in the body of the Ticket.
3.—All the Blanks must be correctly filled in, and the Ticket must be legibly signed with the Christian names and surname and address in full of the party issuing the same.
4.—The day of the month on which the Ship is to sail must be inserted in words and not in figures.
5.—When once issued, this Ticket must not be withdrawn from the Passenger, nor any alteration, addition, or erasure made in it.

*Ship* Hindostan *of* 833 *Tons Register, to take in Passengers at* South West India Docks London *for* Auckland New Zealand *on the* eleventh *day of* September 1873.

I engage that the persons named in the margin hereof shall be provided with a Steerage Passage to, and shall be Landed at, the Port of Auckland in the Province of Auckland New Zealand, in the Ship Hindostan with not less than Fifteen Cubic Feet for Luggage for each Statute Adult, and shall be victualled during the voyage and the time of detention at any place before its termination, according to the subjoined Scale, for the sum of £ 56 . 0 . 0 including Government dues before embarkation, and head money, if any, at the place of landing, and every other charge * except Freight for excess of Luggage beyond the quality above specified, and I hereby acknowledge to have received the sum of £ 20 . 0 . 0 in { ~~part~~ full } payment.

| NAMES. | AGES. | Equal to Statute Adult. |
|---|---|---|
| Wake Ann | 21 | 1 |
| " Emma | 19 | 1 |
| " Charles James | 13 | 1 |
| " Harriett | 50 | 1 |

The following quantities, at least, of Water and Provisions (to be issued daily) will be supplied by the Master of the Ship, as required by Law, viz., to each Statute Adult Three Quarts of Water daily, and an additional Quart of Water daily while the Ship is within the Tropics, exclusive of what is necessary for cooking the articles required by the Passenger Act, to be issued in a cooked state, and a Weekly Allowance of Provisions according to the following Scale:—

*Scale of Dietary for each Adult Passenger per Week.*

| ARTICLES. | Steerage. | ARTICLES. | Steerage. |
|---|---|---|---|
| Preserved Meats | 1 lb. | Onions | 8 oz. |
| Salt Beef | 1¼ " | Molasses (W. India) | ½ lb. |
| Salt Pork | 1 " | Raisins | ½ " |
| Cheese | 6 oz. | Suet | 6 oz. |
| Biscuit | 2 lb. 10 oz. | Pickles | ½ pint. |
| Flour | 3½ lb. | Mustard | ½ oz. |
| Rice or Oatmeal | 1½ " | Pepper | ½ " |
| Peas | ½ pint. | Salt | 2 " |
| Sugar, raw | 1 lb. | Potatoes, Fresh, or | 2 lb. |
| Tea | 1½ oz. | Ditto Preserved | ½ " |
| Coffee | 2 " | Water | 21 quarts |
| Butter | 6 " | Lime Juice (while in Tropics) | 6 oz. |
| Carrots | 8 " | | |

Children between one and four years of age to receive preserved meat, instead of salt meat, every day; and in addition to the articles to which they are entitled by the above-written scale, a quarter of a pint of preserved milk daily, and every alternate day one egg, and 8 ozs. of arrowroot or sago weekly. Children under one year, 3 pints of water daily; and if above four months old, half a pint of preserved milk daily, and every alternate day one egg; also 3 ozs. preserved soup, 12 ozs. biscuit, 4 ozs. oatmeal, 4 ozs. sago or arrowroot, 8 ozs. flour, 4 ozs. rice, and 10 ozs. sugar weekly.

Signature in full William Z McKellar

LONDON, September 1st 1873

† Deposit .... £ —

Balance .... £ 20 . 0 . 0 ~~to be~~ paid at 7, Westminster Chambers on ~~or before~~ September 1st 1873

Advance in Aid by the New Zealand Government. } £ 36 . 0 . 0 ~~£ to be repaid to the Government in the Colony.~~

Total.... £ 56 . 0 . 0 ~~Promissory Notes to be signed before sailing.~~

**NOTICES TO PASSENGERS.**

1.—If Passengers, through no default of their own, are not received on board on the day named in their Contract Tickets, or fail to obtain a passage in the Ship, they should apply to the Government Emigration Officer at the Port, who will assist them in obtaining redress under the Passenger Act.
2.—Passengers should carefully keep this part of their Contract Ticket till after the end of the voyage. If lost, no second Ticket will be issued.

*N.B.—If Passengers are not maintained on Board after the above named date, they will be paid Subsistence Money after the rate of 1s. 6d. per day for each Statute Adult.*
*N.B.—This Contract Ticket is exempt from Stamp Duty.*

* All charges on board the vessel between embarkation and disembarkation.
† It is understood that this Deposit will be absolutely forfeited in case the parties named herein fail to embark in a fit state of health for the voyage at the above-mentioned place and date.

HINDOSTAN (1) — a passengers' contract ticket issued after NZS purchase but before renaming as WAITARA *(WAL)*

WAITARA

(NMM, negative No. G.1796)

## 1. WAITARA (1873—1883) Iron Ship

Official Number: 47634
Tonnages: 883 gross, 833 net. Dimensions: 182.4 x 34.2 x 20.9 feet.
Passengers: c.200 emigrants.

*12.11.1863:* Launched by J. Reid & Co., Port Glasgow, (Yard No. 3D), for D. & J. Macdonald, Liverpool, as HINDOSTAN. *1864:* Transferred to the British & Eastern Shipping Co. Ltd, Liverpool. *28.7.1873:* Sold to C.W. Turner for NZS service and first registered at London in his name on 26.8.1873. *12.9.1873:* Left London for Auckland on her first NZS voyage. *29.1.1874:* Flagship at the Auckland Anniversary Regatta. *15.7.1874:* Renamed WAITARA, still registered in Turner's name.

*21.5.1879:* Registry transferred to Lyttelton in the name of NZS. *11.3.1881:* Grounded at Bluff when outward bound in tow. Refloated and arrived at Port Chalmers on the 13th where docked for repairs. She sailed again on the 25th. *22.6.1883:* Foundered off Portland Bill after collision with the HURUNUI (No. 11), having left Gravesend on the 19th for Wellington with 16 passengers, 25 crew and a full cargo. 4 cabin and 8 steerage passengers and 13 crew were lost.

MATAURA at Port Chalmers before the adoption of painted ports

(ATL/NZA)

## 2. MATAURA (1873—1895) Iron Ship, reduced to Barque from 1878-1889 and from 1895-1900

Official Number: 60398
Tonnages: 898 gross, 853 net. Dimensions: 199.4 x 33.3 x 20.3 feet.
Passengers: c.250 emigrants.
Refrigerated space fitted in 11.1881 for 6,000 carcasses, increased to 10,000 carcasses in 6.1889.

*3.12.1868:* Launched by Aitken & Mansel, Glasgow, (Yard No. 34), as DUNFILLAN for William Ross, Glasgow. Completed

12.1868. *9.1873:* Sold to C.W. Turner for NZS service and first registered at London in his name on 2.10.1873. *27.10.1873:*
*Continued overleaf*

*2. MATAURA — continued*
Left London for Dunedin on her first NZS voyage. *3.7.1874:* Renamed MATAURA, still registered in Turner's name. *21.5.1879:* Registry transferred to Lyttelton in the name of NZS. *12.6.1882:* Left Port Chalmers for the United Kingdom with her first cargo of frozen meat. *26.5.1883:* Left Auckland for the United Kingdom with the first shipment of frozen meat from that port. *22.5.1888:* Registry transferred to London.

*1.1895:* Sold for £2,800 to Rederi A/S Alida, Drammen, (Bruusgaard, Kiosterud & Co., managers), and renamed ALIDA. *24.8.1900:* Dismasted in a hurricane off Cape Horn, bound Levuka to Nantes with copra, and abandoned when her cargo shifted. Two lives were lost and the survivors were rescued by the barque COMLIEBANK (2,283g, 1890) and landed at Valparaiso on 24.9.1900.

RANGITIKI under tow in Otago harbour

*(WAL)*

## 3. RANGITIKI (1873-1898) Iron Ship, reduced to Barque in 1889

Official Number: 47395
Tonnages: 1,227 gross, 1,188 net, 1,650 deadweight. Dimensions: 212.0 x 35.0 x 22.8 feet.
Passengers: 20 1st class and 300 emigrants.

*7.1863:* Launched by the Humber Iron Works Co. (Martin Samuelson), Hull as SCIMITAR and registered at London for their own account. *1863:* Sold to Finlay, Campbell & Co. (registered owners J.H., H.H. and C.H. Allan) *1865:* Registry transferred to Bombay; same owners. *25.3.1871:* Sold to A.H. Campbell, London. *1871:* Sold to J.K. Welch, London. *12.1873:* Sold to NZS for £25,000, remaining registered at London. *24.12.1873:* Sailed from Plymouth for Dunedin on her first NZS voyage. *17.10.1874:* Renamed RANGITIKI. *21.5.1879:* Registry transferred to Lyttelton. *7.11.1882:* Suffered a fire in her wool cargo in the South Atlantic, bound Lyttelton to London. The fire was extinguished the same day. *22.5.1888:* Registry transferred to London. *5.12.1890:* Broke adrift and collided with

the ship BALCLUTHA (1889g, 1886) at Napier. She was towed to Wellington for repairs. *1.1897:* Struck by heavy weather in the Napier roadstead. Captain Pottinger was killed by being thrown against the mainmast. *10.1898:* Sold to A/S Dalston (H.C.A. Michelsen, manager), Sandefjord, and renamed DALSTON. *1899:* Sold to Skibs A/S Dalston (A.J. Grefstad, manager), Arendal. *1905:* Her owners' home port was moved to Kristiansand. *1909:* Sold to Paul Ballande et Fils of Noumea. *12.1.1910:* Arrived at Noumea from Callao, dismantled to a hulk and renamed PAUL BOUQUET. *1919:* Left Noumea in tow of steamer SAINT JOSEPH (1,162g, 1908) for Sydney to be recommissioned. She broke adrift and, after drifting for 40 hours, was recovered and towed back to Noumea to continue as a hulk.

## 4. WAIMEA (1873—1895) Iron Ship, reduced to Barque in 1897

Official Number: 68507
Tonnages: 871 gross, 848 net. Dimensions: 194.3 x 31.7 x 19.0 feet.

*1868:* Built by Reiherstieg Schiffswerft, Hamburg, (Yard No. 172), for C.L. Melosch, Altona, as DORETTE (739 tons gross). *12.1873:* Sold to NZS and first registered at London on 14.1.1874. *5.5.1875:* Renamed WAIMEA. *21.5.1879:* Registry transferred to Lyttelton. *22.5.1888:* Registry transferred to London. *26.4.1893:* Suffered an explosion in her accommodation, bound New Zealand to New York and Boston

and put into Rio de Janeiro where repairs took 2 weeks. One crew member was killed. *7.1895:* Sold for £2,450 to A/S Waimea (J. Westergaard & Co., managers), Christiania. *1.9.1902:* Wrecked in a south-east gale at Algoa Bay with the loss of her master and 7 crew. She had arrived from Fremantle with a full cargo of jarrah.

WAIMEA at Port Chalmers  (ATL)

## 5. RAKAIA (1873—1892) Iron Ship, reduced to Barque in 1889

Official Number: 68499
Tonnages: 1,057 gross, 1,022 net. Dimensions: 210.2 x 34.0 x 19.2 feet.
Passengers: 25 First class; 300 emigrants.

*19.11.1873:* Launched by J. Blumer & Co., Sunderland, (Yard No. 30), at a cost of £14,000 and first registered at London on 19.12.1873. *21.5.1879:* Registry transferred to Lyttelton. *22.5.1888:* Registry transferred to London. *29.1.1889:* Rammed the wharf when berthing at Lyttelton from London doing it considerable damage. *7.1892:* Sold for £5,800 to J.N. Rodbertus, Barth, Germany and renamed MARIE. *27.9.1906:* Driven ashore in a hurricane and sank at Pensacola with a cargo of pitchpine. Salved and sold to E.E. Saunders & Trobach, Pensacola. *1909:* Sold to J.C. McKown, Montevideo. *1910:* Transferred to Donnell & McKown, Montevideo. *20.6.1911:* Sold to D. Cozier, Bridgetown, Barbados. *27.6.1911:* Sold to G.S. Manning, Bridgetown, Barbados. *22.8.1911:* Sold at auction in New York by the District Marshall, having been seized by the United States Government. Her purchaser was B.H. Condon of Nova Scotia who retained her Barbados registry and renamed her RAKAIA in March 1912. *25.3.1912:* Sold to Revere & Co. Ltd, Digby, Nova Scotia, (Crowell & Thurlow, Boston, managers), but remained registered at Bridgetown, Barbados. *26.4.1915:* Transferred to Crowell & Thurlow, Boston, and renamed RUTH STARK. *12.1915:* Dismasted in 06°59'N-15°19'W bound Boston to Sekondi. *8.11.1916:* Sold to the Federal Forwarding Co., New York (Frank F. Boulton, Jules E. Bernard and Adolph Judae). *21.2.1918:* Sold to Agence Francaise de Transports Maritimes, Brest, (R. van Hemelryck & Cie, managers) and renamed MONTE CARLO. *12.6.1918:* Wrecked at the entrance to Quiberon Bay, bound Brest to Nantes.

RAKAIA in Otago harbour  (ATL/NZA)

WAIKATO in Port Chalmers dry dock      (ATL/NZA)

## 6. WAIKATO (1874—1888) Iron Ship, reduced to Barque in 1896 and to Barquentine in 1909

Official Number: 68518
Tonnages: 1,053 gross, 1,021 net, 1,500 deadweight. Dimensions: 210.5 x 34.1 x 19.2 feet.
Passengers: 320 emigrants.

*19.1.1874:* Launched by J. Blumer & Co., Sunderland, (Yard No. 31), at a cost of £14,000 and first registered at London on 18.2.1874. *21.5.1879:* Registry transferred to Lyttelton. *22.5.1888:* Registry transferred back to London. *7.1888:* Sold for £6,800 to J.C. Pfluger & Co, Bremen, and renamed J.C. PFLUGER. *11.7.1900:* Left San Francisco for Queenstown with wheat, but lost her main and mizzen masts in heavy weather and arrived at Santa Barbara on the 16th in tow of GREENWOOD (196g, 1886). She was then towed back to San Francisco by the tug RELIEF (204g, 1884), arriving on the 28th. *10.9.1900:* Condemned and sold at auction for $15,200 to J. Rosenfeld's Sons, San Francisco, and registered at Corinto,

Nicaragua. *4.5.1901:* Registered at San Francisco in the name of Henry Rosenfeld. *11.5.1901:* Sold to J.D. Spreckels & Bros Co. Inc., San Francisco and renamed CORONADO on 21.8.1901. *13.8.1912:* Sold to W.S. Dwinnel, (J. Griffiths & Sons, managers), Minneapolis, but remained registered at San Francisco. *1913:* Sold to the Canadian Pacific Railway Company for use as a coal barge. Her intended change of registry from San Francisco to Vancouver had not been effected at the time of her loss. *20.11.1913:* Foundered 2 miles from White Rocks, near Sechelt, B.C., in tow from Union Bay to Vancouver with coal.

## 7. WAITANGI (1874—1899) Iron Ship, reduced to Barque in 1897

Official Number: 70592
Tonnages: 1,161 gross, 1,128 net, 1,550 deadweight. Dimensions: 222.0 x 35.1 x 20.8 feet.
Passengers: 312 emigrants.

*6.1874:* Launched by J. Blumer & Co., Sunderland, (Yard No. 33), at a cost of £21,500 and first registered at London on 25.7.1874. *21.5.1879:* Registry transferred to Lyttelton. *12.9.1883:* In collision with an unknown vessel 8 miles southwest of St Catherine's Point, Isle of Wight, bound New Zealand to London. *22.5.1888:* Registry transferred back to London. *3.1899:* Sold for £3,625 to Akt. Agda (J. Wagle, manager), Arendal and renamed AGDA. *1904:* Her manager became J. Klocker, Arendal. *1909:* Her managers became Grefstad & Herlofsen, Arendal. *1911:* Sold to Knutsen & Kirknes, Lillesand. *21.1.1913:* Foundered off Spurn Head after striking the Leman & Ower Bank, bound Stettin to Rio de Janeiro with general cargo. 12 lives were lost, the 3 survivors being picked up by the trawler RECTO (177g, 1904).

WAITANGI at Auckland      (WAL)

WAIMATE at Port Chalmers                    (ATL/NZA)

## 8. WAIMATE (1874—1896) Iron Ship

Official Number: 70629
Tonnages: 1,156 gross, 1,124 net. Dimensions: 219.7 x 35.1 x 20.7 feet.
Passengers: 350 emigrants.

*29.8.1874:* Launched by J. Blumer & Co., Sunderland, (Yard No. 34), at a cost of £21,500 and first registered at London on 1.10.1874. *21.5.1879:* Registry transferred to Lyttelton. *22.5.1888:* Registry transferred back to London. *4.1896:* Sold for £4,150 to G.A. Lindblom, Abo (Russian flag), and renamed VALKYRIAN. *10.8.1898:* Left Newcastle, N.S.W., for Iquique with coal and went missing.

ORARI at Wellington                    (ATL/NZA)

## 9. ORARI (1875—1892) Iron Ship, reduced to Barque in 1892

Official Number: 73568
Tonnages: 1,051 gross, 1,011 net. Dimensions: 204.1 x 34.2 x 20.0 feet.
Passengers: 55 cabin; 300 emigrants.

*21.7.1875:* Launched by Palmers' Shipbuilding & Iron Co. Ltd, Jarrow, (Yard No. 321), and completed in August at a cost of £20,000. Registered at London. *13.8.1875:* Prior to handing over, ''fell over'' while loading coal at Jarrow. Minor damage only. *12.10.1875:* Left London for Lyttelton on her first New Zealand voyage. *21.5.1879:* Registry transferred to Lyttelton. *6.6.1887:* Suffered a fire in her poop at South West India Dock, London. *22.5.1888:* Registry transferred back to London. *7.12.1892:* Sold for £4,850 to J.C. Page & Partners, Liverpool with registry remaining at London. There were numerous minor changes of shareholding over the years. W.W.G. Irvine, who had been a shareholder since 1892 became the manager from 1900 until his death on 12.2.1905. *1906:* Sold to Signora A.V. Canepa fu F. Ved. Boero, Genoa. *6.10.1909:* Suffered an explosion at Swansea while loading anthracite for Genoa. *30.11.1909:* Arrived at Penarth for breaking up, but reported resold to Norris & Co., Liverpool, for use as a hulk.

OTAKI at Picton *(WAL)*

## 10. OTAKI (1875—1891) Iron Ship, reduced to Barque in 1894

Official Number: 73576
Tonnages: 1,053 gross, 1,014 net. Dimensions: 204.1 x 34.2 x 20.0 feet.
Passengers: 274 emigrants.

*19.8.1875:* Launched by Palmers' Shipbuilding & Iron Co. Ltd, Jarrow, (Yard No. 322), at a cost of £20,000 and registered at London. *28.7.1877:* In collision with the ship STAR OF INDIA (1,697g, 1861) while entering Plymouth under tow. *21.5.1879:* Registry transferred to Lyttelton. *22.5.1888:* Registry transferred back to London. *12.1891:* Sold for £6,150 through

F. Basse, Bremerhaven to Franzius, Henschen & Co., Bremen, and renamed DOCTOR SIEGERT in 1.1892. *4.7.1895:* Grounded on Diamond Rocks, bound Port of Spain, Trinidad, to Bremen with asphalt. Beached at Chacachacare, Trinidad, and later abandoned as a total loss.

HURUNUI making sail on leaving Wellington. One of the few views of a company sailing ship under way *(WAL)*

## 11. HURUNUI (1875—1895) Iron Ship, reduced to Barque in 1890

Official Number: 73588
Tonnages: 1,054 gross, 1,012 net. Dimensions: 204.1 x 34.2 x 20.0. feet.
Passengers: 300 emigrants.

*17.9.1875:* Launched by Palmers' Shipbuilding & Iron Co. Ltd, Jarrow, (Yard No. 324), and completed 11.1875 at a cost of £20,000. Registered at London. *23.9.1876:* Left London with 259 emigrants and 40 crew. Put into Portland on the 26th with weather damage and scarlet fever amongst the passengers. Towed into Plymouth 6.10.1876 where the passengers were landed into quarantine and the ship was fumigated. *10.11.1876:* Collided with and sank the Italian barque PATER (515n, 1869) off the Eddystone Light with the loss of 8 lives after leaving Plymouth for Wellington. Returned on the 11th for repairs. *21.5.1879:* Registry transferred to Lyttelton. *3.1.1883:* First vessel to enter the Lyttelton Graving Dock. *22.6.1883:* Collided with and sank the WAITARA (No. 1) off Portland Bill bound London to Port Chalmers. *22.5.1888:* Registry transferred back to London. *5.1893:* Laid up. *5.1895:* Sold for £3,500 to J. Lindblom, Abo (Russian flag); renamed HERMES. *1898:* Transferred to G.A. Lindblom, Abo. *1901:* Sold to Robert Mattson, Mariehamn. *4.4.1915:* Sunk by bombs from U 33 off the Isle of Wight 35 miles south of St Catherine's Point, bound London to Port Arthur in ballast.

HURUNUI opening the Lyttelton dry dock *(WAL)*

WAIPA at Port Chalmers                                                                                    (ATL)

## 12. WAIPA (1875—1895) Iron Ship, reduced to Barque in 1897

Official Number: 73598
Tonnages: 1,057 gross, 1,017 net. Dimensions: 204.1 x 34.2 x 20.0 feet.
Passengers: 300 emigrants.

*16.10.1875:* Launched by Palmers' Shipbuilding & Iron Co. Ltd, Jarrow, (Yard No. 325), at a cost of £20,000 and registered at London. *21.5.1879:* Registry transferred to Lyttelton. *22.5.1888:* Registry transferred back to London. *5.1895:* Sold for £3,500 to Rederi A/S Munter, Sarpsborg, (Brodrene Bjornstad, managers), and renamed MUNTER. *1900:* H. Hansen became manager and re-registered at Lillesand. *10.12.1911:* Left Mauritius for Singapore in ballast and went missing.

WAIROA at Port Chalmers                                                                                   (ATL)

## 13. WAIROA (1875—1895) Iron Ship, reduced to Barque in 1897

Official Number: 73621
Tonnages: 1,057 gross, 1,015 net. Dimensions: 204.1 x 34.2 x 20.0 feet.
Passengers: 300 emigrants.

*13.11.1875:* Launched by Palmers' Shipbuilding & Iron Co. Ltd, Jarrow, (Yard No. 326), at a cost of £20,000 and registered at London. *21.5.1879:* Registry transferred to Lyttelton. *22.5.1888:* Registry transferred back to London. *5.1893:* Laid up. *5.1895:* Sold for £3,500 to A/S Winnipeg (C. Zernichow & O. Gotaas, managers), Christiania, and renamed WINNIPEG. *5.1903:* Sold to J.K. Ahlsten, Nystad, (Russian flag). *1907:* Sold to J. Saarinen, Nystad. *1.12.1907:* Left Pensacola for Buenos Aires with pitch pine and went missing.

OPAWA at Port Chalmers     *(Evening Star/NZA)*

## 14. OPAWA (1876—1899) Iron Ship, reduced to Barque in 1896

Official Number: 73740
Tonnages: 1,131 gross, 1,076 net, 1,500 deadweight. Dimensions: 215.2 x 34.0 x 20.4 feet.
Passengers: 300 emigrants.
Refrigerated space: 11,000 carcasses from 1882 to 1898.

*14.11.1876:* Launched by A. Stephen & Sons, Glasgow, (Yard No. 203), and registered at London. *23.2.1881:* Registry transferred to Lyttelton. *22.5.1888:* Registry transferred back to London. *29.10.1888:* Ran onto her anchor and grounded at Oamaru. Delayed until 20.11.1888. *13-14.7.1897:* Grounded in York Bay, Falkland Islands, but resumed her voyage from New Zealand on the 20th. *2.1899:* Sold for £3,350 to Skibs A/S Aquila (M.F. Stray, manager), Kristiansand, and renamed AQUILA. *1900:* S.O. Stray became manager. *1907:* Svend O. Stray & Co. became managers. *1.1917:* Transferred to A/S Excelsior; same managers. *14.3.1917:* Sunk by gunfire from U 53 in 60°04′N-03°19′W, bound Aberdeen to Savannah in ballast.

PAREORA at Port Chalmers     *(ATL/NZA)*

## 15. PAREORA (1876 — 1887) Iron Ship

Official Number: 31755
Tonnages: 879 gross, 879 net. Dimensions: 203.3 x 32.8 x 20.9 feet.
Passengers: 250 emigrants.
Refrigerated space for 10,000 carcasses installed in 1882.

*3.1855:* Completed by A. Stephen & Sons, Glasgow, (Yard No. 8), for A. Stephen & W.S. Crondace, Glasgow, as WHITE EAGLE. *1856:* Sold to John MacFarlane, Glasgow. *1856:* Sold to John Gavin, London, remaining registered at Glasgow. *1860:* Sold to Robinson, London, remaining registered at Glasgow until 1865. *1866:* Sold to Bilbe & Co., London. *1875:* Sold to W. Perry, London. *1876:* Sold to James Anderson & Partners, Dunedin, and registered there 18.12.1876. *12.1876:* Sold to NZS, remaining registered at Dunedin. *9.1877:* Renamed PAREORA. *12.9.1877:* Registry transferred to London. *21.5.1879:* Registry transferred to Lyttelton. *26.11.1881:* Sailed from London for Auckland but lost her anchors and cables in the Downs and was towed back to London by the tug CAMBRIA (209g, 1870). *17.11.1886:* Registry transferred back to London. *1887:* Sold to J. Livingstone, London. *1888:* Broken up.

PIAKO at Wellington                                    (IJF)

## 16. PIAKO (1876—1891) Iron Ship

Official Number: 73745
Tonnages: 1,136 gross, 1,075 net. Dimensions: 215.3 x 34.0 x 20.5 feet.
Passengers: 317 emigrants.

*5.12.1876:* Launched by A. Stephen & Sons, Glasgow, (Yard No. 204), and first registered at London in January 1877. *11.11.1878:* Suffered a fire in her cargo, bound London to Lyttelton. Her passengers were transferred to the ship LOCH DOON (812g, 1872) and she was scuttled at Pernambuco on the 13th to extinguish the flames. She resumed her voyage on 29.12.1878. *25.12.1879:* Suffered a fire in the Tasman Sea when a case of rockets exploded, bound London to Lyttelton. *4.7.1880:* Suffered a fire in her accommodation at London. *7.2.1881:* Registry transferred to Lyttelton. *22.5.1888:* Registry transferred back to London. *22.12.1891:* Sold for £6,725 to J.E. Schaffer, Elsfleth. *22.11.1900:* Left Melbourne for Delagoa Bay with wheat and went missing.

WANGANUI at Port Chalmers                              (ATL/NJK)

## 17. WANGANUI (1877—1888) Iron Ship, reduced to Barque in 1904

Official Number: 76932
Tonnages: 1,136 gross, 1,077 net. Dimensions: 215.3 x 34.0 x 20.4 feet.
Passengers: 241 emigrants.

*18.1.1877:* Launched by A. Stephen & Sons, Glasgow, (Yard No. 205), and registered at London. *18.8.1881:* Registry transferred to Lyttelton. *22.5.1888:* Registry transferred back to London. *9.8.1888:* Sold to J. Leslie, W. Savill, W. Shirres and J.W. Temple, renamed BLENHEIM and registered at Aberdeen on the 11th. By 1903 Leslie was the sole owner. *11.1903:* Sold to Akt. Blenheim, (H.C.A. Michelsen, manager), Sandefjord. *1909:* Manager became N.A.P. Staubo. *1913:* Manager became A. Olsen, Fredrikstad. *22.2.1917:* Torpedoed and sunk by U 50 30 miles S.S.W. of Fastnet, bound Pensacola to Greenock with pitch pine.

TURAKINA at Port Chalmers                    (ATL/NZA)

## 18. TURAKINA (1882—1899) Iron Ship, reduced to Barque in 1902

Official Number: 60352
Tonnages: 1,247 gross, 1,189 net. Dimensions: 232.5 x 35.4 x 22.2 feet.
Refrigerated space for 10,000 carcasses installed in 1883, increased to 13,000 carcasses in 1889 and removed in 1898.

*23.5.1868:* Launched by C. Connell & Co., Glasgow, (Yard No. 55), for G. Smith & Sons, Glasgow (the City Line), as CITY OF PERTH. *1879:* Sold to J. Clark, Glasgow. *1881:* Sold to W. Service, Glasgow. *14.5.1882:* Grounded in a gale at Timaru. Refloated by the paddle tug LYTTELTON (193g, 1878) on 19.6.1882 and sold for £800 to John Mill, Port Chalmers, where she was towed for repairs, leaving Timaru in tow of the LYTTELTON on 21.6.1882. *9.1882:* Sold to NZS and registered

at Lyttelton on 10.10.1882. *13.4.1883:* Repairs were completed. *4.9.1883:* Renamed TURAKINA. *22.5.1888:* Registry transferred to London. *9.7.1898:* Put into Port Elizabeth for repairs to bulwarks and rigging, bound London to Port Chalmers, following heavy weather off the Cape. *2.1899:* Sold for £3,350 to A/S Elida, (A. Bech, manager), Tvedestrand, and renamed ELIDA. *5.1914:* Sold for £1,860 while in the Tyne and broken up.

TONGARIRO at Lyttelton                                        (WAL)

## 19. TONGARIRO (1883—1899) Barque rig

Official Number: 76067
Tonnages: 4,162 gross, 2,657 net. Dimensions: 389.0 x 46.0 x 23.7 feet.
Inverted C.2 cyl. by the shipbuilders, 4,000 ihp, 13.5 knots.
Passengers: 64 1st class, 36 2nd class and 250 steerage. 1899: 20 1st class.
Refrigerated space for 27,000 carcasses (81,200 cu.ft.)

*23.8.1883:* Launched by John Elder & Co., Govan, (Yard No. 280), and ran trials on 17.10.1883. Cost £140,900. Registered at Lyttelton on 27.12.1883. *25.10.1883:* Left London and sailed from Plymouth on 29.10.1883 on her first New Zealand voyage to Port Chalmers. *14.9.1888:* Registry transferred to London. *5.10.1894:* Rammed Franklin wharf through a telegraph mistake on leaving Hobart, bound London to Wellington. No damage to the ship. *2.6.1895:* Put into Spithead after an engine breakdown, bound London to New Zealand and

delayed 10 days for repairs. *9.12.1897:* Left London on her last New Zealand sailing. *4.1898:* Laid up. *6.8.1898—8.1899:* Chartered to the Beaver Line Associated Steamers Ltd (D. & C. McIver, managers), Liverpool, for its Liverpool—Canada service. *27.7.1899:* Sold with RUAPEHU (No. 21), KAIKOURA (No. 22) and RIMUTAKA (No. 23) for £75,000 for the four to the British India Steam Navigation Co. Ltd, Glasgow, and renamed ZIBENGHLA on 23.9.1899. *28.4.1910:* Sold for demolition at Bombay where scrapping began in 6.1910.

AORANGI at Port Chalmers

*(IJF)*

## 20. AORANGI (1883—1896 and 1899—1910) Barque rig to 1896

Official Number: 76068
Tonnages: 4,163 gross, 2,655 net. 1896: 4,268 gross, 2,782 net.
Dimensions: 389.0 x 46.0 x 23.7 feet.
Inverted C.2 cyl. by the shipbuilders, 4,000 ihp, 13.5 knots. *1896:* T.3 cyl. by the Wallsend Slipway & Engineering Co. Ltd, Newcastle, 4,900 ihp, 14 knots.
Passengers: 61 1st class, 44 2nd class and 250 steerage. *1896:* 100 1st class and 50 2nd class. *1910:* 94 1st class, 52 2nd class, 42 3rd class.
Refrigerated space for 27,000 carcasses (83,100 cu.ft.)

*2.10.1883:* Launched by John Elder & Co., Govan, (Yard No. 281), and ran trials on 17.10.1883. Registered at Lyttelton on 28.1.1884. *29.11.1883:* Left London on her first New Zealand voyage to Wellington. *14.9.1888:* Registry transferred to London. *1894—1895:* Chartered to the Canadian Australian Royal Mail Line (James Huddart, manager), Melbourne. *27.3.1896:* Sailed from Bluff on her final NZS sailing from New Zealand. *8.1896:* Sold to James Huddart, London, and refitted by C.S. Swan & Hunter, Newcastle at a cost of £40,000. *17.3.1897:* Transferred to the newly formed Canadian Australian Royal Mail Steamship Co. Ltd, (James Huddart, manager), London. *5.1897:* Entered the Sydney-Honolulu-Vancouver service. *6.1897:* The forced draft fans broke down, bound Sydney to Vancouver and she had to make the return trip under natural draft at reduced speed. *12.8.1897:* Arrived at Wellington on the Line's first call after that port was added to the itinerary. *2.1898:* Control of the Canadian Australian Line passed to NZS as chief creditor. *16.8.1899:* Sold by the liquidator to NZS. *25.3.1901:* Chartered to and a half share sold to the Union Steam Ship Company of New Zealand Ltd,

Dunedin. *9.11.1901:* Grounded in the Brisbane River inward bound from Vancouver. Refloated undamaged. *15.8.1905:* Returned to Rewa Roadstead, Fiji, with machinery damage, having left Suva that day for Honolulu. *31.12.1909:* Arrived at Sydney at the end of her last voyage in the Vancouver service. *2.1910:* The remaining half share was sold to the Union Steam Ship Company of New Zealand Ltd who became the vessel's sole owners. *14.10.1910:* Left Wellington on her first sailing for Rarotonga, Tahiti and San Francisco. She made her final sailing from San Francisco on 1.4.1914. *1.3.1911:* Suffered a mishap to her engines, bound Auckland to San Francisco and delayed for 5 days for repairs, missing a round voyage. *8.1914—3.5.1915:* Requisitioned as a supply ship by the Royal Australian Navy. *5.11.1914:* Sold to the Admiralty. *10.8.1915:* Sunk as a blockship in Holm Sound, Scapa Flow. *8.9.1920:* The hulk was raised, but went out of control when the tug got a wire round its screw. It went ashore again the same day and was subsequently dispersed during channel clearing operations.

AORANGI at Sydney after rebuilding in 1896

*(IJF)*

RUAPEHU at Port Chalmers       (IJF)

## 21. RUAPEHU (1883—1899) Barque rig

Official Number: 76069
Tonnages: 4,163 gross, 2,655 net. Dimensions: 389.0 x 46.0 x 23.7 feet.
Inverted C.2 cyl. by the shipbuilders, 4,000 ihp, 13.5 knots, (14.9 knots on trials).
Passengers: 64 1st class, 36 2nd class and 250 steerage. 1899: 20 1st class.
Refrigerated space for 27,000 carcasses (90,400 cu.ft.)

*19.11.1883:* Launched by John Elder & Co., Govan, (Yard No. 282), and ran trials on 28.12.1883. Cost £138,600. Registered at Lyttelton on 7.3.1884. *10.1.1884:* Left London on her first New Zealand sailing to Auckland. *10.4.1885:* Grounded at Wellington; refloated undamaged the following day. *25.3.1888:* Grounded on Farewell Spit, bound London to Wellington. *14.9.1888:* Registry transferred to London. *1—4.1.1897:* Grounded on Farewell Spit, bound London to Wellington. The passengers were landed at Wellington by the steamer CORINNA (1,279g, 1882) and the RUAPEHU docked at Lyttelton for repairs on the 13th. *4.1899:* Chartered to the Beaver Line

Associated Steamers Ltd (D & C McIver, managers), Liverpool, for 2 voyages from Liverpool to Canada. *27.7.1899:* Sold with TONGARIRO (No. 19), KAIKOURA (No. 22) and RIMUTAKA (No. 23) for £75,000 for the four to the British India Steam Navigation Co. Ltd, Glasgow, and renamed ZAYATHLA on 14.9.1899. *24.8.1900:* Chartered to the Rajah of Gwalior as a hospital ship for the Boxer Rising in China and renamed GWALIOR the same day. No change of ownership. *1902:* Reverted to her owners retaining the name GWALIOR. *4.6.1911:* Sold to L. Pittaluga and broken up at Genoa in 11.1911.

KAIKOURA at Gravesend awaiting embarking passengers       (IJF)

## 22. KAIKOURA (1884—1899) Barque rig

Official Number: 89627
Tonnages: 4,507 gross, 2,883 net. Dimensions: 430.0 x 46.0 x 24.0 feet.
Inverted C.2 cyl. by the shipbuilders, 4,000 ihp, 13.5 knots.
Passengers: 76 1st class, 58 2nd class and 280 steerage. 1899: 142 1st class and 20 2nd class.
Refrigerated space for 34,000 carcasses (101,100 cu.ft.)

*8.9.1884:* Launched by John Elder & Co., Govan, (Yard No.287) and delivered 17.10.1884 at a cost of £154,200. First registered at London on 23.10.1884. *19.10.1884:* In collision with the Danish barque UNION off Portland, bound Glasgow to London. *24.10.1884:* Sailed from London on her first New Zealand voyage to Auckland. *25.10.1884:* Run into by the steamer BAN RIGH (981g, 1870) off Gravesend. *4.1885:* Taken up as an Armed Merchant Cruiser during the Russian war scare of that year, but requisition cancelled before implementation. *17.2.1889:* Suffered a fire in her bunkers at Lyttelton. *18.1.1894:* Put into Teneriffe with a fire in No. 5 hold, bound

London to Wellington. The hold was flooded and the fire put out the following day. *21.9.1896:* Grounded on arrival at Bluff due to a defect in the steering gear. *4.8.1897:* Broke her crankshaft in 22°38'S-40°48'W. 3 days later she was picked up by the German steamer WOLFSBURG (2,489g, 1896) and towed 176 miles to Rio de Janeiro where they arrived on the 8th. *27.7.1899:* Sold with the TONGARIRO (No. 19), RUAPEHU (No. 21) and RIMUTAKA (No. 23) for £75,000 for the four to the British India Steam Navigation Co. Ltd, Glasgow, and renamed ZAIDA on 15.8.1899. *9.1.1907:* Sold to L. Pittaluga, Genoa, and broken up there.

RIMUTAKA

*(WAL)*

## 23. RIMUTAKA (1884—1899) Barque rig

Official Number: 89652
Tonnages: 4,514 gross, 2,859 net, 4,500 deadweight. Dimensions: 430.0 x 46.0 x 25.0 feet.
Inverted C.2 cyl. by the shipbuilders, 4,000 ihp, 13.5 knots.
Passengers: 76 1st class, 58 2nd class and 280 steerage. 1899: 168 1st class and 26 2nd class.
Refrigerated space for 34,000 carcasses (101,700 cu.ft.)

*19.11.1884:* Launched by John Elder & Co., Govan, (Yard No. 288), and delivered 12.1884 at a cost of £152,800. First registered at London on 10.1.1885. *15.1.1885:* Sailed from London on her first New Zealand voyage to Wellington. *28.2.1883:* Rammed the COPTIC (4,448g, 1881) when berthing at Lyttelton through failure of the engine room telegraph. Little damage. *8.9.1895:* Suffered a cargo fire in the South Atlantic Ocean. Arrived at Cape Town on 14th and resumed her voyage to Hobart. *15.4.1896:* Put into Montevideo with machinery damage, bound Wellington to London. *5.3.1897:* Took the ship DERWENT (1,970g, 1884), damaged in collision with the steamer MILO (1,743g, 1892), in tow for Plymouth where arrived on the 6th. *26.8.1899:* Sold with the TONGARIRO (No. 19), RUAPEHU (No. 21) and KAIKOURA (No. 22) for £75,000 for the four to the British India Steam Navigation Co. Ltd, Glasgow, and renamed ZAMANIA on 7.9.1899. *14.7.1911:* Sold to Japanese buyers and presumed scrapped soon afterwards, though she remains in the registers until 1923.

# The New Zealand Shipping Company, Limited

Head Office:
**CHRISTCHURCH,**
New Zealand.

London Branch:
**ROCHESTER BUILDINGS,**
138 Leadenhall St., E.C.

*THE COMPANY'S FLEET COMPRISES THE FOLLOWING MAGNIFICENT FULL-POWERED*

## STEAMERS

|  | TONS. | HORSE-POWER. | COMMANDER. |
|---|---|---|---|
| AORANGI | 4163 | 3600 | W. A. TURPIN. |
| KAIKOURA | 5000 | 4000 | W. C. CRUTCHLEY, R.N.R. |
| RIMUTAKA | 5000 | 4000 | E. O. HALLETT, R.N. |
| RUAPEHU | 4163 | 3600 | C. C. BROUGH. |
| TONGARIRO | 4163 | 3600 | J. E. BONE. |

The above are all new steamers, built of steel, and commanded by men of great experience.

The Passenger accommodation is replete with every modern convenience, and the dietary scale, such as will sustain the well earned reputation of the Company.

A Steamer is despatched from London and the Colony every four weeks.

The Homeward route will be viá the Straits of Magellan if weather permits, and the time occupied is not expected to exceed 40 days.

An experienced Surgeon will accompany each steamer.

PASSAGE MONEY.—Saloon, from 60 guineas upwards; Second Cabin, 40 guineas; Steerage from 18 to 22 guineas.

Arrangements can be made for the passages of friends from London to the Colony.

## IRON CLIPPER SHIPS

| | TONS. | | TONS. | | TONS. |
|---|---|---|---|---|---|
| HURUNUI | 1054 | PIAKO | 1136 | WAIMEA | 871 |
| MATAURA | 898 | RAKAIA | 1057 | WAIPA | 1054 |
| OPAWA | 1131 | RANGITIKI | 1225 | WAIROA | 1057 |
| ORARI | 1054 | TURAKINA | 1247 | WAITANGI | 1161 |
| OTAKI | 1053 | WAIKATO | 1053 | WANGANUI | 1136 |
| PAREORA | 879 | WAIMATE | 1157 | | |

The Saloon and State Cabins are superbly fitted and arranged, and provided with every requisite for the comfort of Passengers.

The Dietary Scale is most liberal; Second Class and Steerage Accommodation is all that can be desired; and the ships are commanded by experienced Masters.

The Company also charters ships of the highest class as required, and vessels are despatched from London to each of the principal ports in the Colony with strict punctuality every month. The Company has always ships loading homewards from New Zealand.

*Further particulars on application at any of the following Branches:*

| | | | |
|---|---|---|---|
| AUCKLAND | LONDON | NELSON | TIMARU |
| DUNEDIN | LYTTELTON | OAMARU | PORT CHALMERS |
| INVERCARGILL | NAPIER | TARANAKI | WELLINGTON |

OR AT THE HEAD OFFICES, CHRISTCHURCH.

An 1884 company advertisement from the brochure for the "Fair of All Nations" at Dunedin in November/December 1884

*(IJF)*

# Chapter 3: Financial Crisis, London Takeover and A New Fleet

As the 1880's progressed, New Zealand sank deeper into depression, reducing the demands for both imports and migrants, and the amount of export cargoes for the return passage. But the costs of the expensive steam fleet remained constant while the earnings of the sailing vessels were unable to bridge the gap. The Company was headed on a course for disaster. Yet for the meantime optimism remained high. Although the first rumblings of shareholder discontent had surfaced publicly in England in June 1886, the Annual Report released the following month showed a paper profit of £42,059 for the year but without adequate provision for depreciation. More ominously there was no dividend, but a further call of £1 per share was made to reduce the liability to the shipbuilders. The deaths of J.L. Coster and Sir William Pearce within the space of two years were to have a profound effect on the Company's future. The first was that of Coster on 17 December 1886. Originally on the staff of the Bank of New Zealand which with the associated New Zealand Loan & Mercantile Agency were the major financial backers of the Company in New Zealand, Coster had played a prominent part in NZS affairs from its foundation, occupying the chair for all but a year. It was his flamboyant personality that had provided much of the drive in the transition from sail to steam, and he had been very much the Company's public face in keeping a positive image for it. As recently as February of that year he had emphasised to the London Board its place as an advisory one only, but with his departure from the scene the hard facts were soon to emerge.

Even before Coster's death, a meeting of the London shareholders had demanded the removal of control to London. The response of the New Zealand Board was to send its solicitor, Leonard Harper, to London to investigate, but also authorised to take action if required. Harper was not slow to appreciate that with the Company's debts exceeding its assets, some drastic action was needed and in July 1887 he agreed to the transfer of control subject to constitutional changes in New Zealand. There, dissatisfaction which Coster had managed to keep under control had broken out with a meeting of Wellington shareholders in October 1886 demanding a local board, and other New Zealand shareholders passing what was in effect a vote of no confidence in the directors. The turmoil continued during Harper's London mission in 1887 with the Bank of New Zealand, faced with major liquidity problems of its own, bringing heavy pressure to bear for reduction of debt, refusing further credit and threatening winding up proceedings.

Although the shareholders at the Annual General Meeting in September 1887 endorsed the directors' view that control should remain in New Zealand, the creditors' pressure was too great, and at an Extraordinary General Meeting held in Christchurch on 28 December 1887 the shareholders approved Harper's recommendations. There were to continue to be two boards with the New Zealand Board retaining local control, but the key parts of the resolutions were that the Head Office should be moved to London and that the London Board should have "supreme financial control and management of the administrative and commercial affairs".

Events had been moving in other directions also. In 1886 it had been decided that G.D. Tyser & Company should become the Company's London freight brokers. Tysers had a long connection with New Zealand, having been responsible for the despatch of the first migrant ship to Wellington in 1839. They had displeased both NZS and Shaw Savill earlier in 1886 by entering into a contract with the freezing works proprietors, Nelson Bros, to ship their frozen meat from Hawkes Bay to London which resulted in the formation of the Colonial Union Line. To counter this threat, in return for Tysers agreeing not to participate in the outward trade, they were given the NZS brokerage contract. It proved an uneasy partnership, and particularly when the following year Tysers acquired the share of the founder, J.H. Flint, in the similarly named Colonial Line in the Australian trade. Another firm involved in the Colonial Line was J.B. Westray & Company whose partners included E.S. Dawes of Gray Dawes & Company. The brokerage interests of Dawes were in direct competition with those of Tysers, and with J.B. Westray a member of the newly empowered NZS London Board, a clash was inevitable.

During the crisis of 1887 the steady hand of Sir William Pearce, who as the largest British creditor wished to protect his investment, had kept the Company clear of disaster. It was his unexpected death on 18 December 1888 that precipitated another crisis just when events seemed to be taking a more settled path. Dawes moved swiftly, and by February 1889 had reached agreement to take over the debt and the shares from the Pearce estate, thus effectively giving him control of NZS. The shipping journal "Fairplay", which at that time was never slow to indulge in controversy, leapt into the fray in March with an article suggesting that Dawes was simply a stooge of Shaw Savill whose objective was to foreclose on the mortgage, hand the New Zealand business over to Shaw Savill and use the ships on the Queensland service where he was already involved with the British India Associated service and more directly with the ships of the Ducal Line. Dawes hotly denied these allegations, asserting that he was committed to the independence of NZS and pointing to his insistence on the reinstatement of the Company's long serving London manager, O.R. Strickland, who had been suspended by Sir John Gorst, the London Chairman. He also stated that Tysers would continue to act as brokers for NZS.

But the controversy would not go away. In November 1889 a circular was issued by some London shareholders led by Thos Johnson claiming again that the Company's policy was inimical to its interests and was playing into the hands of Shaw Savill. Sir John Gorst emphatically denied this claim, and Johnson's motion of censure failed at the Annual General Meeting the following month. Dawes had also taken steps to acquire the outstanding NZS debt to the Bank of New Zealand which was refinanced by a debenture issue in October 1890. Such was the renewed confidence in the Company that the debenture issue was fully subscribed and the capital base was further strengthened the following June when an Extraordinary General Meeting authorised the writing off of £2 per share in order to enable the resumption of dividend payments.

There remained the Tyser situation to be addressed. Dawes opened the battle by obtaining a Court order in October 1890 compelling the surrender by Tysers of the Company's books and documents. This was followed by the termination of the Tyser contract and the launching of a writ claiming damages against Tysers for mismanagement. In return Tysers claimed damages for wrongful termination. The litigation dragged on for over three years, the result being inconclusive. The practical outcome was the appointment of J.B. Westray & Company as the NZS London brokers, an arrangement which was to continue for the rest of the Company's existence, the boards of the two concerns, particularly in later years, being largely comprised of the same people.

The Company's financial crises of the late 1880's were only the foreground commanding the most publicity to the many other problems facing Dawes after he obtained control. The most pressing was to put the Company on a new course which would ensure financial stability and success for the future. The way was made a little easier by the expiry of the mail contract with the New Zealand Government in December 1889. Although it provided some financial security, its income was insufficient to meet the costs involved in the then state of naval architecture in providing fast ships on a demanding regular timetable encircling the world. Basically the five ships in the mail fleet were too small, the fuel for their compound engines took a disproportionate space that could otherwise have been used for paying cargo, and the speed that they were required to make was uneconomic. The freeing of the Company from this burden, with the mails in future being carried on a poundage basis, removed a major financial drag.

OTARAMA (24) at Port Chalmers
*(Otago Early Settlers' Museum/NZA)*

The way ahead was now perceived as based on the twin foundations of extensive refrigerated cargo capacity for the northward voyage combined with moderate speed. To implement this new policy as soon as possible, a newly built ship the SEA KING was purchased and made her first round voyage under that name before being renamed OTARAMA in November 1890. Another was purchased on the stocks and delivered that month as TEKOA. The major step though was the ordering from Dennys of a new passenger steamer to supplement the original five. She bore a name which was to become one of the most famous in the fleet, RUAHINE, and set a basic pattern for the next 20 years. At 6,217 tons gross she was half as big again as the pioneers, her quadruple expansion engines were far more economical than the earlier compounds, and her refrigerated cargo capacity was double theirs. Yet

RUAHINE (26) in original guise with square rig on both masts
*(IJF)*

she remained a lone ship as six steamers were ample for the passenger trade and the Company did not have the resources to build consorts for her until the original ships had earned sufficient depreciation to justify their disposal at a price the market would bear. Despite the increase in size and power, the RUAHINE and her cargo consorts retained square rig on both masts in their early years. The Company's route followed the Roaring Forties outward and homeward and it would have been foolish to have ignored the free assistance to fuel economy provided by the prevailing westerly winds on both legs.

Further and larger cargo ships followed with the WAIKATO, RAKAIA, MATAURA and WAIMATE from 1892 to 1896 as the sailing ships were gradually phased out, the last, the WAITANGI, being sold in August 1899. The wreck of the MATAURA in the Magellan Straits in 1898 was the Company's first steam disaster. As well as the loss of the mails and freight, the loss of the ship also caused untold anguish to many students of the University of New Zealand whose final examination papers she was carrying for marking in England as was then the practice.

## Ships 24 to 31: OTARAMA—WAIMATE

OTARAMA with a white hull, at Lyttelton early in her career                                    (ATL/WAL)

### 24. OTARAMA (1890—1902)
Official Number: 98081
Tonnages: 3,808 gross, 2,460 net. Dimensions: 365.0 x 44.2 x 19.4 feet.
T.3 cyl. by the shipbuilders, 1,600 ihp, 10 knots.
Passengers: 12.
Refrigerated space for 53,000 carcasses (157,300 cu.ft.) installed in 1890.

*8.3.1890:* Launched by Wm Doxford & Sons, Sunderland, (Yard No. 194), and first registered 21.4.1890 to W. Ross & Co., London, as SEA KING. *16.7.1890:* Sold for £50,000 to J.B. Westray & W.C. Dawes of NZS. Refrigeration machinery installed, renamed OTARAMA on 7.11.1890 and registered at Plymouth on 20.11.1890. *22.4.1892:* Collided with the sailing barge QUEEN BEE (70g, 1890) in the Thames. *29.9.1894:* Sailed from London for Auckland but collided with the steamer NAWORTH CASTLE (1,713g, 1878) in the Thames Estuary and arrived back for repairs on 1.10.1894. *2.7.1898:* Broke her high pressure cylinder off the Crozets, bound London to Port Chalmers and completed the voyage with the engine compounded. *21.4.1902:* Ownership transferred to NZS. *8.10.1902:* Sold for £24,000 to Nelson Line (Liverpool) Ltd (H & W Nelson, managers), London and renamed HIGHLAND GHILLIE on 10.10.1902. *7.1912:* Sold to M. Jebsen, Hamburg, and renamed CONSTANTIN. *11.1913:* Sold to M. Gumuchdjian, Varna. *1924:* Transferred to M. Gumuchdjian Ltd, London, and renamed RIVER TYNE. *1925:* Sold to Cie Internationale de Commerce et d'Armement (M. Gumuchdjian, manager), Antwerp, and renamed SPA. *4.1930:* Laid up at Antwerp. *1.1933:* Sold to F. Rijsdijk's Industries Ltd, Hendrik-Ido-Ambacht, and broken up at Dordrecht.

### 25. TEKOA (1890—1902)
Official Number: 97473
Tonnages: 4,050 gross, 2,646 net, 5,400 deadweight. Dimensions: 365.1 x 47.1 x 26.5 feet.
T.3 cyl. by Central Marine Engine Works, West Hartlepool, 1,600 ihp, 10 knots.
12 passengers.
Refrigerated space for 60,000 carcasses (170,100 cu.ft.)

*2.8.1890:* Launched by Wm Gray & Co. Ltd, West Hartlepool, (Yard No. 394), for NZS. She had originally been ordered by Christopher Furness, West Hartlepool, and was purchased by NZS on the stocks for £50,500. She ran her trials on 18.11.1890 and was first registered at Plymouth on 24.11.1890. *8—9.6.1897:* Grounded on the Shipwash Sands, bound London to the Tees. *8.4.1898:* Suffered a fire in her cargo in No. 3 hold, bound London to Dunedin, but it was extinguished and she arrived at Port Chalmers on the 10th. *7.8.1899:*
*Continued overleaf*

*25. TEKOA — continued*

TEKOA at Port Chalmers                                    *(ATL/NZA)*

Grounded on a rock in the Straits of Le Maire between Staten Island and the mainland, bound Wellington to London. It was at first thought that the only survivors were from a boat that got away at the time, until she arrived at Port Stanley, Falkland Islands on the 10th. Arrived at Montevideo 23.10.1899 for temporary repairs and sailed with cement box and empty forehold on 17.12.1899. *5.1902:* Sold for £27,000 to Nelson Line (Liverpool) Ltd, (H & W Nelson Ltd, managers), London, and renamed HIGHLAND CORRIE on 7.6.1902. *4.1909:* Sold to F. Rijsdijk's Industries Ltd, Hendrik-Ido-Ambacht, and broken up.

RUAHINE and her contemporary Shaw Savill/White Star rival GOTHIC of 1893 berthed side by side at Lyttelton                                    *(WAL)*

## 26. RUAHINE (1891—1900) Brig rig

Official Number: 99257
Tonnages: 6,127 gross, 3,926 net, 6,690 deadweight. Dimensions: 430.0 x 50.1 x 31.6 feet. Draft: 27.9 feet.
Q.4 cyl. by Denny & Co., Dumbarton, 4,518 ihp, 67 rpm, 14.57 knots (trials). 1,725 tons coal bunkers.
Passengers: 74 1st class, 36 2nd class and 300 steerage.
Refrigerated space for 71,000 carcasses (212,450 cu.ft.)

*20.10.1891:* Launched by Wm Denny & Bros, Dumbarton, (Yard No. 458), and delivered 18.12.1891 at a cost of £115,800. First registered at Plymouth on 14.1.1892. *14.1.1892:* Sailed from London on her first voyage. This was to Australia under charter to Allport & Hughes. She left London on her first New Zealand voyage on 23.6.1892. *18.10.1892:* Suffered a breakdown in her machinery off Cape Upstart, Queensland. *21.2.1893:* Put into St Helena with a fire in No. 4 hold. She continued to Cape Town where she arrived on the 28th and the cargo was discharged. She continued her voyage to New Zealand on March 8th. *1.3.1893:* All 64 shares in the ship were sold to J.B. Westray and W.C. Dawes. They were transferred back to NZS piecemeal between 5.7.1893 and 17.5.1900. *8.1894:* Broke a blade off her screw and damaged her steering gear off Cape Horn, bound New Zealand to London. *27.1.1897:* Arrived at Freetown with a broken main shaft, having previously broken her thrust shaft on the 20th, bound London to Wellington and put into Dakar. She sailed again from Freetown on 21.2.1897. *4.1897:* Carried the New Zealand contingent to London for Queen Victoria's Diamond Jubilee

RUAHINE                                    *(WAL)*

*26. RUAHINE — continued*

celebrations. *22.5.1900:* Sold for £68,720 to the Compania Trasatlantica, Barcelona, and renamed ANTONIO LOPEZ. *10.6.1909:* Grounded on Point Oswoods, Fire Island, off Long Island, New York, bound Genoa and Naples to Vera Cruz.

Refloated 3 days later and arrived at New York on the 16th. *20.11.1926:* Arrived at Havana, bound Galveston to Barcelona with a fire in No. 2 hold. *1936:* Laid up at Cadiz during the Spanish Civil War. *7.1945:* Broken up at Bilbao.

WAIKATO at Port Chalmers (IJF)

## 27. WAIKATO (1892—1905)

Official Number: 99263
Tonnages: 4,767 gross, 3,071 net, 7,000 deadweight. Dimensions: 400.0 x 48.0 x 21.7 feet.
T.3 cyl. by the shipbuilders, 1,600 ihp, 12.5 knots.
Refrigerated space for 70,000 carcasses (213,300 cu.ft.)

*25.6.1892:* Launched by Wm Doxford & Sons Ltd, Sunderland, (Yard No. 213), and completed in 10.1892 for NZS at a cost of £47,250. First registered at Plymouth on 11.10.1892. *3.12.1892:* Transferred to J.B. Westray and W.C. Dawes. All 64 shares were resold to NZS from 12.10.1894 to 8.10.1896. *18.5.1896:* Fire broke out in the after hold off Cape Leeuwin but was brought under control after 3 hours. *5.6.1899:* Broke her shaft 180 miles south of the Cape of Good Hope bound London to New Zealand. In late July, when in 39°S-39°E, the barquentine TACORA (911g, 1888) attempted to take her in tow. On 15.9.1899 the steamer ASLOUN (2,828g, 1890) took

her in tow and they arrived at Fremantle on 9.10.1899 after transferring bunkers off Amsterdam Island. *30.6.1902:* Broke her shaft in the South Atlantic, bound London to New Zealand. Temporary repairs were effected but she was taken in tow by the steamer MICHIGAN (8,001g, 1898) on 27.7.1902 and arrived at Cape Town on the 31st. *1.1905:* Sold for £20,400 to C. Andersen, Hamburg, and renamed AUGUSTUS. *3.1.1911:* Sold to Emil R. Retzlaff, Stettin. *11.1912:* Sold to E. Accame di L., (Fr. Accame di L., managers), Genoa, and renamed TERESA ACCAME. *1914:* Transferred to Fr. Accame di L. *6.1923:* Sold at Spezia for demolition.

RAKAIA at Port Chalmers
*(Otago Early Settlers' Museum/NZA)*

## 28. RAKAIA (1895—1915)

Official Number: 105262
Tonnages: 5,629 gross, 3,660 net. Dimensions: 420.0 x 54.0 x 28.7 feet.
T.3 cyl. by the shipbuilders, 3,500 ihp, 12.5 knots.
Passengers: 12 1st class and 350 emigrants.
Refrigerated space for 90,000 carcasses (223,900 cu.ft.)

*25.4.1895:* Launched by R. & W. Hawthorn, Leslie & Co. Ltd, Hebburn, (Yard No. 330), delivered on 20.6.1895 and first registered at Plymouth to J.B. Westray and W.C. Dawes on

22.6.1895. *5.1.1896:* Grounded on the Warang Bank, Bijouga Islands, Sierra Leone. Refloated on the 8th and continued to Cape Town where the leaks were stopped by divers. She

*Continued overleaf*

### 27. RAKAIA — continued

continued her voyage from London to Auckland on 9.2.1896. *20.8.1896:* Ownership was transferred to NZS. *15.10.1902:* Suffered a fire in her flax cargo in the after hold a week out from Plymouth, bound Wellington to London. *15.5.1907:* Suffered a fire in No. 3 hold, bound London to Auckland and arrived at Teneriffe the following day. *6.6.1908:* Collided with the anchored ASTURIAS (12,002g, 1908) off Flores Island, Montevideo, and had to put back for repairs. *24.8.1908:* Suffered a fire in the shelter deck in the Indian Ocean, bound London to Port Chalmers. *22.5.1910:* Sailed from Montreal to open the NZS Eastern Canada to New Zealand service, arriving at Auckland on 27.7.1910. *18.8.1913:* Arrived at Albany with a fire in her bunkers and in the wheat in No.3 hold. The fire was extinguished on the 22nd. *19.11.1914:* Touched a reef off Gisborne when leaving for Tokomaru Bay; no damage. *13.2.1915:* Sold for £50,000 to the Brodmead Steamship Co. Ltd (Blue Star Line Ltd, managers), London, and renamed BRODMEAD. Her registry was transferred to London on 16.2.1916. *31.7.1917 — 27.4.1919:* Taken up under the Liner Requisition Scheme. *7.9.1917:* Torpedoed by UB 49 west of Gibraltar (35°52'N-06°13'W), bound Barry to Port Said with coal and towed into Gibraltar on the 8th. 12 crew were lost, including the Master. *14.4.1920:* Transferred to the Union Cold Storage Co. Ltd. (Blue Star Line (1920) Ltd, managers) and renamed ROMANSTAR on 22.9.1920. *4.5.1923:* Suffered a fire in the poop, bound London to Rio de Janeiro. *6.6.1925:* Suffered a fire in No. 3 hold at Liverpool. *11.1.1928:* Collided with the American tanker KEWANEE (3,550g, 1919), bound

RAKAIA at Auckland *(WAL)*

Vancouver to London. *5.1929:* Renamed ROMAN STAR, and transferred to the Blue Star Line Ltd on 3.9.1929. *8.1934:* Sold for £8,000 to S.A. Ricuperi Metallici and arrived at Savona for demolition on 29.9.1934.

MATAURA at Port Chalmers *(IJF)*

## 29. MATAURA (1896—1898)

Official Number: 105273
Tonnages: 5,764 gross, 3,756 net. Dimensions: 421.0 x 54.6 x 29.1 feet.
T.3 cyl. by the shipbuilders, 2,965 ihp, 66 rpm, 12.25 knots on trials.
Passengers: 12 1st class and 350 emigrants.
Refrigerated space for 90,000 carcasses (226,100 cu.ft.)

*15.2.1896:* Launched by Barclay, Curle & Co. Ltd, Glasgow, (Yard No. 399), and ran trials on 4.4.1896. First registered at Plymouth on 7.4.1896 to J.B. Westray and Sir Andrew Maclean. Transferred to Westray and W.C Dawes on 2.6.1896. *27.8.1896:* Transferred to NZS. *1897:* Brought the New Zealand Contingent back from England after Queen Victoria's Diamond Jubilee celebrations. Two days after leaving Cape Town the intermediate cylinder cover broke and the rest of the voyage was completed as a compound.

*12.1.1898:* Struck an uncharted rock off Desolation Island, bound Wellington to London with 18,000 bales of wool and 30,000 frozen carcasses and beached in Sealer's Cove. The ORCANA (4,803g, 1893) carried her passengers and crew to Montevideo, and part of the cargo was salvaged during 1898. The ship had broken in two by March 1898 and cargo salvage was abandoned in December.

PAREORA at Sydney after 1908          (Dufty/WAL)

## 30. PAREORA (1896—1903)

Official Number: 104735
Tonnages: 650 gross, 355 net. Dimensions: 180.0 x 29.2 x 11.1 feet.
T.3 cyl. by G. Clark Ltd, Sunderland, 480 ihp, 8 knots.

26.2.1896: Launched by Wood, Skinner & Co., Newcastle, (Yard No. 60), for W. Kinnear, Dundee, as BREEZE and first registered at Dundee on 25.5.1896. 8.1896: Sold for £9,300 to NZS, still registered at Dundee; renamed PAREORA in 1897. 6.10.1896: Chartered to the Black Ball Coal Mining Company of New Zealand Ltd, London. 25.9.1899: Struck a rock off Oamaru; minor damage only. 7.1903: Transferred to the Blackball Coal Company Ltd, London, but remained registered at Dundee. 28.7.1908: Sold to D. George (W.A. Firth, manager), Dundee, and registry transferred to London. 31.7.1908: Transferred to W.A. Firth, Sydney. 29.8.1908: Collided with the steamer COLAC (1,480g, 1884) off Sydney Heads. 30.6.1911: Collided in fog with the ferry BINNGARRA (442g, 1905) in Sydney Harbour. 28.12.1911: Fire at Sydney. Damage was confined to the timber cargo. 15.11.1917: W.A. Firth died and probate granted to his widow, Mrs A.C. Firth. 10.2.1918: Sold to E.G. Weyland, Sydney. 2.9.1918: Sold to the Electrolytic Zinc Company of Australia Pty Ltd, Hobart, but remained registered at Sydney. 18.9.1919: Wrecked on Althorpe Island, South Australia, bound Port Pirie to Hobart with 700 tons of zinc concentrate. 11 crew were lost.

WAIMATE at Port Chalmers
(Otago Early Settlers' Museum/NZA)

## 31. WAIMATE (1896—1925)

Official Number: 105276
Tonnages: 5,610 gross, 3,629 net. Dimensions: 420.0 x 54.0 x 28.6 feet.
T.3 cyl. by the shipbuilders, 2,731 ihp, 62 rpm, 11.81 knots on trials.
Passengers: 12 1st class and 350 steerage.
Refrigerated space for 90,000 carcasses (221,600 cu.ft.)

11.7.1896: Launched by R. & W. Hawthorn, Leslie & Co. Ltd, Hebburn, (Yard No. 335), and ran trials on 2.10.1896. First registered at Plymouth on 7.10.1896 to J.B. Westray and W.C. Dawes. 2.1.1897: Ownership transferred to NZS. 31.1.1900: Left Wellington for South Africa with part of the 5th New Zealand Contingent to the Boer War. 3.12.1901: Suffered a fire in her flax cargo in Nos. 4 and 5 holds at Napier. It was extinguished after 3 days. 28.6.1902: Grounded on a mudbank at Auckland when leaving for Wellington. The action was taken to avoid another vessel and she was soon refloated and continued her voyage. 2.9.1904: Collided with the steamer MUNCHEN (4,536g, 1889) near the Owers Light in the River Thames. 16.1.1905: Suffered a fire in her flax cargo in No. 5 tween deck, bound Wellington to London. Put into Montevideo where she arrived on the 30th. 31.5.1906: Suffered a fire in her wool cargo in No. 4 hold which was smothered and she arrived at Teneriffe on 2.6.1906. She sailed again on the 3rd and the fire broke out once more on the 5th but she reached Plymouth safely on the 8th. 5.1.1910: Grounded in Barrow Deep, Thames Estuary, inward bound. 16.12.1910: Burst a steam pipe when leaving Sydney for Auckland. She returned for repairs and sailed again on the 18th. 22.5.1914: Suffered a fire in her wool, hemp and tow cargoes in 57°17'S-79°51'W, bound New Zealand to London. She put into Port Stanley on the 26th where the fire was extinguished 2 days later. 1.3.1917: Collided with the steamer ARAHURA (1,596g, 1905) in the Gisborne roadstead, as she left for Auckland. 29.8.1917 – 6.5.1919: Taken up under the Liner Requisition Scheme. 18.5.1925: Sold to S.A. Alti Forni Fonderei Acciaierie e Ferriere Franchi Gregorini, Genoa. 18.6.1925: Wrecked 5 miles north-east of Cape St. Vincent, bound Glasgow to Genoa with coal on her last voyage prior to demolition.

# Chapter 4: Expanding Empire and the First World War

The second half of the 1890's and the years of the 20th century leading up to the outbreak of the First World War were generally a period of economic recovery and unbroken prosperity in New Zealand. The development of the Company's ships and services reflect this encouraging background. It was the era when coal was king, and Dawes became increasingly unhappy with the dependence on other concerns for the supply of bunkers to the Company's ships in New Zealand. At first this was dealt with by the acquisition through the English associated company, the Black Ball Coal Mining Company of New Zealand Limited, of the Blackball coal mine on the west coast of the South Island and the provision of the feeder colliers PAREORA and HESKETH, owned by the parent company but chartered to Black Ball. Following the reconstruction of the company as the Blackball Coal Company Ltd, the ships involved were transferred to that company in 1903. (See Blackball chapter, P.181)    Another new direction for the Company came about by accident rather than design. In 1894 the AORANGI had been chartered to James Huddart of Melbourne who required a third ship for his Canadian Australian Royal Mail Line between Sydney and Vancouver. Huddart was continually short of ready cash for this service, and part of the charter payments were still outstanding when in 1896 the ship was sold to Huddart and underwent an expensive reconstruction and re-engining at Newcastle-on-Tyne. To protect its investment, NZS had been obliged to subscribe for shares in the company that Huddart formed in 1896 to take over the ships and service, the Canadian Australian Royal Mail Steamship Company Ltd, and to agree to leave the balance owing to it as a debt from the new company. There was no improvement in the results from the service during 1897, and considerable friction developed between Huddart and Dawes over the former's alleged failure to provide proper and adequate accounts.

WARRIMOO (35) at Port Chalmers in her original colours for James Huddart's New Zealand & Australasian Steam Ship Co.                    *(IJF)*

Matters came to a head at the end of the year when NZS as a principal creditor applied for a court order for winding up Canadian Australian R M S S Co. and in January 1898 was appointed manager by the Official Receiver. NZS was ill equipped for this new role. Its offices and infrastructure were in England and New Zealand, two centres at which the ships did not call. Burns, Philp & Company were appointed managing agents in Sydney, while Huddart's existing arrangements with the Canadian Pacific Railway at the Canadian end were continued. For want of any real alternative, NZS purchased the assets of Canadian Australian from the Receiver in August 1899, but Dawes' heart was never in an operation which he did not want and which had no real connection with NZS's services. The opportunity came at the end of 1900 when the Union Steam Ship Company of New Zealand Ltd, forced out of its San Francisco service by the American navigation laws, was seeking an alternative. With its already extensive Pacific services, Union was far better placed to control Canadian Australian, and in January 1901 agreed to purchase a half interest and assume the management. The remaining interest and ownership of the ships was acquired by Union over the following decade, leaving NZS to concentrate on its real interests.    A further debenture issue of £300,000 in August 1896 had provided a more solid base for NZS. It was a measure of the Company's rehabilitation in London financial circles that the issue was 50% oversubscribed. With this backing a programme to replace the original passenger steamers was undertaken resulting in the delivery over 1898/1902 of six new liners completed in pairs and rising in size from 6,582 to 8,027 tons gross. The three island hull of the RUAHINE was replaced by a flush deck design with prominent side houses near the bow and a double tier of deck houses amidships containing the main passenger accommodation. The principal innovation came with the second ship, the PAPAROA of 1899, which introduced twin engines and screws instead of the single plant in the PAPANUI the previous year. Broken shafts had been an ever present hazard on the long distances covered by the Company's ships, and the added security offered by a twin installation was a major reassurance to passengers, all the Company's subsequent passenger liners being so designed.

The cargo fleet received similar upgrading with the K twins of 1903 and the O trio of 1906/08, of equal size to the passenger fleet and all twin screw except for the last, the OTAKI, delivered by Dennys in 1908 as a triple screw vessel with a low pressure turbine driving the centre shaft and reciprocating engines on the wings. This combination machinery is now almost always associated with Harland & Wolff's Belfast yard and the major liners it built for the North Atlantic such as the White Star Line's OLYMPIC, TITANIC and BRITANNIC. It is often forgotten that it was

PAPAROA (37) in dock at Lyttelton

*(IJF)*

the New Zealand Shipping Company and Dennys who were responsible for the first ship of this type, its particular appeal to NZS being the added economy or extra power on the long ocean hauls without any increase in bunker requirements.

NZS was also actively pursuing new services for its cargo fleet in these years. Endeavours with various other companies to obtain New Zealand Government contracts for a service to South Africa came to nothing, perhaps fortunately in view of the unhappy experience of those that succeeded. More successful was a joint bid with Shaw Savill for a service from Montreal to New Zealand under contract to the Canadian Government, the first sailing being taken by the RAKAIA in June 1910. This could be seen as a successor to a much earlier but short-lived venture with the sailing fleet of a service to New York from New Zealand in 1889.

A development on a much more minor scale reflected the widespread building in New Zealand of small freezing works to serve local farming communities. NZS was involved with a number of these in the Gisborne area, but that coast offered no ports able to berth ships of the size of the Company's cargo carriers. The operation was a roadstead one, so to serve the deep water ships at anchor in Tokomaru or Tolaga Bays the Company established woolstores ashore and had built at Auckland two small wooden powered lighters, the KIRITONA of 1909 and KOUTUNUI of 1911. They were the only ships built for the Company in New Zealand and were subsequently chartered to, followed by eventual sale to, Richardson & Co. of Napier. NZS was also heavily involved with the development of the flax industry, centred around Foxton in the Manawatu.

The Company had failed in its bid for the New Zealand Government contract for a service from West Coast of England ports in 1903, the successful tenderer being a consortium of the Federal, Houlder and Scottish Shire Lines. Each of these companies had major interests in the Australian trade, though all were involved in New Zealand as well. 1911 was to prove a watershed year for all concerned. From its commencement, negotiations had been proceeding in utmost confidence between W.C. Dawes of NZS and Allan Hughes of Federal for an amalgamation of interests. Efforts became concentrated

KOUTUNUI (52) loading meat carcasses at Tokomaru Bay. The WAKANUI (34) awaits her cargo in the roadstead *(Auckland Museum/WAL)*

when it became known that J.R. Ellerman who had secured control of Shaw Savill the previous year was starting to buy NZS shares. Hughes had already in 1910 made a bid which would have secured control of the entire Houlder operation, but it was hotly disputed by some of the Houlder family and had to be withdrawn. Control of Houlders effectively passed to Furness Withy in July 1911, a concern that then had little interest in services to Australia. Agreement was reached in December 1911 for the acquisition by NZS of the Houlder Australian interests, and the following month the merger with Federal was made public.

This domino progress led to strained relations with Turnbull Martin & Company, the owners of the other partner in Federal-Houlder-Shire, and in July 1912 the former Houlder interest in the combination with the four ships involved was sold to the Union Steam Ship Company of New Zealand Ltd which had long been seeking a footing in the direct United Kingdom trade. Now named Federal-Shire, the combination continued as a three member operation, all with British territorial names - the Federal English counties, the Turnbull Martin Scottish shires and the Union Irish counties — though it was NZS which had given the former Houlder Granges their Irish names before the resale. It was an uneasy combination though as Turnbull Martin resented the perceived NZS/Federal dominance since Union was content to leave the management of a trade of which it had no experience largely in Federal hands. The Turnbull Martin unease was to erupt in acrimonious litigation during the First World War which dragged on into the mid 1920's after the combined service had effectively ceased.

Launch of the RUAHINE (50) at Dumbarton in 1909
*(NZA)*

During this corporate activity the Company had placed in service three new liners which marked the culmination of its own designed steam passenger vessels. All came from the Denny yard at Dumbarton, being successively the largest vessels completed by that builder and in that town and the first in the fleet to top 10,000 tons gross. The class began with the second RUAHINE in 1909 followed by the ROTORUA in 1910 and the REMUERA in 1911. Names beginning with R had been used for the middle pair of the 1898/1902 group; these deliveries confirmed the practice which was to be followed by the Company for all its subsequent passenger liners.

Accommodation for about 250 passengers in three classes was provided principally in three tiers of decks amidships, while the number could be doubled by temporary emigrant berths in the tween decks on outward voyages. A distinguishing feature, removed from the survivors after the war, was a yard on each mast extending the full beam. The final additions to the fleet pre war were the large cargo liners HURUNUI and HOROTATA, the latter being rigged with three masts. Both could carry 1000 emigrants in their tween decks when required.

Meanwhile as Hughes, who soon proved to be the driving force in the new NZS/Federal combine, was considering the future of the companies which he tended to see more through the eyes of the Federal Australian interest, relations with the New Zealand Board in Christchurch became rather strained. In an effort to pre-empt the locals, early in 1913 Hughes put out feelers to the Union Steam Ship Company of New Zealand Ltd for an amalgamation. The Union response was wary as it feared not only the prospect of control being moved to London, but even more the political repercussions which might flow from such a merger. Discussions were moving away from amalgamation towards the Union Company assuming the local management of NZS when the outbreak of the First World War diverted attention elsewhere.

Although losing three ships by torpedoing, it was surface raiders which dominated the NZS part in the First World War. It began early with the loss of the unarmed KAIPARA to the converted German liner KAISER WILHELM DER GROSSE as she made her way across the Atlantic only two weeks after the declaration of hostilities. It was an encounter of a far different kind in March 1917 when the OTAKI met the raider MOEWE and sailed herself into the legends of both NZS and the merchant service generally. In theory the two ships were completely mis-matched with the OTAKI's single 4.7 inch gun at the stern opposed to the raider's 4 5.9 inch and several smaller weapons.

OTAKI (48) discharging explosives off Motuihi Island, Hauraki Gulf, Auckland    *(Auckland Museum/WAL)*

Nevertheless such was the accuracy of the OTAKI's fire that before she was abandoned she had scored a number of hits causing fires to break out on the MOEWE. For his part in the action Captain A. Bisset Smith received the posthumous award of the Victoria Cross, and NZS established a scholarship in his memory under which pupils from his old school, Robert Gordon's Colleges at Aberdeen, were granted free passages in the Company's ships to New Zealand and supported during their study there. The Company was heavily involved with the movement of both troops and cargo from the beginning of the conflict. The RUAPEHU and ORARI were part of the Main Body convoy of troops that left New Zealand in October 1914, and among the transports with Australian troops which joined them in Albany was the HORORATA.

Two events with a profound impact on the Company's future occurred during the war years. The first was the opening of the Panama Canal. The OTAKI was the first Company ship to pass through it in May 1916 and from that year onward the outward and homeward passages through the Southern Ocean were abandoned and voyages in both directions were made via Panama. The second event was the takeover by P&O. Frustrated in his negotiations with the Union Company, Hughes had turned elsewhere. With financial control of the Company already in London, there was no delay in communication to the other side of the world, and given the strong Dawes connection linking NZS with British India which had already merged with P&O in 1914, there was an obvious already existing commonality of interests. On 1 July 1916 the announcement was made of the P&O offer of £10 of its deferred stock for each £10 NZS share. By September the deal was concluded and NZS/Federal were henceforth to be part of a much wider group though in conformity with standard Inchcape practice they were left very much to run their own affairs under the guidance of Allan Hughes, who was described in the P&O minutes as "an exceptionally capable businessman". The P&O Chairman, Lord Inchcape, emphasised that he personally would receive nothing by way of honorarium — "Not a farthing will pass", though acknowledging his expectation of increasing reward from his position in the British India managing partnership. Because of wartime conditions though, the putting into operation of the planned changes following the takeover had to be postponed to the coming of peace.

## Ships 32 to 59: HESKETH—HORORATA

### 32. HESKETH (1896—1899)

Official Number: 89225
Tonnages: 640 gross, 393 net. Dimensions: 180.4 x 28.1 x 13.6 feet.
Twin screw, One C.2-cyl. by Kincaid & Co., Greenock, each cylinder driving its own shaft, 80 nhp, 10 knots.

HESKETH at Greymouth                    (WAL)

*6.1883:* Launched by the Queenstown & Passage West Docks Co., Cork, (Yard No. 2), for the Australasian Steam Navigation Company, Sydney. *24.1.1887:* Transferred to James Munro and then from 23.2.1887 to Duncan Mackinnon & G.S. Mackenzie, all on behalf of the British India & Queensland Agency Company Ltd, Brisbane, but remained registered at Sydney. *27.4.1887:* Transferred to the Australasian United Steam Navigation Company Ltd, Brisbane, remaining registered at Sydney. *14.7.1890:* Collided with and sank the steamer ROYAL SHEPHERD (269g, 1853) off Sydney Heads. *12.1894:* Chartered to the Black Ball Coal Mining Company of New Zealand Ltd, London, for operation on the New Zealand coast. *11.1896:* Sold for £4,000 to NZS, remaining chartered to Black Ball but registry was transferred to London in 7.1897. *26.10.1899:* Grounded 200 yards north of the North Tip Head, at the entrance to Greymouth when inward bound from Lyttelton. She was driven broadside on and was abandoned to the underwriters on 27.10.1899. The wreck was sold to a Greymouth syndicate for £197 on 6.11.1899.

### 33. PAPANUI (1898—1910)

Official Number: 108562
Tonnages: 6,372 gross, 4,099 net, 9,440 deadweight. Dimensions: 430.0 x 54.1 x 30.1 feet. Draft: 27.0 feet.
T.3 cyl. by Denny & Co., Dumbarton, 4,124 ihp. 70.5 rpm, 13.64 knots on trials.
Passengers: 34 1st class, 45 2nd class, 400 steerage.
Refrigerated space for 100,000 carcasses (225,900 cu.ft.)

*1.11.1898:* Launched by Wm Denny & Bros, Dumbarton, (Yard No. 602), and delivered 26.12.1898 to NZS at a cost of £90,700. Left London on her first New Zealand sailing to Wellington on 12.1.1899. *18.3.1901:* Arrived at Vigo with the French barque MARTHE MARGUERITE (592g, 1884), disabled after losing her rudder, in tow. *22.9.1901:* Put into Vigo with a bunker fire, bound New Zealand to Plymouth. *28.4.1909:* Suffered a minor fire in Victoria Dock, London. 38,000 carcasses were destroyed and 1 life lost. *13.12.1909:* Struck a rock off North Waterhouse Island, inward bound to Beauty Point, Tasmania, and after repairs there arrived at Melbourne on 19.1.1910. *23.5.1910:* Sold at auction to H.A. Visbord, Melbourne, but the sale fell through. *5.7.1910:* Registry transferred to Melbourne by NZS. *13.10.1910:* Sold at a second auction and registered on 14.10.1910 to J. Paterson, Melbourne. *21.11.1910:* Registration closed and re-registered in Nicaragua to enable the ship to leave Melbourne in an unseaworthy state. The Premier of Victoria was reported as saying that he could not stop her as there was no warship in port and he had no control over her crew of Filipinos. *5.12.1910:* Left Melbourne without a pilot for Nagasaki. She was later reported passing Sydney "with a large hole in her bottom and floating on her double bottom tanks". She arrived at Nagasaki
*Continued overleaf*

### 33. PAPANUI — continued

PAPANUI leaving Wellington       (ATL/NZA)

on 3.1.1911. *17.4.1911:* Arrived back at Melbourne from Nagasaki via Hobart and registered at Melbourne on 21.4.1911 to H.C. Sleigh and H.B. Black. *1911:* Carried passengers from Melbourne to London for the coronation of King George V. *5.9.1911:* Suffered a fire in the bunker coal in No. 3 hold, bound London to Cape Town and Fremantle with 364 emigrants and 108 crew. She arrived at St Helena on the 11th and was beached in Jamestown Bay, being abandoned the next day. The fire was reported to be out on the 19th. The passengers were picked up by the OPAWA (No. 47) on October 14th and taken to Cape Town. A plaque on the library wall at Jamestown recorded the thanks of the rescued to the islanders for looking after them for 5 weeks.

WAKANUI arriving at Wellington       (IJF)

## 34. WAKANUI (1899—1913)

Official Number: 108566
Tonnages: 5,824 gross, 3,256 net. Dimensions: 420.0 x 54.0 x 28.6 feet.
T.3 cyl. by the shipbuilders, 3,500 ihp, 13 knots. 1919: New boilers.
Passengers: 26 1st class and 350 steerage.
Refrigerated space for 90,000 carcasses (221,300 cu.ft.)

*15.11.1898:* Launched by R. & W. Hawthorn, Leslie & Co. Ltd, Hebburn, (Yard No. 360), and ran trials 25.2.1899. Cost £74,000. First registered at Plymouth to J.B. Westray and W.C. Dawes on 25.2.1899. *14.8.1899:* Transferred to NZS. *1.2.1901:* Grounded while inward bound in the Thames. *27.2.1906:* Suffered damage to a main engine cylinder 300 miles north of the Cape Verde Islands. Arrived at St Vincent on 2.3.1906. *1.1.1908:* Struck by the steamer HUGO (1,422g, 1907) while berthed at Hull. *16.3.1911:* Arrived at Saint John, N.B., after grounding in the approaches. *15.9.1912:* Suffered a fire in No. 4 hold at Montreal. *3.2.1913:* Sold for £40,000 to the Brodmead Steamship Company Ltd, then transferred on 8.4.1913 to the Brodmount

Steamship Company Ltd, London, (Blue Star Line Ltd, managers) having been renamed BRODMOUNT on 1.4.1913. *29.5.1917—16.5.1919:* Taken up under the Liner Requisition Scheme. *23.1.1920:* Renamed STUARTSTAR. *14.4.1920:* Transferred to the Union Cold Storage Company Ltd, (Blue Star Line (1920) Ltd, managers). *4.10.1923:* Grounded at the Hook of Holland, inward bound from Zarate, Argentina, to Rotterdam with frozen meat. She was moved by a heavy swell onto a connection dam to the New Waterway breakwater on 19.12.1923 and abandoned as a total loss. The remains were removed by explosives by order of the Dutch Government.

WARRIMOO in Union Company colours          *(WAL)*

## 35. WARRIMOO (1899—1901)

Official Number: 101901
Tonnages: 3,526 gross, 1,897 net. Dimensions: 345.0 x 42.2 x 25.1 feet.
T.3 cyl. by the Wallsend Slipway & Engineering Co. Ltd, Wallsend, 4,000 ihp, 15 knots.
Passengers: 233 1st and 127 2nd class. 1895: 112 1st and 60 2nd class.
Refrigerated space (from 1895): 18,000 cu.ft.

*28.5.1892:* Launched by C.S. Swan & Hunter, Wallsend, (Yard No. 175), for the New Zealand & Australasian Steam Ship Co., London & Melbourne, (James Huddart, manager). Ran trials on 23.7.1892 when averaged 17 knots. Registered at London. *3.9.1892:* Left London for Sydney and 15.10.1892 left Sydney for Auckland on her first trans-Tasman voyage. *4.1893:* Transferred to the Canadian Australian Royal Mail Line, London & Sydney, (James Huddart, manager) and left Sydney on her first voyage to Vancouver on 17.6.1893. *9.8.1895:* Grounded on Carmanah Point, inward bound to Vancouver from Honolulu. Refloated the same day; repairs were carried out at Sydney. *17.3.1897:* Transferred to the Canadian Australian Royal Mail Steamship Co. Ltd, London. *2.1898:* Management taken over by NZS which assumed control of the Line on behalf of the Receiver. *16.8.1899:* Sold to NZS. *3.1901:* Sold to the Union Steam Ship Company of New Zealand Ltd, Dunedin, and transferred to trans-Tasman service. *8.3.1905:* Fire broke out in the forehold 8 miles off Cape Schanck, bound Melbourne to Hobart. She returned to Melbourne where the cargo was found to be badly damaged. *25.11.1905:* Collided with and sank the tug SQUIRREL, (32g, 1884), off Goat Island, Sydney Harbour, when outward bound for Wellington. The WARRIMOO was undamaged, but the tug was raised and broken up as a total loss. *15.9.1907:* Ashore near Cape Farewell, bound Lyttelton to Newcastle, N.S.W. Towed off by the steamer ROTOITI (1,159g,

1898) on the 16th and proceeded to Port Chalmers for inspection and repair. *14.10.1907:* Grounded on a sandbank at Bluff, outward bound for Melbourne. Refloated undamaged. *31.3.1909:* Went aground in Otago harbour while passing the dredge No. 404 (478g, 1893), outward bound to Sydney. Refloated on the rising tide the same day. *15.11.1909:* Fire broke out in No. 1 hold while berthed at Dunedin and the hold had to be flooded to extinguish it. The cargo was seriously damaged. *20.12.1909:* Touched on a mudbank at Bluff, outward bound for Dunedin. Refloated undamaged. *9.3.1911:* Ashore on a mudbank at Newcastle. Refloated undamaged. *10.7.1911:* Collided with the steamer ARCHER (694g, 1882) when berthing at Newcastle. No damage. *15.7.1912:* Deck fittings were damaged and the smokeroom flooded in a gale, bound Sydney to Wellington. *8.9.1914:* Collided with Queens Wharf, Wellington, when berthing from Sydney. 16 feet was cut off the corner of the wharf but the ship was undamaged. *18.11.1914:* Stranded at Bluff but refloated undamaged. *1915-1916:* Served as a New Zealand transport making 3 voyages to Suez. *18.10.1916:* Sold to Khiam Yik & Co. Ltd, Singapore, (Tan Kah Kee, manager) and delivered to the purchaser on 29.1.1917. *18.5.1918:* Collided with the escorting destroyer CATAPULTE (300 tons, 1903) 12 miles S.W. of La Galite, Algeria, bound Singapore to Marseilles with 1,700 Chinese troops. Her bottom was blown out when depth charges from the destroyer exploded and she sank with the loss of 1 life.

MIOWERA at Sydney in Union Company colours *(IJF)*

## 36. MIOWERA (1899—1908)

Official Number: 101935
Tonnages: 3,345 gross, 1,911 net. Dimensions: 345.0 x 42.2 x 25.1 feet.
T.3 cyl. by the Wallsend Slipway & Engineering Co. Ltd, Wallsend, 4,000 ihp, 15 knots.
Passengers: 233 1st and 127 2nd class passengers.
Refrigerated space (from 1894): 18,000 cu.ft.

*27.5.1892:* Launched by C.S. Swan & Hunter, Wallsend, (Yard No. 176), for the New Zealand & Australasian Steam Ship Co., London & Melbourne, (James Huddart, manager). Completed 8.10.1892 and registered at London. *25.10.1892:* Left London for Sydney and 17.12.1892 left Sydney for Auckland on her first trans-Tasman voyage. *4.1893:* Transferred to the Canadian Australasian Royal Mail Line, London & Sydney, (James Huddart, manager) and left Sydney on 18.5.1893 on her first sailing to Vancouver. *2.10.1893:* Grounded at Honolulu, bound Sydney to Vancouver. Refloated on 23.10.1893 and arrived at Esquimalt on 6.2.1894. After temporary repairs there, she then returned to her builders for permanent repairs and the installation of refrigerated space. *6—8.1894:* Made 3 cruises to the Norwegian fjords. *31.7.1894:* Ran aground on an uncharted rock at Askevold near the entrance to Dalsfjord while on a cruise. She was beached and the passengers put ashore, but was then refloated and returned to the builders for further repairs. *1.9.1894:* Left London for Sydney where she re-entered the Vancouver service. *13.5.1895:* Arrived at Vancouver having broken the high pressure piston and completing the last 1,200 miles from Honolulu partly with the main engine compounded and partly under sail. *26.1.1896:* Suffered an engine breakdown soon after leaving Sydney for Vancouver and returned to port the same day for repairs. *17.3.1897:* Transferred to the Canadian Australian Royal Mail Steamship Co. Ltd, London. *16.9.1897:* Suffered gale damage, bound Sydney to Wellington with cabin doors and boats smashed. *2.1898:* Management taken over by NZS which assumed control of the Line on behalf of the Receiver. *16.8.1899:* Sold to NZS. *4.1901:* Chartered to and a half share sold to the Union Steam Ship Company of New Zealand Ltd, Dunedin, which became the managers. *27.10.1904:* Grounded on a sandbank in English Bay when arriving at Vancouver from Sydney. 10 plates had to be replaced. *2.1908:* The remaining half share was sold for £7,000 to the Union Steam Ship Company which renamed the vessel MAITAI. *7.5.1908:* Sprang a leak through a fractured plate, bound Melbourne to Hobart and docked at Hobart for repairs on the 12th. *6.2.1910:* Damaged the piston rod of the high pressure cylinder, bound Wellington to Sydney where repairs were completed on arrival. *8.5.1910:* Cabins and alleyways were flooded by heavy seas, bound Sydney to Wellington. *16.11.1910:* Left Wellington on her first voyage in the Sydney—San Francisco service. *30.5.1913:* Cabins, saloons and engineroom were partly flooded by heavy seas off Portland Island, bound Napier to Gisborne. *19.8.1913:* Suffered engine damage at Wellington. *14.8.1914:* Registry transferred to London for war risk insurance purposes. *25.12.1916:* Wrecked on the South Reef at Avarua, Rarotonga, due to the anchor cable parting, bound San Francisco to Wellington.

PAPAROA at Wellington

*(WAL)*

## 37. PAPAROA (1899–1926)

Official Number: 111346
Tonnages: 6,563 gross, 4,262 net, 8,360 deadweight. Dimensions: 430.0 x 54.2 x 30.0 feet.
Twin screw, two T.3 cyl. by Denny & Co., Dumbarton, 3,551 ihp, 75 rpm, 13.6 knots on trials, 1,446 tons coal fuel.
Passengers: 37 1st class, 40 2nd class and 78 3rd class. 1911: Reduced to 3rd class only. 1921: 2nd and 3rd class.
Refrigerated space: 100,000 carcasses (226,500 cu.ft.)

23.8.1899: Launched by Wm Denny & Bros, Dumbarton, (Yard No. 613), and delivered on 19.10.1899 at a cost of £108,400. First registered at Plymouth that day in names of J.B. Westray and W.C. Dawes. 9.11.1899: Left London on her first New Zealand sailing to Wellington. 21.5.1900: Ownership transferred to NZS. 26.10.1902: Suffered a bunker fire at Montevideo, bound Wellington to London. 18.12.1908: Suffered a fire in her bunkers and in No. 3 hold, bound Wellington to London. Put into St Vincent on the 26th, the hold was flooded on the 29th and she sailed again on the 30th. 17.5.1916: Suffered a cargo fire at New York. 17.7.1917 – 25.2.1919: Taken up under the Liner

Requisition Scheme. 21.11.1917: Suffered a bunker fire at London. 27.3.1919: Suffered a fire in the engineroom at Glasgow while loading for New Zealand. 26.5.1921: Re-entered the main passenger service from Southampton until reverted to the secondary service in 1923. 17.3.1926: Caught fire in the bunkers and No. 3 hold off St Helena (29°38'S-14°02'E), bound Liverpool to Brisbane and abandoned. She was scuttled by HMS BIRMINGHAM (5,440 tons, 1914) as a danger to navigation in 28°26'S-13°42'E on 18.3.1926. The passengers and crew were taken on board the P&O steamer BARRABOOL (13,148g, 1922) and landed at Cape Town.

WHAKATANE at Adelaide

(IJF)

## 38. WHAKATANE (1900–1924)

Official Number: 111348
Tonnages: 5,715 gross, 3,659 net. Dimensions: 420.0 x 54.0 x 28.7 feet.
T.3 cyl. by the shipbuilders, 3,500 ihp, 13 knots.
Passengers: 26 1st class and 350 steerage (to 1920).
Refrigerated space for 90,000 carcasses (221,000 cu.ft.)

3.11.1899: Launched by R. & W. Hawthorn, Leslie & Co. Ltd, Hebburn, (Yard No. 372), and delivered 23.1.1900. Registered at Plymouth in the names of J.B. Westray & W.C. Dawes. 2.8.1901: Ownership transferred to NZS. 3.1902: Suffered a fire in wool trans-shipped from the WAIMATE (No. 31), bound Napier to Wellington. 2.9.1902: Grounded on leaving Bluff for Timaru. 4.9.1902: Touched ground lightly 1½ miles north of Timaru, inward bound in heavy fog. 2.5.1904: Collided with the steamer RANGOON (3,891g, 1897) while sailing from London. 19.1.1905: Arrived at Teneriffe with steering gear disabled and rammed by the steamer ATHENIC (12,234g, 1901) while berthed there on the 20th. 4.10.1905: Run into by the steamer MERION (11,621g, 1902) while berthed at Liverpool. 25.9.1906: Suffered a fire in the forehold while berthed in Poplar Dock, London. 4.7.1909: In collision in fog with the steamer CIRCE (2,770g, 1891) off Dungeness. She was towed to Dover and beached. 15.4.1910:

Collided with the steamer DETTINGEN (4,221g, 1899) in Victoria Dock, London. 3.5.1911: Steering gear carried away in a gale off Cuvier Island bound Tokomaru Bay to Auckland and completed the voyage under jury rig. 28.9.1912: Grounded at Port Pirie endeavouring to avoid collision with a collier. 3.9.1913: Collided with the wharf and grounded while arriving in fog at Quebec from Sydney, C.B. 26.12.1915: Collided with the steamer REPTON (2,881g, 1894) in the Downs. 28.8.1917 – 26.9.1919: Taken up under the Liner Requisition Scheme. 1920–1924: Served as a cadet ship for 20 cadets. 18.5.1921: Collided with the steamer ADMIRAL CODRINGTON (6,629g, 1918) off Gisborne after her anchor dragged in a gale. She proceeded to Auckland for repairs. 13.3.1924: Sold for £30,000 to S.A. Nav. Alta Italia, Genoa, and renamed MONCENISIO. 4.1929: Sold to Soc. Italiana di Nav. e Transporti, Genoa, arrived at Savona 24.4.1929 and broken up later that year.

## 39. PETONE (1900–1903)

Official Number: 112654
Tonnages: 708 gross, 388 net. Dimensions: 185.4 x 29.2 x 11.8 feet.
T.3 cyl. by McKie & Baxter, Glasgow, 500 ihp, 9 knots.

6.11.1899: Launched by Taylor & Mitchell, Greenock, (Yard No. 3), and completed 1.1.1900 for John White, London as GRESHAM. 6.2.1900: Sold for £13,400 to NZS and renamed PETONE for

charter to the Blackball Coal Co. Ltd. 7.1903: Sold for £13,725 to the Blackball Coal Co. Ltd, London & Christchurch. 4.11.1904: Broke her shaft off Cape Egmont, bound Wellington to Kaipara.

*Continued overleaf*

### 39. PETONE — continued

*14.9.1906:* Discovered on arrival at Greymouth that the crowns of the boiler furnaces were sagging. Left Greymouth 19.9.1906 in tow of the tug DUCO (130g, 1892) for Wellington for repairs. *15.8.1908:* Broke her crankshaft 3 hours after leaving Lyttelton for Greymouth and was towed back to port by the tug LYTTELTON (193g, 1878) the next day. *9.9.1908:* Machinery damage off Cape Foulwind. *1910:* Sold to James Watt, London. *25.10.1910:* Sold to the Canterbury Steam Shipping Co. Ltd, Lyttelton. *28.6.1913:* Fractured her tail shaft off Timaru and towed into port by the dredge No. 350 (941g, 1906). She was towed to Lyttelton for permanent repairs on 29.6.1913 by the steamer BREEZE (547g, 1909). *8.3.1916:* Sold to John Montgomery & R. C. Todhunter, Lyttelton. *1.9.1916:* Sold to Cunningham, Shaw & Co. Ltd, London, (V.S. Lovell, manager), but remained registered at Lyttelton. *1917:* Sold to the Petone Shipping Co. Ltd, Cardiff, but registered at London. *1917:* Sold to the Zenith Steam Shipping Co. Ltd, Cardiff, and remained registered at London, (Loane, Williams & Co., managers). *9.9.1918 — 31.3.1919:* Requisitioned to carry coal. *8.10.1921:* Went ashore 4 miles east of Fecamp in fog, bound Blyth to Rouen. She was refloated on the 9th. *10.10.1921:* Sold to the Bennett Steam Ship Co. Ltd, Goole, and renamed SPARTA. *17.6.1940:* Evacuated troops from Brest to Falmouth. *10.3.1941:*

Mined and sunk in 50°55'N-00°35'E, bound Blyth to Southampton with 750 tons of coal. 9 of her crew were lost.

PETONE, right, at Picton in Canterbury S.S. Co. ownership. RUAPEHU (41) is on the far side of the wharf *(Marlborough Historical Society)*

RIMUTAKA at Nelson                                                                 *(WAL)*

## 40. RIMUTAKA (1900—1930)

Official Number: 111355
Tonnages: 7,765 gross, 4,983 net, 9,570 deadweight. Dimensions: 457.7 x 58.2 x 30.8 feet.
Twin screw, two T.3 cyl. by Denny & Co., Dumbarton, 4,740 ihp, 79 rpm, 13.8 knots on trials. 1,700 tons coal fuel.
Passengers: 40 1st, 50 2nd and 80 3rd class. 170 steerage. 1911: Reduced to 3rd class only. 1920: 2nd and 3rd class.
Refrigerated space: 263,000 cu.ft., increased to 331,900 cu.ft. in 1919.

*11.10.1900:* Launched by Wm Denny & Bros, Dumbarton, (Yard No. 634), and delivered 15.12.1900 at a cost of £142,900. First registered at Plymouth on 1.1.1901 to J.B. Westray & W.C. Dawes. *3.1.1901:* Sailed from London on her first New Zealand voyage to Wellington. *16.3.1901:* Ownership transferred to NZS. *31.8.1902:* Suffered a fire bound Teneriffe to London. *23.6.1906:* Suffered a fire in her wool cargo in No. 5 hold in Victoria Dock, London. *27.11.1908:* Collided with the steamer DRUMLANRIG (4,306g, 1906) off the East Goodwin Lightvessel, collided with the East Pier as she put into Dover where she was beached. *17.2.1915:* Arrived at Dakar with a fire in No. 3 hold. The hold was flooded and the fire extinguished by the following day.

*27.7.1917 — 16.9.1919:* Taken up under the Liner Requisition Scheme. *27.12.1917:* Arrived at Aden with a fire in her bunkers and in No. 3 hold which had to be flooded. 2 lives were lost. *23.12.1920:* Returned to the passenger service from Southampton to New Zealand, her last sailing being from London on 15.11.1929. *5.11.1926:* Suffered a fire in No. 1 tween deck bound Auckland to Panama. *24.4.1928:* Burst a main steam pipe and had to put into Bahia for repairs. *23.6.1929:* Collided with the steamer MARGHA (8,278g, 1917). *29.4.1930:* Sold for £14,000 to T.W. Ward Ltd and broken up at Pembroke Dock where work began on 5.5.1930.

RUAPEHU at Lyttelton                                    (IJF)

## 41. RUAPEHU (1901—1931)

Official Number: 111357
Tonnages: 7,705 gross, 4,943 net, 9,320 deadweight. Dimensions: 457.3 x 58.2 x 30.8 feet. Draft: 27.5 feet.
Twin screw, two T.3 cyl. by Denny & Co, Dumbarton, 5,045 ihp, 83 rpm, 14.33 knots on trials. 1,700 tons coal fuel.
Passengers: 40 1st, 50 2nd and 90 3rd class. 170 steerage to 1906. 1911: 2nd and 3rd class only.
Refrigerated space: 283,000 cu.ft.

*21.2.1901:* Launched by Wm Denny & Bros, Dumbarton, (Yard No. 639), and delivered on 18.4.1901 at a cost of £147,000. Registered at Plymouth on 20.4.1901 in the names of J.B. Westray and W.C. Dawes. *5—11.1901:* Chartered to the Allan Line Steamship Co. Ltd, Glasgow, and made 5 round voyages to Canada. She was renamed AUSTRALASIAN while on charter from 18.5.1901 to 25.11.1901. *5.12.1901:* Left London on her first New Zealand sailing to Wellington. *2.6.1902:* Grounded briefly off West Africa, bound London to Wellington. *12.10.1904:* Collided successively in fog in the Thames with the spritsail barge ALBERT, (52 tons, 1865), the LOCH ELVIE and the ketch THOMAS STRATTEN (68 tons, 1871) and a barge. *17.3.1905:* 48 shares were transferred to NZS, the remaining 16 following on 19.3.1906. *16.10.1914—3.12.1914:* Sailed with the Main Body of New Zealand troops in the first convoy from Wellington to Alexandria via Albany. *21.1.1915:* In collision at Cardiff, bound London to Lyttelton. *2.6.1917—22.5.1919:* Taken up under the Liner Requisition Scheme. *12.8.1917:* Suffered a bunker fire at Auckland. *3.12.1918:* Suffered a fire in a storeroom while in drydock in the Royal Albert Dock, London. *13.10.1920:* Suffered a fire in No. 4 tween deck at Lyttelton. *14.1.1921:* Resumed

passenger sailings to New Zealand, her last being from London on 20.12.1930. *15.5.1925:* Suffered a fire in drydock at Millwall, London. It began in No. 3 hold and spread to Nos. 1 and 2 holds and the bridge. *29.4.1931:* Laid up at Falmouth. *5.8.1931:* Sold for £5,000 to S.A. Cant. di Porto Venere for breaking up. While in course of demolition at Savona on 10.9.1931 she damaged a wharf in a gale.

RUAPEHU in Wellington harbour as HMNZT No. 5, October 1914        (WAL)

TONGARIRO leaving Wellington                          (ATL/WAL)

## 42. TONGARIRO (1901—1916)

Official Number: 111356
Tonnages: 7,600 gross, 4,917 net.
Dimensions: 457.0 x 58.0 x 30.5 feet. Draft: 29.5 feet.
Twin screw, two T.3 cyl. by the shipbuilders, 5,000 ihp, 14 knots.
Passengers: 40 1st, 50 2nd and 80 3rd class. 179 steerage. 1911: 2nd and 3rd class only.
Refrigerated space: 273,900 cu.ft.

*24.11.1900:* Launched by R. & W. Hawthorn, Leslie & Co. Ltd, Hebburn, (Yard No. 358), and completed in 2.1901. Registered

at Plymouth 23.2.1901 in the names of J.B. Westray & W.C. Dawes. She had been laid down as RANGITIKEI. *26.2.1901:* Left

*Continued overleaf*

### 42. TONGARIRO — continued

London with troops for Cape Town. *16.3.1901:* Took in tow the disabled steamer NORHAM CASTLE (4,392g, 1883) and arrived with her at Ascension on the 18th. *31.3.1901:* Sailed from Cape Town with returning troops for Fremantle, Sydney and New Zealand. *9.12.1901:* Sailed from London for Auckland on her first normal New Zealand voyage. *18.3.1902:* 32 shares were transferred to NZS, with a further 16 on 7.4.1904 and the remaining 16 on 16.3.1905. *1911:* Reduced to secondary passenger services. *6.10.1911:* Struck the Standard Oil pier at Purfleet and grounded inward bound in the River Thames from Newcastle. *30.8.1916:* Grounded on Bull Rock, Portland Island, Hawkes Bay, bound London, Newport News and Auckland to Wellington with general cargo. She broke in two on 6.9.1916 after 300 tons of cargo had been salved and completely disintegrated on the 14th.

TURAKINA leaving Wellington

*(ATL/IJF)*

## 43. TURAKINA (1902—1917)

Official Number: 114620
Tonnages: 8,210 gross, 5,289 net.
Dimensions: 473.0 x 59.6 x 31.0 feet. Draft: 29.5 feet.
Twin screw, two T.3 cyl. by the shipbuilders, 5,000 ihp, 14 knots.
Passengers: 40 1st, 54 2nd and 74 3rd class. 170 steerage.
Refrigerated space: 294,000 cu.ft.

*23.4.1902:* Launched by R. & W. Hawthorn, Leslie & Co. Ltd, Hebburn, (Yard No. 382), and completed in 8.1902 at a cost of £158,000. Registered at Plymouth on 26.8.1902 in the names of J.B. Westray & W.C. Dawes. *2.9.1902:* Left London on her first New Zealand sailing to Wellington. *16.3.1905:* 40 shares were transferred to NZS, the remaining 24 following on 19.3.1906. *27.10.1905:* Suffered a fire in the flax cargo in No.4 hold at Wellington. *25.5.1907:* Struck the dock wall in the Royal Albert Dock, London. *26.9.1907:* Left Auckland for London and 3 days later a fire broke out in the flax and tow cargo in No. 1 hold. She put back to Wellington, arriving on 4.10.1907, assisted by the tug TERAWHITI (260g, 1907). *4.3.1913:* Fire broke out in the bunkers and No. 3 hold as she left Rio de Janeiro. The hold was flooded and she was beached on the 6th when fire was also found in No. 2 hold which was also flooded on the 7th. The fire was out by the 10th by which time No. 1 hold was also affected and further smoulder fires broke out in Nos.1, 2 and 3 holds as cargo was discharged on the 14th. Most of the refrigerated cargo was spoiled. The ship was refloated on 25.3.1913 and sailed on 23.4.1913 for Britain for repairs. *5.8.1917:* Taken up under the Liner Requisition Scheme. *13.8.1917:* Torpedoed by U 86 120 miles south-west of the Scilly Isles (48°30'N-08°34'W) bound London to New York and New Zealand in ballast. Four of the crew were lost.

## 44. KAIKOURA (1903—1926)

Official Number: 114629
Tonnages: 6,998 gross, 4,477 net. Dimensions: 460.0 x 58.2 x 30.9 feet.
Twin screw two T.3 cyl. by the shipbuilders, 4,500 ihp, 14.3 knots on trials.
Passengers: 22 1st class and 200 steerage.
Refrigerated space: 281,500 cu.ft.

*27.6.1903:* Launched by John Brown & Co. Ltd, Clydebank, (Yard No. 360), and ran trials on 11.9.1903. Registered at Plymouth on 11.9.1903 to J.B. Westray & W.C. Dawes. *29.11.1907:* Grounded at Harington Bend, Otago Harbour, inward bound to Port Chalmers from London. After lightening, refloated the same day. *8.4.1911:* Ownership transferred to NZS. *17.8.1917—1.8.1919:* Taken up under the Liner Requisition Scheme. *10.5.1919:* Run into by the lighter AGNES MARTIN (41g, 1882) at Napier. A small fire was caused but soon extinguished. *9.4.1923:* Suffered a fire in the wool and tallow cargo in No. 4 hold, bound Wellington to Opua. Arrived at Auckland on the 10th where the fire was put out. *13.9.1924:* Suffered a fire in the copra cargo in Nos.4 and 5 shelter decks at Wellington. *12.11.1925:* Collided with the steamer HALO (2,365g, 1919) in the Thames, inward bound from Avonmouth. *12.8.1926:* Sold to Ditta L. Pittaluga, Genoa, and renamed GIANO on 16.8.1926. *1927:* Renamed FERRANIA; same owner. *1929:* Sold to Neomontana S.A. and arrived at Savona 1.3.1929 for demolition.

KAIKOURA at Wellington

(ATL/NZA)

KAIPARA at Port Chalmers

(WAL)

## 45. KAIPARA (1903—1914)

Official Number: 114630
Tonnages: 7,596 gross, 4,886 net. Dimensions: 460.4 x 58.2 x 30.9 feet.
Twin screw, two T.3 cyl. by the shipbuilders, 4,500 ihp, 14.4 knots on trials.
Passengers: 22 1st class and 200 steerage.
Refrigerated space: 281,500 cu.ft.

*9.9.1903:* Launched by John Brown & Co. Ltd, Clydebank, (Yard No. 361), and ran trials on 11.11.1903. Registered at Plymouth on 3.11.1903 to J.B. Westray & W.C. Dawes. *17.6.1905:* Grazed a patch of coral off Ascension Island, bound London to Port Chalmers. *8.9.1908:* Touched by the steamer WAIKARE (3,071g, 1897) at Wellington while the WAIKARE was leaving port. Minor damage only. *14.1.1910:* Grounded in Rangitoto Channel, leaving Auckland for London. Refloated on the 20th and beached in Hobson Bay. Again refloated on the 26th and docked for repairs at Auckland on the 27th. *12.4.1910:* Suffered a bunker fire at Auckland. It was put out on the 14th. *8.4.1911:* Ownership transferred to NZS. *16.8.1914:* Captured by the German raider KAISER WILHELM DER GROSSE (13,952g, 1897) 170 miles south-west of Teneriffe when bound Lyttelton to Liverpool and London, and sunk by gunfire and scuttling charges in 25°10'N-17°18'W.

KAIPARA ashore in Rangitoto Channel, Auckland in 1910

(WAL)

ORARI at Wellington

*(ATL/NZA)*

## 46. ORARI (1906—1927)

Official Number: 119350
Tonnages: 7,207 gross, 4,564 net, 10,690 deadweight. Dimensions: 460.7 x 60.2 x 31.3 feet. Draft: 28.6 feet.
Twin screw, two T.3 cyl. by Denny & Co., Dumbarton, 5,386 ihp, 83 rpm, 14.64 knots on trials. 2,070 tons of coal fuel.
Passengers: 6 1st class.
Refrigerated space: 286,650 cu.ft.

*25.6.1906:* Launched by Wm Denny & Bros, Dumbarton, (Yard No. 769), and ran trials on 13.9.1906. Cost £113,700. Registered at Plymouth on 21.9.1906 to G.T. Haycraft & T.R Westray. *5.7.1908:* Ownership transferred to NZS. *16.8.1909:* Collided with the barque LOUDON HILL (2,139g, 1887) off Flores Island, Montevideo and repaired there. *1.1.1912:* Collided with and sank the tug ATLAS (259g, 1907) while leaving Antwerp. *9.4.1914:* Grounded at Montevideo, outward bound for London. Refloated undamaged with the help of 4 tugs. *16.10.1914:* Sailed with the Main Body of New Zealand troops in the first convoy from Wellington to Alexandria via Albany. *25.5.1917—28.4.1919:* Taken up under the Liner Requisition Scheme. *12.12.1917:* Struck a submerged object, outward bound in the Thames. *1920—1927:* Served as a cadet ship for 20 cadets. *3.4.1924:* Grounded entering La Plata from Wallaroo. *19.6.1926:* Collided with the steamer FERDINAND (550g, 1883) while leaving Hamburg for London. *18.1.1927:* Sold for £18,250 to the West of Scotland Shipbreaking Co. Ltd. While being broken up at Troon she caught fire on 25.1.1927 and again on 7.7.1927.

OPAWA at Adelaide

*(IJF)*

## 47. OPAWA (1906—1928)

Official Number: 124566
Tonnages: 7,230 gross, 4,588 net, 10,620 deadweight. 1928: 9,593 gross, 5,523 net. Dimensions: 460.7 x 60.2 x 31.3 feet. Draft: 28.6 feet.
Twin screw, two T.3 cyl. by Denny & Co., Dumbarton, 5,652 ihp, 85 rpm, 14.64 knots on trials. 2,108 tons coal fuel.
Passengers: 6 1st class.
Refrigerated space: 286,650 cu.ft.

*5.11.1906:* Launched by Wm Denny & Bros, Dumbarton, (Yard No. 774), ran trials and delivered 18.12.1906 at a cost of £120,700. Registered at Plymouth on 1.1.1907 to G.T. Haycraft & T.R. Westray. *5.5.1908:* Ownership transferred to NZS. *24.12.1915:* Collided with the steamer MANCHESTER INVENTOR (4,247g, 1902) while coming down the Manchester Ship Canal. *6.4.1917—11.4.1919:* Taken up under the Liner Requisition Scheme. *28.10.1920:* Grounded near Cape Henry, Chesapeake Bay, bound London to New Zealand. *12.3.1924:* Collided with the steamer MABRITON (6,694g, 1920) in the River Scheldt, bound Townsville to London. *18.2.1925:* Suffered a fire in No.3 hold and bunkers, bound Australia to Trieste and Genoa and put into Perim. The bunker fire was out on the 21st but the hold fire not until 7th March. She sailed again on the 9th. *25.3.1926:* Suffered a fire in the bunkers, bound Adelaide to Sydney. *9.1927:* Laid up at Falmouth. *8.2.1928:* Sold for £20,000 to Hvalfangerslsk Antarctic A/S, Tonsberg, (Bruun & von der Lippe, managers). Converted to a whale factory ship by Akers M.V., Oslo; renamed ANTARCTIC and had a fire in the hold on 29th March while under conversion. *1934:* Sold to Nippon Hogei K.K., Tokyo, and renamed ANTARCTIC MARU. *1935:* Renamed TONAN MARU. *1936:* Sold to Kyodo Gyogyo K.K., Tokyo. *1937:* Owners renamed Nippon Suisan K.K., Tokyo. *28.11.1943:* Sunk by the U.S. submarine BOWFISH 25 miles off Nah Trang, Vietnam (12°46'N-109°42'E), while operating as a tanker.

OTAKI at Wellington

*(ATL/NZA)*

## 48. OTAKI (1908–1917)

Official Number: 124576
Tonnages: 7,420 gross, 4,611 net, 10,630 deadweight. Dimensions: 465.4 x 60.3 x 31.3 feet. Draft: 28.6 feet.
Triple screw, two T.3cyl. on the wing shafts, 4,444 ihp, 103 rpm. Parsons low pressure turbine on the centre shaft, 2,414 shp, 227.5 rpm. All by Denny & Co., Dumbarton, 15.07 knots on trials. 2,054 tons coal fuel.
Passengers: 6 1st class.
Refrigerated space: 290,000 cu.ft.

*15.8.1908:* Launched by Wm Denny & Bros, Dumbarton, (Yard No. 835), ran trials on 2.11.1908 and delivered on 5.11.1908 at a cost of £123,900. First registered at Plymouth on 12.11.1908 to G.T. Haycraft & T.R. Westray. *27.10.1909:* Arrived at London with a fire in No.3 hold. *14.3.1910:* Ownership transferred to NZS. *11.11.1911:* Grounded in the Thames outward bound. Rammed by the steamer BITINIA (3,125g, 1900) while aground and returned to Tilbury for repairs. *20.7.1915:* Stood by the burning steamer BENALLA (11,118g, 1913) 800 miles east of Durban.

*23.9.1915:* Suffered a fire in the bunkers at Auckland. *30.5.1916:* Made the first NZS transit of the Panama Canal, bound Wellington to London. *10.3.1917:* Sunk by gunfire and torpedoes from the German raider MOEWE (4,595g, 1914) 420 miles west by south of Lisbon, bound London to New York and New Zealand in ballast. The master and 5 of the crew were lost. Captain A. Bisset Smith was posthumously awarded the Victoria Cross for the action against the raider.

KIRITONA in Richardson colours

*(ATL)*

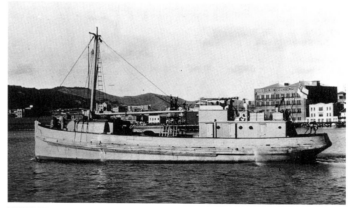

KIRITONA at Wellington in naval service during World War II

*(ATL/IJF)*

## 49. KIRITONA (1909–1925)

Official Number: 121592
Tonnages: 136 gross, 75 net. Dimensions: 87.0 x 24.5 x 8.5 feet.
6 cyl. 4 S.C.S.A. semi-diesel by the Standard Oil Engine Co., San Francisco, 150 bhp, 7 knots. Powered lighter; wood hull, auxiliary ketch rig.

*16.10.1909:* Launched by C. Bailey Jnr, Auckland, for NZS for lightering at Tokomaru Bay. First registered at Napier on 6.12.1909. *9.1912:* Bareboat chartered to Richardson & Co. Ltd, Napier, who were the NZS lightering contractors at that port and at Gisborne. *29.11.1912:* Suffered a fire in the cargo at Port Ahuriri, Napier. *6.3.1918:* Suffered at fire at Port Ahuriri, Napier. *13.12.1918:* Grounded off East Cape. *10.9.1919:* Engine room fire at Gisborne. *1.8.1922:* In collision with the lighter FANNY (94g, 1884) at Napier. *13.10.1925:* Sold to Richardson & Co.

Ltd, Napier. *26.3.1926:* Broke her foremast at Waikokopu. It was replaced in April. *14.4.1942:* Requisitioned by the Government of New Zealand and purchased by it on 16.10.1942. She served in the Royal New Zealand Navy as a degaussing vessel (ZO 8) and later as a repair ship. *10.1945:* Her engines were removed and she was converted to a dumb store lighter. *6.1955:* Dismantled and the hull sold to Parry Bros Ltd, Auckland, as a store ship for barge gear. *1961:* Broken up at Auckland.

RUAHINE at Wellington in her original rig

*(WAL)*

## 50. RUAHINE (1909—1949)

Official Number: 124582
Tonnages: 10,758 gross, 6,283 net, 9,940 deadweight. 1920: 10,839 gross, 6,856 net. 1926: 10,870 gross, 6,872 net.
Dimensions: 480.6 (497.0 overall) x 60.3 x 32.1. Draft: 29.5 feet.
Twin screw, two T.3cyl. by Denny & Co., Dumbarton, 7,815 ihp, 96 rpm, 15.9 knots on trials. 1,828 tons coal fuel. 1923: 2,562 tons oil fuel.
Passengers: 56 1st, 88 2nd and 126 3rd class. 250 emigrants. 1933: 220 tourist class. 1946: 140 tourist class.
Refrigerated space: 291,000 cu.ft., increased to 324,900 cu.ft. in 1931.

*19.8.1909:* Launched by Wm Denny & Bros, Dumbarton, (Yard No. 880), and delivered on 6.11.1909 at a cost of £169,100. First registered at Plymouth on 25.10.1909 to G.T. Haycraft & T.R. Westray. *25.11.1909:* Left London on her first New Zealand sailing to Wellington. *27.1.1911:* Collided with the steamer BEACON GRANGE (4,237g, 1898) at Las Palmas, bound London to Wellington. *28.6.1911:* Ownership transferred to NZS. *16.3.1912:* Attempted to tow the sinking P&O liner OCEANA (6,610g, 1888) into shallow water after she had been in collision off Beachy Head. *22.12.1913:* Struck near the stern by the steamer MAORI (3,399g, 1907) while berthed at Wellington. *24.10.1914:* Sailed from Wellington for London but returned on the 25th leaking through a meat port door which had been damaged in the collision with the MAORI and not properly repaired. *13.3.1917—8.5.1919:* Taken up under the Liner Requisition Scheme. *17.3.1917:* Missed by a torpedo from U 81 170 miles south-west of the Fastnet. *29.3.1917:* In collision with the steamer VESLA (1,107g, 1913) at New York while both vessels were at anchor. *27.7.1920:* In collision with the harbour ferry DUCHESS (308g, 1897) at Wellington. *1920:* The accommodation was rebuilt. *2.12.1920:* Sailed from London to resume passenger service to New Zealand. *1923:* Her boilers were converted for oil fuel. *21.6.1924:* Suffered a fire at London. *23.9.1926:* Collided with the steamer AUTOMEDON (7,628g, 1922) in the Thames when outward bound for Wellington. *15.1.1938:* Collided with the steamer CORSEA (2,764g, 1921) at London. *4.2.1938:* Collided with the tanker BROOMDALE (8,334g, 1937) at Glasgow. *1938:* Reduced to cargo only and then laid up in the Fal from 4.5—6.10.1939. *30.3.1940—6.4.1946:* Requisitioned for the Liner Division of the Ministry of Shipping, later Ministry of War Transport, but served as a Personnel Ship from 24.1.1941—10.11.1941. *2.9.1948:* Left London on her last New Zealand sailing to Auckland and laid up at Hull on her return. *5.4.1949:* Sold for £50,000 to Ragruppamento Armatore Fratelli Grimaldi, Genoa, renamed AURIGA on 7.4.1949 and registered at Naples. She was rebuilt at Genoa for the Naples - South America service. *1954:* Chartered to Chargeurs Reunis for Far East service. *18.1.1957:* Laid up at Naples. *22.3.1957:* Arrived at Savona and sold for £247,000 to be scrapped there by ARDEM.

RUAHINE leaving Auckland in her final NZS days

*(MP/NZA)*

ROTORUA at Wellington

(WAL)

## 51. ROTORUA (1910–1917)

Official Number: 124587
Tonnages: 11,130 gross, 7,094 net, 10,600 deadweight. Dimensions: 484.2 x 62.3 x 41.1 feet. Draft: 29.4 feet.
Triple screw, two T.3 cyl. on the wing shafts, 5,350 ihp, 104 rpm. Low pressure Parsons turbine on the centre shaft, 3,281 shp, 225 rpm. All by Denny & Co., Dumbarton, 15.77 knots on trials. 2,030 tons coal fuel.
Passengers: 52 1st, 72 2nd and 156 3rd class. 280 supplementary 3rd class.
Refrigerated space: 299,500 cu.ft.

*9.7.1910:* Launched by Wm Denny & Bros, Dumbarton, (Yard No. 915), and ran trials on 5 & 6.10.1910. Cost: £172,500. Registered at Plymouth on 6.10.1910 to G.T. Haycraft & T.R. Westray. *27.10.1910:* Left London on her first New Zealand sailing for Wellington. *13.11.1912:* Ownership transferred to NZS. *22.3.1917:* Torpedoed and sunk by UC 17 24 miles east of Start Point, bound Wellington and Newport News to London with general cargo. 1 life was lost.

KOUTUNUI at Wellington in Richardson colours

(DNB)

KOUTUNUI as a hulk in Fiordland

(Brian Saunders)

## 52. KOUTUNUI (1911–1925)

Official Number: 121594
Tonnages: 171g, 98 net. Dimensions: 96.7 x 24.0 x 8.4 feet.
Twin screw, two C.2 cyl. by G. Fraser & Sons, Auckland, 128 ihp, 7 knots. 1929: Two 3 cyl. 2 S.C.S.A. diesels by the Fairbanks, Morse Co., Detroit. 90 bhp, 9 knots. Wood hull; powered lighter.

*22.10.1910:* Launched by C. Bailey Jnr, Auckland, for NZS. Ran trials 4.1.1911 and first registered at Napier on 4.2.1911. *9.1912:* Bareboat chartered to Richardson & Co. Ltd, Napier, who were the NZS lightering contractors at that port and at Gisborne. *6.11.1914:* Grounded on Peria Reef, Orete Point. Refloated on the 9th. *13.10.1925:* Sold to Richardson & Co. Ltd, Napier. *24.12.1925:* Stranded at Table Cape. *7.6.1930:* Machinery damage at Palliser Bay. *16.12.1934:* Machinery damage at Tora Landing. *31.1.1940:* Collided with the schooner MIRO (75g, 1925) at Napier and beached. *8.7.1940:* Minor strandings at Port Ahuriri. *22.1.1945:* Struck a floating log in Cook Strait. *9.7.1946:* Grounded on Kaiti Reef, Gisborne and slipped for repairs. *30.1.1949:* Grounded on Schnapper Point Reef 10 miles from Nelson, inward bound from Picton. *15.5.1950:* Collided with a launch at Motueka. *20.1.1953:* Sold to the Gisborne Lightering & Stevedoring Co. Ltd, Gisborne; remained registered at Napier until 1970. *9.1.1968:* Sold to Luggate Game Packers Ltd, Dunedin, and converted at Port Chalmers to a dumb freezer depot based in Nancy Sound, Fiordland. *28.8.1970:* Sold to Koutunui Fisheries Ltd, Dunedin. *3.10.1985:* Sold to the Koutunui Syndicate (D.B. Edmonds & others), Dunedin. Still in existence.

REMUERA in the Bay of Biscay in her original rig*(WAL)*

## 53. REMUERA (1911–1940)

Official Number: 124590
Tonnages: 11,276 gross, 7,154 net, 10,595 deadweight. 1920: 11,158 gross, 7,113 net. 1927: 11,383 gross, 7,246 net.
Dimensions: 485.0 x 62.3 x 41.0 feet. Draft: 29.4 feet.
Twin screw, two T.3 cyl. by Denny & Bros, Dumbarton, 7,314 ihp, 94 rpm, 15.65 knots on trials, 2,167 tons coal fuel. 1920: 2,506 tons oil fuel.
Passengers: 52 1st, 92 2nd, 128 3rd and 258 supplementary 3rd class. 1933: Cabin and tourist class only.
Refrigerated space: 317,000 cu.ft.

*31.5.1911:* Launched by Wm Denny & Bros, Dumbarton, (Yard No. 929), ran trials on 5 & 6.9.1911 and delivered on 8.9.1911 at a cost of £176,100. Registered at Plymouth on 16.8.1911 to G.T. Haycraft & T.R. Westray. *28.9.1911:* Sailed from London on her first New Zealand sailing to Wellington. *18.2.1912:* Collided with the steamer NIOBE (1,319g, 1905) off the Lizard. *5.5.1915:* Ownership transferred to NZS. *15.7.1916:* Made the first NZS passenger sailing through the Panama Canal, bound Wellington to London. *14.8.1917–19.2.1919:* Taken up under the Liner Requisition Scheme. *1920:* Boilers converted to oil fuel and accommodation rebuilt before re-entering the New Zealand service on 3.3.1921. *21.7.1922:* Collided with the steamer

MARENGO (6,302g, 1910) 12 miles south of Bolt Tail, Devon, bound Southampton to Wellington with general cargo. She arrived at Portland the same day and returned to Tilbury for repairs on the 25th. *9.9.1925:* Collided with the tanker MATINA (2,698g, 1924) at Willemstad. *23.12.1926:* Suffered a fire in No. 1 tween deck, bound Southampton to Wellington. She arrived at Wellington on 10.1.1927. *1927:* Accommodation further reconstructed with 20 additional cabins on the old boat deck and the boats raised. *19.4.1940:* Requisitioned for service in the Liner Division. *26.8.1940:* Sunk by aerial torpedoes off the Moray Firth (57°50′N-01°54′W), bound Wellington to London. All 93 crew and 1 gunner were saved.

REMUERA at Lyttelton after rebuilding                                                                                       *(IJF)*

## 54. HURUNUI (1912–1918)

Official Number: 132751
Tonnages: 8,901 gross, 5,638 net. Dimensions: 495.0 x 63.1 x 31.7 feet.
Twin screw, two Q.4 cyl. by D. Rowan & Co., Glasgow, 1,142 nhp, 15.65 knots on trials.
Refrigerated space: 390,000 cu.ft.

*25.9.1911:* Launched by Russell & Co., Port Glasgow, (Yard No. 624), ran trials on 27.12.1911 and delivered in 1.1912. Her completion had been delayed by a fire in the forehold on 27.9.1911. First registered at Plymouth on 27.12.1911 to G.T. Haycraft & T.R. Westray. *22.2.1915:* Ownership transferred to

NZS. *2.3.1917:* Taken up under the Liner Requisition Scheme. *26.3.1917:* Struck a pier on arriving at Avonmouth. *18.5.1918:* Torpedoed and sunk by U 94 48 miles south-west of the Lizard (49°08′N-05°00′W) with the loss of 1 life, bound Wellington to London.

HURUNUI at Port Chalmers

*(Otago Early Settlers' Museum/IJF)*

WESTMEATH at Wellington

*(ATL/IJF)*

## 55. WESTMEATH (1911—1912)

Official Number: 117381
Tonnages: 8,096 gross, 5,212 net. Dimensions: 475.0 x 56.1 x 32.4 feet.
Twin screw, two T.3cyl. by Richardsons, Westgarth & Co. Ltd, Hartlepool, 3,500 ihp, 12 knots.
Passengers: 204 3rd class.
Refrigerated space: 292,800 cu.ft.

*15.2.1903:* Launched by Furness, Withy & Co. Ltd, West Hartlepool, (Yard No. 265), and first registered on 15.8.1903 at Greenock to the Empire Transport Co. Ltd, (Houlder Bros & Co. Ltd, managers), as EVERTON GRANGE. *20.6.1907:* Struck rocks at Duiker Point near Cape Town, bound Liverpool to Australia. *30.8.1907:* Struck and sank the schooner OSCAR ROBINSON (61g, 1883) when proceeding down the river at Port Adelaide. *6.1.1911:* Stranded at Kangaroo Point, Kingscote, South Australia. She was refloated on 13.1.1911. *24.12.1911:* Sold to NZS and renamed WESTMEATH on 26.4.1912. *11.7.1912:* Sold to the Union Steam Ship Co. of New Zealand Ltd, Dunedin (still registered at Greenock), although the sale was not recorded in the register until 26.4.1915. *7.8.1914—6.11.1914:* Requisitioned as a transport and took the 1st Battalion of the Honorable Artillery Company to France. They now have her bell. *15.5.1915:* Suffered a fire in her bunkers, bound Wellington to London. She put into St Vincent with some damage to the meat cargo. *22.3.1917—21.5.1919:* Taken up under the Liner Requisition Scheme. *15.7.1917:* Torpedoed by UC 48 off Cherbourg, bound Buenos Aires to Havre, but reached Falmouth for repairs. *26.5.1920:* Suffered a fire in No. 4 tween deck 6 days out of Panama, bound Liverpool to Auckland. *29.1.1923:* Her deck fittings were damaged and the engineroom and stokehold flooded in a gale, bound Liverpool to Auckland. *9.3.1925:* Sold to the Soc. Ligure di Nav. a Vapore, Genoa and renamed NORDICO. *12.1926:* Picked up and towed the broken down steamer ELISA CAMPANELLA (4,808g, 1899) from 200 miles out in the Atlantic into Queenstown. *1927:* Sold to D. & E. Fratelli Bozzo, Genoa. *29.3.1930:* Laid up at Genoa. *5.1932:* Sold for £5,000 to G. Pittaluga, Genoa and arrived at Savona on 2.5.1932 for breaking up.

## 56. LIMERICK (1912—1912)

Official Number: 109983
Tonnages: 5,790 gross, 3,793 net. Dimensions: 420.0 x 54.2 x 29.5 feet.
T.3 cyl. by the shipbuilders, 3,000 ihp, 12 knots.
Passengers: 26 1st and 230 2nd class.
Refrigerated space: 257,000 cu.ft.

*18.4.1898:* Launched by Workman, Clark & Co. Ltd, Belfast, (Yard No. 148), and first registered on 8.10.1898 to the Rippingham Grange Steamship Co. Ltd, London, (Houlder Bros & Co. Ltd, managers), as RIPPINGHAM GRANGE. *1.6.1899:* Transferred to the Houlder Line Ltd, (Houlder Bros & Co. Ltd, managers). *1.9.1899:* Went ashore on Tipara Reef, bound Port Pirie to United
*Continued overleaf*

*56. LIMERICK — continued*

LIMERICK leaving Wellington as HMNZT No. 7 in 1914

(ATL/IJF)

Kingdom. She had to jettison 1,500 tons of lead concentrates before refloating on the 4th with the aid of 2 tugs. *1905:* Went ashore at Cape Naturaliste, Western Australia. *1.9.1905:* Went ashore on Scraper Shoal off Kangaroo Island, South Australia, when the wheel chain carried away. She was refloated undamaged the same day. *8.1906:* Damaged her shaft bound Glasgow to Auckland and put into St Vincent for repairs. *26.4.1912:* Sold to NZS; renamed LIMERICK on 19.6.1912.

*11.7.1912:* Sold to the Union Steam Ship Company of New Zealand Ltd, Dunedin (still registered at London), although the sale was not recorded in the register until 26.4.1915. *16.10.1914:* Sailed with the Main Body of New Zealand troops in the first convoy from Wellington to Alexandria via Albany. *28.5.1917:* Torpedoed and sunk by U 86 140 miles south-west of Bishop Rock (48°53'N-09°45'W) with the loss of 8 lives, bound Sydney to London with refrigerated and general cargo.

TYRONE at Timaru. The only known photo of the ship under this name other than as a wreck

(Port Chalmers Museum)

## 57. TYRONE (1912—1912)

Official Number: 114064
Tonnages: 6,592 gross, 4,246 net. Dimensions: 450.5 x 55.2 x 30.6 feet.
Twin screw, two T.3 cyl. by the shipbuilders, 3,500 ihp, 13 knots.
Passengers: 46 1st and 48 3rd class.
Refrigerated space: 210,900 cu.ft.

*3.10.1901:* Launched by Workman, Clark & Co. Ltd, Belfast, (Yard No. 181), and first registered at Greenock on 12.12.1901 to Houlder Line Ltd, London, (Houlder Bros & Co. Ltd, managers), as DRAYTON GRANGE. *4.1902:* Took the 10th Boer War Contingent from Wellington. On the way she rescued the crew of the wrecked Dutch barque GEERTRUIDA GERARDA (1,410g, 1890). *26.4.1912:* Sold to NZS, renamed TYRONE on 19.6.1912 and registry transferred to London. *11.7.1912:* Sold to the Union Steam Ship Company of New Zealand Ltd, Dunedin (still

registered at London), although the sale was not recorded in the register up to the time of her loss. *9.1913:* The Federal emblem was removed from her funnel at Auckland prior to her intended entry into the Australasia - North American Pacific coast trade on the completion of her outward voyage. *27.9.1913:* Went ashore on Rerewahine Point, one mile south of Taiaroa Head, Otago, bound Manchester to Auckland, Lyttelton and Dunedin. She became a total loss, only about 30 tons of cargo being salved.

ROSCOMMON in the Queensland trade under B.I. charge
*(W.A. Schell)*

## 58. ROSCOMMON (1912—1912)

Official Number: 114066
Tonnages: 6,591 gross, 4,245 net. Dimensions: 450.5 x 55.2 x 30.6 feet.
Twin screw, two T.3 cyl. by the shipbuilders, 3,500 ihp, 13 knots.
Passengers: 46 1st and 320 3rd class passengers.
Refrigerated space: 278,000 cu.ft.

*23.1.1902:* Launched by Workman, Clark & Co. Ltd, Belfast, (Yard No. 182), ran trials on 27.2.1902 and first registered at Greenock on 4.3.1902 to the Oswestry Grange Steamship Co. Ltd, (Houlder Bros & Co. Ltd, managers), as OSWESTRY GRANGE. *26.4.1912:* Sold to NZS; renamed ROSCOMMON on 19.6.1912. *11.7.1912:* Sold to the Union Steam Ship Company of New Zealand Ltd,

Dunedin (still registered at Greenock), although the sale was not recorded in the register until 26.4.1915. *24.7.1917:* Taken up under the Liner Requisition Scheme. *21.8.1917:* Torpedoed and sunk by U 53 20 miles north-east of Tory Island (55°27'N-08°00') bound Manchester to Australia with general cargo.

## (FALLS OF ORCHY)

In July 1914 NZS entered into a conditional agreement with Wright, Graham & Co. Ltd, Glasgow, to purchase the steamer FALLS OF ORCHY (4,904g, 1907) which that company

managed for the Falls Line Steamship Co. Ltd. The conditions of sale were not met and the sale fell through in August, the ship never having entered NZS service.

HORORATA at Adelaide
*(IJF)*

## 59. HORORATA (1914—1939)

Official Number: 132757
Tonnages: 9,461 gross, 5,613 net, 10,687 deadweight. Dimensions: 511.1 x 64.2 x 32.0. feet. Draft: 28.6 feet.
Twin screw, two Q.4 cyl. by Denny & Co., Dumbarton, 8,493 ihp, 89 rpm, 15.73 knots on trials, 1,876 tons coal fuel.
1925: Experimented with pulverised coal firing, then converted to oil fuel.
Passengers: 5 1st class and 1,066 steerage.
Refrigerated space: 380,000 cu.ft.

*29.12.1913:* Launched by Wm Denny & Bros, Dumbarton, (Yard No. 993), and delivered 23.5.1914 at a cost of £214,000. First registered at Plymouth to NZS on 3.6.1914. *24.8.1914—11.9.1917:* Requisitioned as the Australian Expeditionary Force transport A 20 (67 officers, 2,000 other ranks, 124 horses), leaving Albany with the first convoy for Alexandria on 1.11.1914. *12.9.1917—12.4.1919:* Taken up under the Liner Requisition Scheme. *20.3.1918:* In collision. *19.1.1927:* Grounded on the North Foreland and run into the following day while aground by the steamers CORNESS (1,553g, 1909) and REIHER (975g, 1909) *8.1930—1.1931:* Laid up at London. *7.1932—2.1933:* Laid up in the Fal. *1934—1939:* Served as a

cadet ship for 20 cadets. *6.6.1939:* Sold for £10,000 to the British India Steam Navigation Co. Ltd, London, and renamed WAROONGA on 21.7.1939 (still registered at Plymouth). Her cadet accommodation was increased to 43 until she ceased as a cadet ship in 9.1939. *7.3.1940:* Requisitioned to serve in the Liner Division. *5.4.1943:* Torpedoed by U 630 in the North Atlantic (57°10'N-35°30'W) and sank the following day, bound Sydney and New York to London in Convoy HX 231 with refrigerated and general cargo. 12 crew, a gunner and 6 passengers were lost from 110 crew, 8 gunners and 14 passengers.

# Chapter 5: The Inter-War Years

The Company's primary objective following the Armistice was the replacement of lost tonnage. To this end the AJANA was transferred from the associated Australind fleet in 1920 and renamed OTARAMA, two standard G class ships were taken over from The Shipping Controller and completed as the OTAKI and PIAKO while the German reparations steamer TASMANIA was acquired without change of name in 1921. The HURUNUI which had been laid down to a company design but taken over by The Shipping Controller was completed in 1920 while 3 further vessels to a basically similar design but with the centrecastle extended over Nos. 2 and 4 hatches, the TEKOA, TURAKINA and TONGARIRO were delivered over 1922/25. All four were distinguished by their telescopic upper masts and removable funnel top with staging half way up to enable passage of the Manchester Ship Canal, the NZS ships now being involved in the west of England service in the same way as the Federal ships.

HORORATA (59) arrives at Wellington with returning troops, 1919    (WAL)

The replacement of the ROTORUA of 1910 in the passenger fleet was less easy, the directors baulking at the cost of new tonnage in the immediate post-war years. The decision was finally made to rebuild the fire damaged Federal liner SHROPSHIRE as a passenger vessel and she emerged in March 1923 as the second ROTORUA.

ROTORUA (66) in the Panama Canal with her original 5 topmasts    (WAL)

Meanwhile the changes on shore forestalled by the war were put into place. Although the New Zealand Board remained, the Head Office of the Company for New Zealand was moved from Christchurch to Wellington, the local branches were closed and management in the Dominion was vested in the Union Steam Ship Company which in effect created an NZS section in each of its principal offices. Thus was the move planned by Hughes in 1913 effected, but on a rather different basis. It had been facilitated by the Union Company itself being taken over by P&O in 1917, a move largely effected through the intermediacy of Hughes and made easier by New Zealand's attention being diverted to the war effort. By the Armistice the take-over was a known fact, so the association of the two concerns at a local level caused little comment. Other rationalisations which took place were the gradual transfer of the Union Company's interest in Federal-Shire to NZS/Federal while, with an associated coal supplier to hand, the Blackball Coal subsidiary was no longer necessary and from April 1st 1922 that company's 3 colliers were placed on long term charter to the Union Company which assumed their management and acquired the coal hulks outright.

A further change at the other end of NZS activities was the removal of the passenger embarking and landing port in England from Plymouth to Southampton as from January 1920. This had actually been announced in May 1914 but deferred on the outbreak of war. The move was a recognition that safety in the English Channel was no longer a real problem, but that ease and speed of rail access to London was. The Southampton call continued until November 1932 when passenger working was concentrated in London where the ships loaded and discharged. There was a final period of Southampton calls from 1949 to 1963 when the terminal again became London.

The NZS Royal Albert Dock ferry ENTERPRIZE. Note the Company white riband between hull and boot-topping
*(D.F. Raines)*

From August 1924 Curacao became the Company bunkering port for all oil fired ships in the fleet. That remained a minority of the steamers throughout the inter-war years, though unrewarding experiments with pulverised coal were made in the HORORATA in 1925.

The major matter confronting the Company's directors and managers in the mid-1920's was the replacement of the ageing passenger fleet, none of which was less than 15 years old. Plans for new ships were prepared in 1925 but were deferred on account of cost. Following the Union Company experience with the trans-Pacific liner AORANGI, they were to have been diesel engined ships of some 20,000 tons, but it was not until 1927 that orders for somewhat smaller ships were finally placed. The RANGI class as it became generally known produced three of the finest and probably the best remembered of all the Company's passenger liners. An air of modernity was given by the sweeping passenger decks amidships running aft to a full cruiser stern. What made the RANGIs particularly memorable to the travelling public though were their two imposing yellow funnels, the only such ships in the Company's history. Although they were to have long and satisfactory careers, all at first was far from well. The first ship, the RANGITIKI,

RANGITIKI (69) as built with additional kingposts, flying bridge and tall funnels
*(P&O)*

proved excessively tender and virtually unstable in ballast condition necessitating the removal of two sets of samson posts and derricks before she sailed on her maiden voyage. Even this was not enough and was followed by the demolition of the flying bridge, the shortening of the funnels and the installation of further permanent ballast after the first round voyage. Hasty changes were made to the RANGITATA and RANGITANE in the course of construction and thereafter all three ships performed very creditably and economically, though like all early motorships they tended to suffer from excessive vibration when pushed.

The exigencies of the great depression of the early 1930's precluded any major initiatives, the efforts of the Company's management being concentrated on keeping it viable. Fortunately the first steps towards renewal of the cargo fleet had been taken before the worst of the depression struck with the delivery over 1930/31 of the OTAIO, ORARI and OPAWA, the first motor cargo ships in the fleet and the first to berth all the crew amidships rather than in the forecastle or poop. They were a very successful trio whose basic layout and concept were followed in the Company's ships over the next 30 years.

As the depression eased, the Company ventured a return to the North America/Australasian trade which had been abandoned during the First World War. An attempt to revive it had been made in 1928, but soon lapsed in the face of strenuous competition from the Government owned Canadian National Line. By 1936 things were different. The Canadian authorities had wearied of the continual financial drain of subsidised shipping and were ready to sell out. Three British companies with interests in Australasia decided to pool their resources resulting in the formation of the Montreal Australia New Zealand Line Ltd (popularly known as the MANZ Line) and owned one third each by NZS, Port Line and Ellerman & Bucknall. Although 10 of the Canadian National ships were purchased by MANZ, they were considered unsuitable and were disposed of over the next 3 years, after which the trade was maintained by ships allocated from the fleets of the participating companies. As its contribution to the new trade, NZS introduced the KAI class, all diesel engined of which the KAIMATA was acquired from Trinder, Anderson who managed the KAI ships, 3 were built over 1937/39 and the KAITUNA was a Transatlantic Steamship Company design acquired on the stocks from the Swedish concern. The KAI class at 5,800 tons average was considerably smaller and slower than the Company's main line ships, and the minimal refrigerated space provided reflected the differing requirements of the North American trade.

Apart from the MANZ Line ships, no new tonnage had been built for NZS in the later 1930's, the ships then commissioned joining the Federal fleet. Ashore though there had been changes when it was concluded that the management arrangements with the Union Company in New Zealand were not serving as well as had been hoped and it was decided to revert to separate offices concentrating solely on NZS/Federal business. This change had only partly been put into place when the outbreak of the Second World War again diverted all efforts towards national survival.

## Ships 60 to 80: OTARAMA—KAIPAKI

OTARAMA arriving at Wellington          *(ATL/WAL)*

### 60. OTARAMA (1919—1928)

Official Number: 132712
Tonnages: 7,759 gross, 4,873 net, 10,400 deadweight. Dimensions: 454.0 x 56.2 x 36.0 feet.
Twin screw, two Q.4 cyl. by D. Rowan & Co., Glasgow, 817 nhp, 13 knots.
Passengers: 20 1st class.
Refrigerated space: 158,300 cu.ft.

*22.2.1912:* Launched by Russell & Co., Port Glasgow, (Yard No. 631), and first registered on 7.5.1912 to the Australind Steam Shipping Co. Ltd, London, (Trinder, Anderson & Co., managers), as AJANA. *28.10.1914—12.5.1917:* Requisitioned as an Australian Expeditionary Force transport (17 officers, 410 other ranks, 304 horses). *14.4.1917:* Attacked by a submarine in the English Channel but escaped. *13.5.1917—12.4.1919:* Taken up under the Liner Requisition Scheme. *29.7.1917:* Chased by a submarine off the north-west coast of Ireland but escaped. *25.11.1919:* Sold for £290,000 to NZS. Taken over at Avonmouth in 4.1920, renamed OTARAMA on 6.4.1920 and registered at Plymouth on 12.4.1920. *16.11.1925:* Grounded at Eastham. *17.12.1927—22.2.1928:* Laid up in the Fal. *29.2.1928:* Sold for £27,500 to D. & E. Fratelli Bozzo, Genoa, and renamed AMARANTO. *11.1932:* Broken up at Genoa.

### 61. OTAKI (1920—1934)

Official Number: 132763
Tonnages: 7,976 gross, 4,985 net, 10,200 deadweight. Dimensions: 449.1 (465.0 overall) x 58.2 x 37.1 feet. Draft: 29.3 feet.
Twin screw, two T.3 cyl. by the shipbuilders, 5,500 ihp, 13 knots.
Passengers: 12 1st class.
Refrigerated space (from 1923): 205,100 cu.ft.

*29.10.1919:* Launched by Barclay, Curle & Co. Ltd, Glasgow, (Yard No. 574), ran trials 23.1.1920 and delivered to NZS on 4.2.1920. She had been laid down for The Shipping Controller as the G class standard ship WAR JUPITER. She was first registered at Plymouth on 22.1.1920. *28.6.1924:* Arrived at Las Palmas with a fire in No. 4 hold, bound Wellington to London. *2.1931—2.1932, 7.1932—2.1933* and *7—12.1933:* Laid up in the Fal. *16.5.1934:* Collided with the steamer REDCAR (1,475g, 1920) at London. *31.5.1934:* Sold for £17,500 to The Clan Line of Steamers Ltd, Glasgow, (Cayzer, Irvine & Co. Ltd, managers), and renamed CLAN ROBERTSON on 15.6.1934. *2.12.1938:* Sold to the Stanhope Steamship Co. Ltd, London, (J.A. Billmeir & Co.

OTAKI at Adelaide

(IJF)

Ltd, managers), and renamed STANFLEET on 8.12.1938. *5.7.1939:* Sold to the Zubi Shipping Co. Ltd, London. *20.11.1939:* Sold for £65,000 to the Blue Star Line Ltd, London, and renamed PACIFIC STAR. *24.4.1940:* Requisitioned for the Liner Division. *27.10.1942:* Torpedoed by U 509 south-west of the Canaries (29°16'N-20°57'W) and abandoned the following day in 29°21'N-19°28'W. She was sighted again on the 30th, but is presumed to have sunk soon afterwards. She had been bound from Rosario and Freetown to Liverpool in Convoy SL 125 with refrigerated and general cargo.

HURUNUI at Wellington

(IJF)

## 62. HURUNUI (1920—1940)

Official Number: 145100
Tonnages: 9,266 gross, 5,876 net. Dimensions: 470.0 (482.00 overall) x 62.5 x 37.7 feet.
High pressure and low pressure turbines double reduction geared to a single shaft, by Richardsons, Westgarth & Co. Ltd, Hartlepool, 4,500 shp, 15 knots.
Refrigerated space: 402,200 cu.ft.

*1915:* Ordered by the Federal S.N. Co. Ltd as NORFOLK from Sir Raylton Dixon & Co. Ltd, Middlesbrough, (Yard No. 596a). The order was requisitioned by The Shipping Controller, (J.W. Glover, manager), but was handed back in 1919. *20.4.1920:* Launched as HURUNUI, but still in Federal ownership. She ran preliminary trials in 11.1920 and was delivered on 20.1.1921 following final trials on 18.1.1921. Registered at London to Federal. *18.9.1922:* Transferred to NZS and registered at Plymouth. *7.8.1925:* Suffered slight damage in a collision at Adelaide. *14.3.1931:* Suffered a bunker fire soon after leaving port and returned to Brisbane. *7—12.1933, 9.1934—2.1935, 10.1935—1.1936* and *7—9.1936:* Laid up in the Fal. *19.11.1937:* Collided with and sank the Lowestoft drifter REGAIN (87g, 1914) 5 miles off Smith's Knoll with the loss of 9 lives. *21.2.1940:* Requisitioned for the Liner Division. *14.10.1940:* Torpedoed by U 93 and sank the following morning 150 miles west of Cape Wrath (58°58'N-09°54'W), bound in ballast from London and Newcastle to Auckland in Convoy OB 227. 2 crew were lost.

## 63. PIAKO (1920—1941)

Official Number: 132766
Tonnages: 8,283 gross, 5,127 net. Dimensions: 450.0 x 58.2 x 37.2 feet.
High pressure and low pressure turbines single reduction geared to a single shaft, by the shipbuilders, 5,000 shp, 13 knots.
Refrigerated space: 317,000 cu.ft.

*17.6.1920:* Launched by A. Stephen & Sons Ltd, Glasgow, (Yard No. 492), registered at Plymouth to NZS on 14.12.1920 and ran trials on 20.12.1920. She had been laid down originally for The Shipping Controller as the modified G class standard ship WAR ORESTES. *13.2.1922:* Collided with the steamer ENDA (863g, 1911), bound London to Barry. *5.12.1924:* Struck the wharf while
*Continued overleaf*

*63. PIAKO — continued*

PIAKO at Adelaide                                                                                  *(IJF)*

leaving Brisbane and damaged in No. 1 hold. She was delayed in port for 3 weeks for repairs. *16.5.1929:* Suffered a hold fire bound Oamaru to London. *8.1931—1.1932* and *7.1934—2.1935:* Laid up at Falmouth. *8.1935—3.1936:* Laid up at Liverpool. *9.1936—1.1937:* Laid up at Truro. *6—9.1939:* Laid up at Falmouth. *16.5.1940:* Requisitioned for the Liner Division. *18.5.1941:* Torpedoed and sunk by U 107 west of Monrovia (07°52′N-14°57′W), bound Albany to Freetown and Liverpool with refrigerated and general cargo. 10 crew were lost.

TASMANIA at Adelaide                                                                               *(IJF)*

## 64. TASMANIA (1921—1936)

Official Number: 143348
Tonnages: 7,514 gross, 4,688 net, 10,475 deadweight. 1923: 9,008 gross, 5,765 net. Dimensions: 484.5 x 62.7 x 29.4 feet. Draft: 27.2 feet.
Q.4 cyl. by the shipbuilders, 4,500 ihp, 12 knots. Low pressure turbine of 500 shp connected to the shaft through double reduction gearing and Bauer-Wach couplings installed in 1930.
Refrigerated space (from 1923): 412,000 cu.ft.

*26.6.1913:* Launched by the Flensburger S.G., Flensburg, (Yard No. 333), for the Deutsch-Australische D.G., Hamburg, and completed 17.9.1913 as TASMANIA. *5.8.1914:* Seized by the Belgian Government at Antwerp. *9.10.1914:* Returned to her owners. *3.5.1919:* Surrendered to the British Government and registered at London in the name of The Shipping Controller, (F. & W. Ritson, Sunderland, managers). *1920:* Management transferred to NZS. *18.1.1921:* Sold to NZS without change of name. *26.8—4.11.1921:* Laid up at Falmouth. *3.5.1922:* Grounded on arriving at Wellington from Brisbane. *26.3.1923:* Registry transferred to Plymouth. *16.12.1928:* Collided with the motorship PACIFIC SHIPPER (6,304g, 1924) in the Manchester Ship Canal off the Old Quay Lock Layby, bound Newport to Brisbane. *19.1.1932:* Struck a wreck, bound London to Brisbane. *6.3.1932:* Lost a blade from her propeller, bound Sydney to Brisbane. *16.3.1932:* Suffered a fire in the port boiler at Sydney. *23.4.1932:* Touched the bank of the Yarra River when proceeding to her berth at Melbourne. *3.10.1933—19.1.1934, 18.7.1934—15.2.1935* and *11.7.1935—27.1.1936:* Laid up at Falmouth. *27.1.1936:* Sold for £14,000 through W.P. Jobson & Co. to Metal Industries Ltd. *31.1.1936:* Arrived at Rosyth where demolition commenced on 19.2.1936.

TEKOA at Adelaide

(IJF)

## 65. TEKOA (1922—1958)

Official Number: 145994

Tonnages: 8,526 gross, 5,369 net, 11,670 deadweight. Dimensions: 460.6 (483.0 overall) x 62.8 x 35.0 feet. Draft: 30.2 feet. High, intermediate and low pressure turbines double reduction geared to a single shaft, by the shipbuilders, 5,500 shp, 15 knots. Refrigerated space: 348,900 cu.ft.

*20.9.1921:* Launched by Earle's Shipbuilding & Engineering Co. Ltd, Hull, (Yard No. 626), registered at Plymouth to NZS on 16.2.1922, ran trials on 21.2.1922 and delivered on 3.3.1922. *17.10.1923:* In collision off Austruweel, River Scheldt with the steamer MAMARI (8,114g, 1904), when inward bound to Antwerp from Brisbane. *1924:* Boilers converted to oil fuel. *26.8.1925:* Struck the quay wall and sank several barges when berthing at Curaçao, bound Wellington to London. *31.1.1932:* Collided with the steamer MAGNE (1,226g, 1912) off Saltend, bound Townsville to Hull. *5—9.1931* and *2.1932—7.1932:* Laid up at Falmouth. *15.5.1935:* Collided with the wharf while berthing at Brisbane and docked for repairs. *30.3.1940—18.4.1946:* Requisitioned for the Liner Division. *17.3.1943:* Rescued the survivors from the steamers SOUTHERN PRINCESS (12,156g, 1915) and IRENEE DU PONT

(6,125g, 1941) sunk in convoy HX 229. *20.8.1946:* Collided with the wharf while berthing at Melbourne. *16.6.1955:* Put into Fremantle with engine trouble, bound Swansea to Adelaide. Sailed again on the 19th but engines broke down 8 miles off Cape Leeuwin the same day. Carried out repairs at sea and proceeded. *8.5.1958:* Arrived back at Wellington after developing trouble in the brine system on the 5th, bound Wellington to London. She sailed again on the 13th. *27.5.1958:* Sold for £140,000 to Hector Whaling Ltd, London, (Bugge & Krogh-Hansen, managers), and converted by Swan, Hunter & Wigham Richardson Ltd, Wallsend, to the whale oil and meat transport ENDERBY. *21.11.1960:* Sold to Kyokuyo Hogei K.K., Tokyo, and renamed KYOKUREI MARU. *4.1969:* Sold to Nichimen & Co. and demolition commenced at Mihara-shi on 21.8.1969.

ROTORUA leaving Wellington after the loss of her main topmast

(WAL)

## 66. ROTORUA (1923—1940) See SHROPSHIRE (No. F.17)

## 67. TURAKINA (1923—1940)

Official Number: 145998

Tonnages: 8,565 gross, 5,373 net. Dimensions: 460.5 x 62.7 x 35.2 feet. High and low pressure turbines single reduction geared to a single shaft, by D. Rowan & Co. Ltd, Glasgow, 5,500 shp, 15.8 knots on trials. Refrigerated space: 336,700 cu.ft.

*4.5.1923:* Launched by Wm Hamilton & Co. Ltd, Port Glasgow, (Yard No. 322), registered at Plymouth to NZS on 8.9.1923 and ran trials on 13.9.1923. *15.10.1925:* Suffered a fire in the copra

in Nos. 4 & 5 shelter decks at Wellington when about to sail for Napier. She was delayed for 10 days. *2.9.1932:* Collided with the motorship SEGUNDO (4,414g, 1925) and the steamer

*Continued overleaf*

*67. TURAKINA — continued*

TURAKINA at Brisbane *(VHY/NZA)*

CHILTON (2,125g, 1925) and struck several tugs in the River Tyne when arriving at Newcastle. *24.12.1933:* Collided with the motorship EKNAREN (5,243g, 1922) at Brisbane. *11.4.1940:* Requisitioned for the Liner Division. *20.8.1940:* Sunk by gunfire and torpedoes from the German raider ORION (7,021g, 1930) in the Tasman Sea (38°27'S-167°35'E), bound Port Pirie and Sydney to Wellington with refrigerated and general cargo. 38 crew were lost and the remainder taken prisoner.

TONGARIRO in Otago harbour *(Bain-Wright Collection)*

## 68. TONGARIRO (1925—1960)

Official Number: 146002
Tonnages: 8,729 gross, 5,501 net, 12,537 deadweight. Dimensions: 460.5 (480.7 overall) x 62.7 x 35.2 feet. Draft: 31.3 feet.
High and low pressure turbines single reduction geared to a single shaft, by D. Rowan & Co. Ltd, Glasgow, 5,500 shp, 16.1 knots on trials. Oil fuel.
Refrigerated space: 332,000 cu.ft.

*13.11.1924:* Launched by Wm Hamilton & Co. Ltd, Port Glasgow, (Yard No. 323), ran trials on 25.2.1925 and delivered to NZS on 2.3.1925. *17.7.1929:* Grounded 5 miles south-east of Ras al Ara, Perim, bound Bowen to London. Refloated the next day. *30—31.3.1932:* Suffered rudder damage in rough weather off Oamaru; repaired in dry dock at Port Chalmers. *26.8.1936:* Grounded in the Clyde near Dumbarton. *4.12.1939:* Lost her rudder in 49°40'N-10°58'W, bound Southampton to Auckland and arrived back at Falmouth on the 12th. *25.4.1940—20.3.1946:* Requisitioned for the Liner Division but spent the period from 7.10.1945—16.2.1946 as a victualling stores issuing ship. *7.8.1941:* Grounded when leaving Buenos Aires. *9.9.1941:* Collided with and sank the tanker SOCONY (4,404g, 1936) in 51°03'N-41°32'W with the loss of 2 lives while in convoy, bound Halifax to London. She arrived at Belfast for repair on the 17th. *3.3.1942:* Suffered a gunfire attack from a submarine off Cape Naturaliste having left Fremantle the previous day for the United Kingdom with wool and general cargo. *6.7.1943:* Grounded in the Panama Canal, but refloated the following day. *17.10.1947:* Mainmast collapsed at Lisbon and new one fitted. *14.8.1954:* Touched the bank of the Yarra when arriving at Melbourne. *26.8.1954:* Suffered a failure of her steering gear, bound Melbourne to Adelaide and towed back to Williamstown by the tugs HOWARD SMITH (496g, 1952) and TOORONGA (246g, 1922). *27.4.1960:* Sold for £112,000 to Far East Metal Industry & Shipping Ltd, London, and renamed FAR EAST TRADER (still registered at Plymouth). *25.7.1960:* Arrived at Hong Kong for demolition by Far East Metal Industry Corp. who began work 29.8.1960.

RANGITIKI at Lyttelton 3/3/35 *(IJF)*

## 69. RANGITIKI (1929 – 1962)

Official Number: 149561
Tonnages: 16,697 gross, 10,271 net, 14,100 deadweight. Dimensions: 531.0 (550.0 overall) x 70.2 x 38.1 feet. Draft: 33.8 feet. Twin screw, two x 5 cyl. 2 S.C.S.A. Sulzer diesels by the shipbuilders, 9,300 bhp, 15 knots. 2,774 tons of oil fuel consumed at 50 tons per day. 1948: two x 6 cyl. 2 S.C.S.A. Doxford diesels by the shipbuilders, 15,000 bhp, 16 knots. Passengers: 100 1st, 86 2nd and 413 3rd class. 1933: 100 1st and 495 tourist class. 1948: 121 1st and 284 tourist class. Refrigerated space: 416,400 cu.ft.

*29.8.1928:* Launched by John Brown & Co. Ltd, Clydebank, (Yard No. 516), and delivered to NZS 31.1.1929 at a cost of £613,500. *15.2.1929:* Sailed from Southampton on her first New Zealand voyage to Wellington. *20.6.1940 – 13.12.1940:* Requisitioned for the Liner Division, and was in the JERVIS BAY convoy from Halifax to Britain in 11.1940. *14.12.1940 – 27.5.1946:* Served as a personnel ship with a capacity for 2,600 troops. *4.9.1946:* Touched the locks at Colon, Panama Canal.

*9.10.1947 – 28.8.1948:* Reconditioned and re-engined by the shipbuilders at a cost of £1,500,000. *26.9.1958:* Briefly grounded on the Goodwin Sands, bound London to Lyttelton, but refloated and continued her voyage. *26.7.1962:* Sold for £141,500 to the Cia. Espanola de Demolicion Naval S.A., Madrid, and arrived at Santander on 26.7.1962. Breaking up by Recuperaciones Submarinas began there in 10.1962.

## 70. RANGITATA (1929 – 1962)

Official Number: 149564
Tonnages: 16,737 gross, 10,315 net. Dimensions: 531.0 (550.0 overall) x 70.2 x 38.1 feet. Draft: 33.8 feet. Twin screw, two x 5 cyl. 2 S.C.S.A. Sulzer diesels by the shipbuilders, 9,300 bhp, 15 knots. 1949: two x 6 cyl. 2 S.C.S.A. Doxford diesels by the shipbuilders, 15,000 bhp, 16 knots. Passengers: 100 1st, 86 2nd and 413 3rd class. 1933: 100 1st and 495 tourist class. 1949: 123 1st and 288 tourist class. Refrigerated space: 418,700 cu.ft.

*26.3.1929:* Launched by John Brown & Co. Ltd, Clydebank, (Yard No. 517), and delivered 19.10.1929 at a cost of £577,300. Registered at Plymouth in the name of the Federal S.N. Co. Ltd, (NZS, managers). *22.11.1929:* Sailed from Southampton on her first New Zealand sailing to Auckland. *17.7.1930:* Rescued the passengers and crew from the burning steamer TARGIS (5,925g, 1915) in 33°56′W-50°11′W and stood by until the vessel sank 2 days later. *1.10.1936:* Ownership transferred to NZS. The sale was not entered in the Plymouth register until 2.3.1937. *4.12.1939 – 15.8.1946:* Requisitioned as a personnel ship with a capacity for 2,600 troops. She spent from 19.3.1940 to 27.12.1940 with the Liner Division and remained on Government charters until 2.11.1948. *11.5.1948:* Suffered a fire in the galley when in the North Atlantic, bound Auckland to London. *8.12.1948 – 3.9.1949:* Reconditioned and re-engined by the shipbuilders. *1.11.1957:* Suffered an engine breakdown, *Continued overleaf*

RANGITATA a view along the wide boat deck *(WAL)*

70. RANGITATA — *continued*

RANGITATA leaving Wellington                                                    (IJF)

bound London to Auckland and put into Falmouth for repairs. 8.3.1958: Suffered a galley fire in the Royal Albert Dock, London. 2.1.1960: Suffered an engine breakdown in the Atlantic 1,600 miles from Land's End, bound Auckland to Southampton. Repairs were effected at sea. 16.5.1962: Sold for £193,500 to N.V.

Holland, Hendrik-Ido-Ambacht, and left London for Rotterdam on 17.5.1962. 29.5.1962: Resold to Brodospas, renamed RANG, Dutch flag, and arrived at Split on 21.7.1962 for breaking up. Demolition began in 9.1962.

RANGITANE at Auckland                                                           (DNB)

# 71. RANGITANE (1929—1940)

Official Number: 149565
Tonnages: 16,733 gross, 10,311 net. Dimensions: 531.0 (550.0. overall) x 70.2 x 38.1 feet. Draft: 33.8 feet.
Twin screw, two x 5 cyl. 2 S.C.S.A. Sulzer diesels by the shipbuilders, 9,300 bhp, 15 knots.
Passengers: 100 1st, 86 2nd and 413 3rd class passengers. 1933: 100 1st and 495 tourist class.
Refrigerated space: 418,800 cu.ft.

27.5.1929: Launched by John Brown & Co. Ltd, Clydebank, (Yard No. 522), and delivered 12.11.1929 to NZS at a cost of £613,500. 20.12.1929: Sailed from Southampton on her first New Zealand sailing to Auckland. 25.4.1940: Requisitioned for the Liner Division. 27.11.1940: Sunk by torpedoes and gunfire from the German raiders ORION (7,021g, 1930) and KOMET (3,287g,

1937) 320 miles north of East Cape (36°43′S-175°27′W), bound Auckland to Panama and London with refrigerated and general cargo. 6 passengers and 7 crew were lost. Of the 299 survivors, 209 were landed at Emirau Island on 12th December and the remainder were kept prisoner on the raiders.

OTAIO at Adelaide

(IJF)

## 72. OTAIO (1930—1941)

Official Number: 149569

Tonnages: 10,048 gross, 6,130 net, 13,000 deadweight. Dimensions: 472.0 (490.0 overall) x 67.2 x 35.7 feet. Draft: 32.4 feet.
Twin screw, two x 4 cyl. 2 S.C.S.A. Doxford diesels by Wm Doxford & Sons Ltd, Sunderland, 9,390 bhp, 16 knots. 2,806 tons oil fuel.
Refrigerated space: 424,700 cu.ft.

*26.8.1930:* Launched by Vickers-Armstrongs Ltd, Barrow, (Yard No. 661), ran trials 12.12.1930 and delivered to NZS 14.12.1930 at a cost of £329,400. *7.2.1940:* Requisitioned for the Liner Division. *7.9.1940:* Struck by a bomb in Victoria Docks, London, which penetrated 3 decks but failed to explode. 12 crew were killed. *28.8.1941:* Torpedoed and sunk by U 558 330 miles west by north of the Fastnet (52°16′N-17°50′W), bound Liverpool to Curacao and Sydney in convoy OS 4 with general cargo. 25 crew and 1 gunner were lost.

ORARI at Auckland post war

(RCP)

## 73. ORARI (1931—1958)

Official Number: 162906

Tonnages: 10,107 gross, 6,070 net, 12,585 deadweight. Dimensions: 471.0 (490.0 overall) x 67.3 x 36.8 feet. Draft: 32.4 feet.
Twin screw, two x 9 cyl. 2 S.C.S.A. Sulzer diesels by Sulzer Bros., Winterthur, 9,000 bhp, 16 knots.
Refrigerated space: 412,450 cu.ft.

*23.10.1930:* Launched by A. Stephen & Sons Ltd, Glasgow, (Yard No. 531), and delivered to NZS 19.2.1931 at a cost of £330,000. *4.11.1932:* Grounded in Otago harbour outward bound to New Plymouth. *23.1.1934:* Suffered an engineroom fire bound Opua to Wanganui. *24.8.1935:* Suffered a fire in No. 2 upper tween deck at Alexandra Dock, Liverpool. *4.1939—9.1939:* Laid up at Falmouth. *17.2.1940—2.3.1946:* Requisitioned for the Liner Division, but spent the period from 18.5.1942—13.10.1942 as a mechanical transport ship. *5.1940:* At Dakar when the French capitulated, but escaped to Freetown. *3.7.1940:* Badly shaken by near misses from 3 bombs in the English Channel off Beachy Head, bound for London. *13.12.1940:* Torpedoed by U 43 450 miles south-west of Ireland (49°50′N-20°55′W), bound Melbourne to Avonmouth with refrigerated and general cargo. There were no casualties and she arrived at Rothesay on the 16th and was repaired by her builders. *10.3.1942:* Encountered the Italian submarine LUIGI TORELLI in 13°N-57°W, bound U.K. to the Plate, but escaped by her speed. *4.6.1942:* Left the Clyde for Malta with military stores in Operation Harpoon and mined off Malta on the 16th without any casualties. She left Malta on 1.8.1942 after completion of temporary repairs. *11.1953—7.1954* and *6—8.1958:* Laid up at Falmouth. *31.7.1958:* Sold to Capo Gallo Cia di Nav. S.p.A., Palermo, and renamed CAPO BIANCO. *1971:* Sold to Euronavi S.p.A., Palermo and laid up at Savona where she arrived on 18.5.1971. *8.1971:* Demolition commenced at Vado by Vado Alti Forni e Acciaierie.

OPAWA at Brisbane                                                                (VHY/NZA)

## 74. OPAWA (1931—1942)

Official Number: 162907
Tonnages: 10,107 gross, 6,068 net, 12,815 deadweight. Dimensions: 471.0 x 67.3 x 36.8 feet.
Twin screw, two x 9 cylinder 2 S.C.S.A. Sulzer diesels by the shipbuilders, 9,000 bhp, 16 knots.
Refrigerated space: 412,050 cu.ft.

*20.1.1931:* Launched by A. Stephen & Sons Ltd, Glasgow, (Yard No. 532) and delivered to NZS 25.4.1931 at a cost of £325,000. *2.7.1931:* Arrived at Auckland on her maiden voyage with the CITY OF KIMBERLEY (6,169g, 1925), having towed her 1,300 miles after the loss of her propeller. *6.7.1940:* Requisitioned for the Liner Division, but spent 14.1.1941 - 8.5.1941 as a mechanical transport ship. *14.1.1941:* Suffered near misses from bombs while at Avonmouth. *6.2.1942:* Torpedoed and sunk by U 106 400 miles north-east of Bermuda (38°21'N-61°13'W), bound Lyttelton to Halifax and the U.K. with refrigerated and general cargo. 56 lives were lost.

OPAWA arrives at Auckland at the end of her maiden voyage in 1931 with Ellerman CITY OF KIMBERLEY in tow                     (NZA)

## 75. KAIMATA (1936—1954)

Official Number: 161958
Tonnages: 5,237 gross, 3,190 net, 9,400 deadweight. Dimensions: 415.5 (430.3 overall) x 56.2 x 25.6 feet. Draft: 26.7 feet.
8 cyl. 2 S.C.S.A. Sulzer diesel by the shipbuilders, 4,042 bhp, 123 rpm, 15.08 knots on trials. 1,168 tons oil fuel.

*14.7.1931:* Launched by Wm Denny & Bros. Ltd, Dumbarton, (Yard No. 1250), and delivered on 31.10.1931 to their own account, (O.G. Trinder, manager), and registered at Glasgow as ARDENVOHR. Her manager employed her in the services of the Australind Steam Shipping Co. Ltd. *11.8.1936:* Sold to NZS for £90,000. *6.10.1937:* Re-registered at Plymouth, renamed KAIMATA on 11.11.1937 and placed on MANZ Line services, (Trinder,Anderson & Co., managers). *4.11.1938:* Grounded twice in the Suez Canal bound London to Port Chalmers. She was refloated undamaged the same day. *2.5.1940—11.4.1946:* Requisitioned for the Liner Division but spent the periods 5.3.1942—28.5.1942, 17.10.1942—9.1.1943 and 1.5.1943—18.10.1943 as a mechanical transport ship. *3/4.5.1941:* Suffered minor damage during an air raid at Liverpool. *30.10.1941:* Suffered a main engine breakdown bound Fremantle to Melbourne and made the 517 mile remainder of her voyage with engines at reduced speed and jury sail. She arrived at Melbourne on 5.11.1941. *1.6.1942:* Nearly had her stern blown off by gunfire from the cruiser USS CHICAGO (9,300 tons, 1930) firing at a Japanese midget submarine in Sydney harbour. *12.1942:* Present at the North African landings where on 9.12.1942 she was narrowly missed by a bomb as she left Algiers. *7.1943:* Present at the Sicilian landings where on 13.7.1943 she was slightly damaged in an air attack at Syracuse. *29.9.1944:* Collided with the motorship TAI SHAN (6,962g, 1929) in the Thames, inward bound from Launceston with general cargo. *15.11.1951:* Suffered a fire in No. 5 shelter deck, bound Liverpool and Cape Town to Melbourne. She put into Fremantle on the 17th and the fire was out 3 days later. *18.11.1954:* Sold for £60,000 to the Avenue Shipping Co. Ltd, (Trinder, Anderson & Co. Ltd, managers), and renamed ANTRIM on 16.12.1954. *17.1.1955:* Returned to Balboa for repairs to the main bearings, bound Britain to New Zealand. Repairs were carried out at Cristobal and she sailed again on 27.1.1955. *8.2.1957:* Sold for £397,500 to the Hong Kong Fir Shipping Co. Ltd, Hong Kong and renamed HONGKONG FIR. *1958:* Transferred to the Cia de Nav. Abeto S.A., Panama, (The Fir Line Ltd, managers). *20.8.1960:* Suffered an engineroom fire at the

KAIMATA at Brisbane                  *(VHY/NZA)*

Taikoo Dockyard, Hong Kong. *1962:* Sold to the Republik Indonesia, (Djawatan Angkutan-Angkatan Darat), Djakarta, and renamed ADRI X. *9.1963:* Sold to P.T. Affan Raya Line, Djakarta and renamed AFFAN-EL-BAHAR. *10.1964:* Transferred to P.T.

Maskapi Pelayaran Sang Saka, Djakarta, and renamed SANG PRATIWI. *12.1967:* Renamed PALA; same owners. *10.5.1969:* Demolition commenced at Hong Kong by the Hung Shing Wire Works Co. Ltd and was completed on 25.6.1969.

KAIKOURA at Adelaide, as built                  *(IJF)*

## 76. KAIKOURA (1937—1954)

Official Number: 165874
Tonnages: 5,852 gross, 3,432 net, 9,544 deadweight. 1952: 6,067 gross, 3,454 net. Dimensions: 446.3 (460.0 overall) x 59.0 x 25.8 feet. Draft: 26.3 feet.
4 cyl. 2 S.C.S.A. Doxford diesel by John Brown & Co. Ltd, Clydebank, 4,250 bhp, 13 knots.
Refrigerated space: 18,100 cu.ft. 1950: 40,347 cu.ft.

*7.9.1937:* Launched by A. Stephen & Sons Ltd, Glasgow, (Yard No. 556) and delivered on 17.11.1937 to NZS, (Trinder, Anderson & Co., managers), for MANZ Line service. *26.4.1940—6.5.1946:* Requistioned for the Liner Division, but spent from 30.1.1943—15.3.1943 as a military store ship. *5.3.1949:* Broke a piston in the main engine shortly after leaving Auckland for Havana and New York. Returned for repairs the same day and sailed again on the 10th. *26.1.1950:* Grounded on a sandbank in Otago harbour, bound Dunedin to Port Chalmers; she was

refloated after 5 hours. *1952:* Accommodation rebuilt by Grayson, Rollo & Clover Docks Ltd, Liverpool, raising the bridge 1 deck higher. *11.1952:* Collided with a barge at New York. *9.11.1954:* Sold for £120,000 to the Avenue Shipping Co. Ltd, (Trinder, Anderson & Co. Ltd, managers), and renamed TYRONE on 19.11.1954, having originally been announced as WICKLOW. *9.1963:* Sold to The Shin Wing Hong, Hong Kong, where she arrived on 15.9.1963 and demolition began on 16.10.1963.

KAIKOURA after rebuilding                  *(JYF/NZA)*

KAIPARA at Adelaide, as built                                                                                    (IJF)

## 77. KAIPARA (1938—1955)

Official Number: 165876
Tonnages: 5,882 gross, 3,454 net, 9,532 deadweight. 1952: 6,032 goss, 3,425 net. Dimensions: 438.9 (454.6 overall) x 58.9 x 25.7 feet. Draft: 26.3 feet.
4 cyl. 2 S.C.S.A. Doxford diesel by the shipbuilders, 4,250 bhp, 13 knots.
Refrigerated space: 39,300 cu.ft.

*21.10.1937:* Launched by Wm Doxford & Sons Ltd, Sunderland, (Yard No. 636), and delivered on 12.1.1938 to NZS, (Trinder, Anderson & Co., managers), for MANZ Line service. *6.4.1940—9.3.1946:* Requisitioned for the Liner Division. *16.7.1943:* Torpedoed by U 306 85 miles from Dakar (13°30'N-17°43'W), bound Buenos Aires to Liverpool. There were no casualties and she arrived at Dakar the following day and was beached. She finally left for the Tyne on 24.2.1944 for repairs. *1952:* Accommodation rebuilt by Mountstuart Dry Docks Ltd, Cardiff, raising the bridge 1 deck higher. *15.7.1953:* Struck the wharf at the entrance to Champlain Dry Dock, Lauzon,

Quebec. *10.11.1955:* Sold for £120,000 to the Avenue Shipping Co. Ltd, (Trinder, Anderson & Co. Ltd, managers), and renamed ROSCOMMON on 21.11.1955. *24.4.1957:* Put into Fremantle for survey after suffering heavy weather damage and a split in the shell plating in No. 1 double bottom tank, bound Melbourne to London. Final repairs at Cardiff took 6 weeks. *1962:* Sold through Mitsui & Co. Ltd to Cris Cia Nav. S.A., Beirut, (A. Halcoussis Shipping Ltd, managers), and renamed CRIS. *10.1967:* Arrived at Kaohsiung prior to the 7th. Demolition was completed there in 2.1968.

RIMUTAKA leaving Auckland                                                                                    (MP/NZA)

## 78. RIMUTAKA (1938—1950)

Official Number: 145517
Tonnages: 16,385 gross, 10,333 net. Dimensions: 551.6 (573.0 overall) x 72.0 x 38.5 feet. Draft: 30.0 feet.
Twin screw, two sets of high, intermediate and low pressure turbines double reduction geared, by the shipbuilders, 13,250 shp, 16 knots. 1928: Converted to oil fuel.
Passengers: 231 1st and 180 2nd class. The second class was redesignated 3rd in 1928. 1930: 840 tourist class. 1938: 772 tourist class. 1950: 614 tourist class.
Refrigerated space: 136,100 cu.ft. 1938: 360,700 cu.ft. (removed in 1950).

*24.8.1922:* Launched by Sir W.G. Armstrong, Whitworth & Co. Ltd, Walker-on-Tyne, (Yard No. 964), and delivered on 26.4.1923

at a cost of £1,000,000 to The Peninsular and Oriental Steam Navigation Co., London (registered at Newcastle), as

MONGOLIA. *11.5.1923:* Left London on her first sailing to Sydney. *16.7.1933:* Collided with the tanker BRITISH VENTURE (4,696g, 1930) and a breakwater at Copenhagen and then ran aground, while on a cruise. *3.12.1936:* Collided with the motorship VILLA DE MADRID (6,942g, 1931) off Marseilles, bound London to Brisbane. *7.5.1938:* Chartered to NZS and re-registered at Plymouth on 5.8.1938 as RIMUTAKA. *27.11.1938:* Collided with the steamer CORFLEET (1,803, 1934) off the Nore. *8.12.1938:* Left London on her first New Zealand sailing to Wellington. *9.3.1939:* Suffered a fire in No. 3 hold in 32°16'S-164°32'E, bound London to Auckland. *9.1939:* Requisitioned for conversion to an armed merchant cruiser, but released.

*12.5.1940 — 14.6.1946:* Requisitioned for the Liner Division. *2.3.1950:* Returned to P&O after having been sold 10.1.1950 for £95,000 to Cia. de Nav. Incres S.A., Panama, (Home Lines, managers). Handed over on 8.3.1950 and renamed EUROPA. *16.6.1950:* Left Genoa on her first sailing to New York. *11.1951:* Transferred to the Incres Steamship Co. Ltd, Panama, refitted at Genoa and renamed NASSAU for Caribbean cruising. *1954:* Transferred to the Liberian flag. *10.1961:* Sold to Cia Nav. Turistica Mexicana S.A., Acapulco, rebuilt by the Fairfield Shipbuilding & Engineering Co. Ltd, Glasgow, and renamed ACAPULCO. *19.5.1963:* Laid up at Manzanillo. *15.12.1964:* Arrived at Osaka in tow for demolition which commenced at Sakai on 6.1.1965.

KAITUNA at Wellington

*(NJK/NZA)*

## 79. KAITUNA (1938—1954)

Official Number: 165885
Tonnages: 4,907 gross, 2,854 net, 8,926 deadweight. Dimensions: 413.6 (432.2 overall) x 56.6 x 25.3 feet. Draft: 25.8 feet.
7 cyl. 2 S.C.D.A. B & W diesel by the shipbuilders, 4,550 bhp, 14 knots.

Originally ordered by the Rederi A/B Transatlantic, Gothenburg, (G. Carlsson, manager), sold to NZS on the stocks and launched 10.10.1938 by Eriksbergs M.V., Gothenburg, (Yard No. 285), at a cost of £165,000 for the MANZ Line service, (Trinder, Anderson & Co., managers). *12.1938:* Completed and registered at Plymouth 20.12.1938. *1.6.1940 — 29.5.1946:* Requisitioned for the Liner Division, but spent from 30.4.1943 — 17.7.1943 as a military store ship. *19.7.1943:* Damaged by a limpet mine, bound Mersin to Haifa in ballast (35°15'N-35°35'E). She arrived at Haifa the same day and temporary repairs were made at Alexandria. There were no casualties from the mine which had been attached at Mersin on the 9th. *19.12.1953:* Suffered a fire in the engineroom at Kingston, Jamaica. It was put out after 4 hours. *27.6.1954:* Fractured a main engine piston rod, bound Kingston to Houston and proceeded on the remaining cylinders. *17.9.1954:* Sold for £120,000 to the Avenue Shipping Co. Ltd, (Trinder, Anderson & Co. Ltd, managers), and renamed ARMAGH on the 18th. *29.7.1955:* Holed below the waterline in No. 4 hold at Wellington when a bundle of rails slipped out of the slings.

*21.6.1956:* Suffered a fire in No. 1 hold while loading at Swansea. The fire was put out the following day but there was another outbreak in No. 2 hold on the 26th. *24.4.1960:* Struck the bank in Culebra Cut, Panama Canal, after a steering failure, bound London to Auckland. Repairs were effected at Balboa, and she sailed again on 1.5.1960 but had to put back with a leak in the forepeak for further repairs. She finally sailed on the 5th. *26.5.1961:* Sold for £111,900 to the Kam Kee Navigation Co. Ltd, Hong Kong, (Jebshun & Co, managers), but remained registered at London as SHUN WAH. *7.2.1962:* Arrived at Auckland with 3 cracks in the shelter deck caused by heavy weather, bound Osaka to Auckland. *15.7.1963:* Suffered a fire in the engineroom off Slipper Island, Bay of Plenty, bound Auckland to Tauranga. She drifted to within 10 miles of the coast before the fire was put out and steerage way regained. *1.11.1966:* Collided with the tug GRONINGEN (598g, 1963), bound Moji to Davao in 29°37'N-131°22'E. She arrived at Nagasaki in tow of the tug on the 4th. *28.2.1967:* Delivered at Nagasaki to Iwai & Co. Ltd who began demolition that day.

KAIPAKI as built                                                                                      (DNB)

## 80. KAIPAKI (1939–1955)

Official Number: 165888 Tonnages: 5,862 gross, 3,426 net, 9,544 deadweight. 1952: 6,013 goss, 3,402 net.
Dimensions: 443.9 (458.5 overall) x 59.0 x 25.8 feet. Draft: 26.3 feet.
4 cyl. 2 S.C.S.A. Doxford diesel by Barclay, Curle & Co. Ltd, Glasgow, 4,250 bhp, 13 knots.
Refrigerated space: 45,900 cu.ft.

*7.2.1939:* Launched by A. Stephen & Sons Ltd, Glasgow, (Yard No. 567), and delivered to NZS 20.4.1939 for MANZ Line service, (Trinder, Anderson & Co., managers). *12.6.1940–6.3.1946:* Requisitioned for the Liner Division but spent from 26.11.1942–6.2.1943 as a mechanical transport ship. *7.4.1945:* Collided with the tanker CHRISTIAN HOLM (9,185g, 1927) at New York. *24.9.1946:* Collided with the steamer LIVERPOOL PACKET (2,894g, 1945) in fog 125 miles north-east of Halifax (45°30'N-60°17'W), bound Singapore to Montreal. Repairs were completed at Montreal on 24.10.1946. *1952:* Accommodation rebuilt by Mountstuart Dry Docks Ltd, Cardiff, raising the bridge one deck higher. *19.10.1955:* Sold for £120,000 to the Avenue Shipping Co. Ltd, (Trinder, Anderson & Co. Ltd, managers), and renamed WESTMEATH on 14.11.1955. *18.1.1958:* Arrived at Balboa after suffering an engine breakdown, bound Gisborne to Panama. Repairs were completed at Cristobal on 1.2.1958. *8.11.1962:* Arrived at Antwerp. *26.12.1962:* Demolition commenced by Jos. de Smedt.

KAIPAKI after rebuilding in 1952                                       (IJF)

A close-up of the reconstructed bridge
(Welsh Industrial & Maritime Museum)

# Chapter 6: Second World War and Rebuilding

As in the first conflict, it was enemy surface raiders which were to figure prominently in NZS Second World War losses. On her way across the Tasman Sea on 20th August 1940 the TURAKINA with her single 4.7'' gun aft encountered the German raider ORION armed with 6 5.9'' guns and other smaller weapons. Nothing daunted, Captain J.B. Laird and his crew got a wireless message away before the aerials were brought down and continued firing at their adversary until the TURAKINA was ablaze and sinking. In nearly every way it was a repeat of the OTAKI/MOEWE clash 23 years previously, but in this case Laird and his ship's company never received the recognition for their gallantry that was their due.

TURAKINA (67) leaving Sydney on her last voyage. Note the stern gun which featured in her fight with the raider                                                                        (IJF)

The same raider ORION, having joined up with her consort the KOMET, was also jointly responsible for the Company's major loss of the war 3 months later when the passenger liner RANGITANE was stopped and sunk 2 days out of Auckland. From the passenger fleet, the REMUERA and ROTORUA were also lost in 1940, the former being the first Company vessel to be sunk by a torpedo dropped from an aircraft rather than fired by a submarine. Torpedoes from submarines accounted for the other 4 vessels lost in 1940/42, but the survivals were almost as noteworthy as the losses. Both the ORARI and the HORORATA suffered major torpedo damage but were able to limp into port after epic feats by their crews. Repairs in each case involved massive reconstruction. The RANGITIKI as the largest ship in the famous JERVIS BAY convoy of 1940 narrowly escaped destruction by the pocket battleship ADMIRAL SCHEER, while the ORARI was again to cheat disaster when she was mined in June 1942 nearing the end of a Malta relief voyage, but was able to make port before sinking.

RANGITATA (70) as a troopship                                                                        (Mariners Museum/NZA)

With the conclusion of hostilities, reconstruction of the fleet was again the main priority. The demand for New Zealand produce in a war famished Britain was insatiable, and attention was concentrated on the provision of refrigerated capacity. In these circumstances it was not surprising that the post-war fleet was substantially a repeat of the proven successful designs of the late 1930's with little thought given to whether there might be a need for a new approach. Fortunately the Company had been able to take delivery of the HORORATA and 3 ships of the P class during the war, though it had been obliged to accept turbine machinery for all 4 instead of the diesels it would have preferred, because of the shortage of the latter.

The 8 ships of the H class, 4 of which eventually carried NZS names, were the backbone of the immediate post-war programme, each able to lift over 500,000 cu.ft. of refrigerated cargo and maintain a speed of 16 knots. This time the passenger fleet was not neglected either with orders for two major units which at 21,800 tons were the largest ever owned by the Company. The RANGITOTO and RANGITANE introduced a new concept to the fleet with

Launch of the RANGITANE (90) at Clydebank                                                                 (NJK)

their accommodation for 416 passengers all in one class, the fares being graded according to cabin. Allowing the full run of the ship to all appealed particularly to egalitarian New Zealand passengers and was repeated in the final ship, the rather smaller third RUAHINE, delivered in 1951. The two surviving RANGIs of 1929 were given extensive refits including re-engining with more powerful machinery to enable them to keep pace with the new ships, but in their case the two class configuration in the accommodation was retained. Pending the arrival of the new ships,

TEKOA (65) at Wellington in post-war colour scheme
(VHY/NZA)

RANGITANE (90) passes her sister RANGITOTO (89) on arrival at Auckland at the conclusion of her maiden voyage                    *(New Zealand Herald)*

the demand for berths was met by the veteran second RUAHINE, restored to passenger status after being relegated to cargo only in 1938-39, the RIMUTAKA chartered from the P&O in 1938 and the RAKAIA whose austerity wartime accommodation for 36 cabin class continued to fill a need. The first two had been sold and the last removed from passenger service by the end of 1950.

## Ships 81 to 91: HORORATA—RUAHINE

HORORATA at Port Chalmers                    *(IJF)*

## 81. HORORATA (1942—1966)

Official Number: 165897
Tonnages: 13,945 gross, 8,323 net. 1946: 12,090 gross, 7,146 net, 14,246 deadweight. Dimensions: 532.2 (551.3 overall) x 70.4 x 44.7 feet. Draft: 32.6 feet.
Twin screw, two sets of high, intermediate and low pressure turbines single reduction geared, by the shipbuilders, 12,300 shp, 16 knots.
Refrigerated space: 569,900 cu.ft.

*9.10.1941:* Launched by John Brown & Co. Ltd, Clydebank, (Yard No. 566), and delivered to NZS on 9.4.1942. *10.4.1942 — 10.8.1946:* Requisitioned for the Liner Division. *13.12.1942:* Torpedoed by U 103 north of the Azores (42°09'N-34°31'W), bound Auckland to Liverpool with refrigerated and general cargo. No casualties. She arrived at Santa Cruz on the 14th and at Horta on the 18th for temporary repairs. *17.3.1943:* Left Fayal and arrived at Liverpool on the 23rd. Repairs were completed at Birkenhead by Cammell, Laird & Co. Ltd in 9.1943. *22.12.1954:* Struck the quay while berthing at Newport, Mon. *5.3.1955:* Fire broke out in the boiler room at Wellington, spreading to the general and refrigerated cargo

in No. 3 hold. It was put out on the 6th, temporary repairs were made at Wellington and final repairs at Falmouth. *23.5.1962:* Collided with and sank the tug FORAGER (244g, 1945) at Glasgow. 2 lives lost. *15.1.1966:* Collided with and sank the tug ISELGARTH (152g, 1949) off Penarth, inward bound to Cardiff from Auckland. 3 lives lost. *20.1.1966:* Damaged a propeller against the dock wall at Cardiff. *28.12.1966:* Transferred to the Federal S.N. Co. Ltd, (NZS, managers), but remained in NZS colours. *4.5.1967:* Sold for £134,000 to the Astroguarda Cia Nav. S.A., Piraeus, (Mavroleon Bros & Co., managers) and renamed NOR. *5.9.1967:* Arrived at Kaohsiung and delivered on the 9th for demolition.

PAPANUI at Auckland *(RCP)*

## 82. PAPANUI (1943—1965)

Official Number: 165898
Tonnages: 10,002 gross, 5,890 net, 9,785 deadweight. Dimensions: 477.0 (494.0 overall) x 64.8 x 39.0 feet. Draft: 27.3 feet.
High, intermediate and low pressure turbines double reduction geared to a single shaft, by the shipbuilders, 8,000 shp, 15.5 knots.
Refrigerated space: 483,400 cu.ft.

*27.10.1942:* Launched by A. Stephen & Sons Ltd, Glasgow, (Yard No. 592), and delivered to NZS on 20.5.1943. She was on requisition to the Liner Division until 5.4.1946. *14.7.1945:* Collided in Gravesend Bay, New York, with the steamer JAMES CALDWELL (7,191g, 1942) when outward bound for Pearl Harbor. She sailed again on 17.8.1945 after completion of repairs. *24.12.1951:* Took in tow the steamer THOULA CHANDRIS (2,401g, 1914) and brought her in to Nelson on the 25th. *9.7.1965:* Sold for £101,000 to the Astroguarda Cia Nav. S.A., Piraeus, (Mavroleon Bros & Co., managers), and renamed FLISVOS on the 14th. *5.10.1965:* Arrived at Kaohsiung for demolition.

PAPANUI towing the THOULA CHANDRIS towards Nelson in 1952 *(WAL)*

## 83. PAPAROA (1943—1966)

Official Number: 165899
Tonnages: 10,005 gross, 5,889 net, 9,785 deadweight. Dimensions: 477.0 (495.3 overall) x 64.8 x 39.0 feet. Draft: 27.3 feet.
High, intermediate and low pressure turbines double reduction geared to a single shaft, by the shipbuilders, 8,000 shp, 15.5 knots. Refrigerated space: 483,400 cu.ft.

*20.5.1943:* Launched by A. Stephen & Sons Ltd, Glasgow, (Yard No. 593), and delivered on 8.12.1943. She was on requisition to the Liner Division until 28.3.1946. *30.12.1949—21.2.1950:* Chartered to the Ministry of Food as a store ship. *17.10.1953:* Collided with the steamer ANGUSBRAE (2,905g, 1943) while leaving St John's, N.B. *19.4.1954:* Suffered a fire in No. 2 lower hold at Montreal. It was extinguished the following day. *12.6.1962:* Struck a submerged object off East London, damaging 3 propeller blades and the rudder. She arrived in port the same day and was docked for repairs. *28.12.1966:* Transferred to the Federal S.N. Co. Ltd, (NZS, managers). *11.5.1970:* Sold for £200,000 to the Astroguarda Cia Nav. S.A., Piraeus, (Mavroleon Bros & Co., managers), and renamed MARGARET. She made one outward voyage to Australia on charter to NZS. *24.11.1970:* Sold to the China National Machinery Import & Export Corporation and broken up at Whampoa.

PAPAROA at Dunedin

(IJF)

## 84. PIPIRIKI (1944—1966)

Official Number: 165900
Tonnages: 10,057 gross, 5,918 net, 9,785 deadweight. Dimensions: 477.0 (494.0 overall) x 64.8 x 39.0 feet. Draft: 27.3 feet.
High, intermediate and low pressure turbines double reduction geared to a single shaft, by the shipbuilders, 8,000 shp, 15.5 knots.
Refrigerated space: 481,500 cu.ft.

*28.12.1943:* Launched by A. Stephen & Sons Ltd, Glasgow, (Yard No. 597), and delivered to NZS on 16.5.1944. She was on requisition to the Liner Division until 29.5.1946. *30.11.1955:* Struck the quay wall at Swansea while leaving for Adelaide. *13.6.1956:* Suffered a fire in the insulation while under repair at Falmouth. It was extinguished after 5 hours. *28.12.1966:* Transferred to the Federal S.N. Co. Ltd, (NZS, managers). *14.1.1968:* Shed a propeller blade in mid-Pacific, bound London to Apia and Suva and proceeded under auxiliary sail and slow engine speed to Suva where she arrived on 2.2.1968. She was docked at Wellington for repairs. *3.2.1971:* Arrived at Kaohsiung from Dunedin and delivered on the 5th to the Nan Feng Steel Enterprise Co. Ltd. for the sum of £160,000. Demolition began on the 18th.

PIPIRIKI at Auckland as completed with liferafts and without topmasts (WAL)

PIPIRIKI at Auckland

(RCP)

RAKAIA at Adelaide                                                     *(JYF)*

## 85. RAKAIA (1946—1966)

Official Number: 168539
Tonnages: 8,563 gross, 5,026 net. 1946: 8,213 gross, 4,504 net, 9,633 deadweight. Dimensions: 457.3 (474.2 overall) x 63.3 x 35.0 feet.
8 cyl. 2 S.C.D.A. B & W diesel by the shipbuilders, 7,500 bhp, 15 knots.
Passengers: 45 under war conditions. 1946—1950: 36 cabin class.
Refrigerated space: 367,900 cu.ft.

*30.12.1944:* Launched by Harland & Wolff Ltd, Belfast, (Yard No. 1230), and delivered on 30.6.1945 to the Ministry of War Transport, (NZS, managers), as EMPIRE ABERCORN. Registered at Belfast and on requisition to the Liner Division until 26.6.1946. *26.6.1946:* Sold to NZS for £512,000 and registered at London on 26.11.1946 as RAKAIA. *3—6.1950:* Converted at Liverpool as a cadet ship for 38 cadets, reduced to 28 in 1958. She ceased that role in 1968. *10.10.1957:* Suffered an engine breakdown in the North Atlantic (41°02'N-61°28'W) 700 miles out of New York, bound Bluff and New York to Manchester. She reached Liverpool after 11 days on 6 cylinders and with improvised sail assistance. Repairs by Harland & Wolff Ltd took 4 months. *28.12.1966:* Transferred to the Federal S.N. Co. Ltd, (NZS, managers). *22.8.1971:* Sold for $250,000 to the Lee Sing Shipbreaking Co. Ltd, Hong Kong, where demolition began in 11.1971.

HAPARANGI at Auckland                                               *(RCP)*

## 86. HAPARANGI (1947—1966)

Official Number: 181680
Tonnages: 11,281 gross, 6,650 net, 14,410 deadweight. Dimensions: 541.3 (560.7 overall) x 70.2 x 34.7 feet. Draft: 32.6 feet.
Twin screw, two x 5 cyl. 2 S.C.S.A. Doxford diesels by the shipbuilders, 12,800 bhp, 16 knots.
Refrigerated space: 522,650 cu.ft.

*20.2.1947:* Launched by John Brown & Co. Ltd, Clydebank, (Yard No. 634), and delivered to NZS on 26.8.1947. *28.5.1962:* Grounded in lower Otago harbour outward bound from Port Chalmers for Bluff. She was refloated after 4 hours. *28.12.1966:* Transferred to the Federal S.N. Co. Ltd, (NZS, managers). *1.10.1971:* Management transferred to P&O General Cargo Division. *19.4.1973:* Transferred to The Peninsular and Oriental S.N. Co. *8.9.1973:* Sold through Mitsui & Co. Ltd, London, to the Tung Cheng Steel Manufacturing Co. Ltd, Kaohsiung, where she had arrived on 6.9.1973. Demolition began on 22.2.1974.

HURUNUI at Adelaide

*(IJF)*

## 87. HURUNUI (1948—1966)

Official Number: 181932
Tonnages: 11,276 gross, 6,640 net, 14,940 deadweight. Dimensions: 541.5 (560.8 overall) x 70.3 x 34.8 feet. Draft: 32.6 feet.
Twin screw, two x 5 cyl. 2 S.C.S.A. Doxford diesels by Vickers-Armstrongs Ltd, Barrow, 12,800 bhp, 16 knots.
Refrigerated space: 522,100 cu.ft.

*14.8.1947:* Launched by Vickers-Armstrongs Ltd, Walker-on-Tyne, (Yard No. 105), and delivered to NZS on 14.6.1948 at a cost of £1,250,000. *20.6.1958:* Collided with and sank the tug LAVERNOCK (135g, 1919) at Cardiff when arriving from Lyttelton. 1 life lost. *14.12.1963:* Suffered an engineroom fire at Napier. *28.12.1966:* Transferred to the Federal S.N. Co. Ltd, (NZS, managers). *1.10.1971:* Management transferred to P&O General Cargo Division. *19.4.1973:* Transferred to The Peninsular and Oriental S.N. Co. *8.9.1973:* Sold to the Dongkuk Steel Mill Co. Ltd, Busan, where demolition commenced on 8.11.1973.

HINAKURA at Wellington

*(WAL)*

## 88. HINAKURA (1949—1966)

Official Number: 183041
Tonnages: 11,272 gross, 6,642 net, 14,620 deadweight. Dimensions: 541.3 (560.7 overall) x 70.2 x 34.7 feet. Draft: 32.6 feet.
Twin screw, two x 5 cyl. 2 S.C.S.A. Doxford diesels by the shipbuilders, 12,800 bhp, 16 knots.
Refrigerated space: 522,650 cu.ft.

*21.1.1949:* Launched by John Brown & Co. Ltd, Clydebank, (Yard No. 647). She had been named on the 19th but the launching was delayed by gale force winds. Delivered to NZS on 29.6.1949. *28.12.1966:* Transferred to the Federal S.N. Co. Ltd, (NZS, managers). *1.10.1971:* Management transferred to P&O General Cargo Division. *19.4.1973:* Transferred to The Peninsular and Oriental S.N. Co. *3.4.1974:* Suffered a fire in the engineroom bilges from a boiler blow-back at Wellington. *12.6.1974:* Arrived at Kaohsiung and on the 19th delivered to the Tung Cheng Steel Manufacturing Co. Ltd for breaking up which commenced 14.8.1974.

RANGITOTO at Wellington

(WAL)

## 89. RANGITOTO (1949—1966)

Official Number: 183069
Tonnages: 21,809 gross, 12,424 net, 16,000 deadweight.
Dimensions: 587.5 (609.2 overall) x 78.2 x 48.3 feet. Draft: 32.1 feet.
Twin screw, two x 6 cyl. 2 S.C.S.A. Doxford diesels by Vickers-Armstrongs Ltd, Barrow, 16,000 bhp, 17 knots.
Passengers: 416 one class. 1969: 355 1st class.
Refrigerated space: 494,600 cu.ft.

*12.1.1949:* Launched by Vickers-Armstrongs Ltd, Walker-on-Tyne, (Yard No. 109), and delivered to NZS on 5.8.1949 at a cost of £2,500,000. *25.8.1949:* Left London on her first New Zealand sailing to Wellington. *1965:* Mainmast removed. *28.12.1966:* Transferred to the Federal S.N. Co. Ltd, (NZS, managers). *14.6.1969:* Sailed from Auckland for London on the last NZS passenger voyage. *27.8.1969:* Sold to Oriental South America Lines Inc., Monrovia, (Island Navigation Corp., managers), rebuilt at Hong Kong and renamed ORIENTAL CARNAVAL. She entered round the world service from San Diego in 1970. *7.3.1975:* Laid up at Hong Kong. *18.2.1976:* Delivered to the Lee Sing Shipbreaking Co. Ltd for demolition at Hong Kong. *27.2.1976:* Demolition began.

RANGITOTO in the Panama Canal          (Brownell Collection, WSS)

RANGITOTO at Sydney on a Melbourne Cup cruise

(NJK)

RANGITANE at Auckland

(MP/WAL)

## 90. RANGITANE (1949—1966)

Official Number: 183153

Tonnages: 21,867 gross, 12,456 net, 14,700 deadweight. Dimensions: 587.5 (609.2 overall) x 78.2 x 48.7 feet. Draft: 32.1 feet.
Twin screw, two x 6 cyl. 2 S.C.S.A. Doxford diesels by the shipbuilders, 16,000 bhp, 17 knots.
Passengers: 416 one class. 1969: 350 1st class.
Refrigerated space: 494,600 cu.ft.

*30.6.1949:* Launched by John Brown & Co. Ltd., Clydebank, (Yard No. 648), and delivered to NZS on 15.12.1949. *27.1.1950:* Left London on her first New Zealand sailing to Auckland.

*8.3.1951:* Grounded in the River Scheldt off Terneuzen, inward bound from London to Antwerp. She was refloated by tugs on the 9th. *17.12.1952:* Suffered a fire in the cargo in No. 1 hold

*Continued overleaf*

The small lounge                    (Otago Maritime Society)

The drawing room                    (Otago Maritime Society)

The dining saloon                    (Otago Maritime Society)

A 4 berth pullman cabin                    (Otago Maritime Society)

**90. RANGITANE** — *continued*

at Auckland. *10.7.1953:* Sailed from London for Auckland but suffered a breakdown in the starboard engine and returned on the 11th. She sailed again on the 12th but returned once more on the 13th with a burnt out shaft bearing. She finally sailed on the 19th. *14.2.1956:* Arrived at Balboa after suffering an engine breakdown, bound Wellington to Southampton. She missed a round voyage while repairs were carried out by the shipbuilders. *10.10.1957:* Collided with the steamer HAWAIIAN TOURIST (7,643g, 1945) in San Pablo Reach, Panama Canal, bound London to Wellington. She left Balboa after repairs on the 16th. *6.1965:* Mainmast removed. *28.12.1966:* Transferred to the Federal S.N. Co. Ltd (NZS, managers). *30.3.1968:* Left Auckland on her final New Zealand voyage. *22.5.1968:* Sold for £210,000 to the Astroguarda Cia Nav. S.A., Piraeus, (Mavroleon Ship Management Ltd, managers), and renamed JAN. Chartered back to the Federal S.N. Co. Ltd for a cargo only voyage to Australia. *8.1968:* Sold to Taiwanese shipbreakers for demolition and arrived at Kaohsiung prior to 11.9.1968. *9.1968:* Resold to Oriental Latin America Lines Inc, Monrovia, (Island Navigation Corp., managers), and left Kaohsiung on 31.12.1968 as ORIENTAL ESMERALDA. *1—4.1969:* Refitted at Hong Kong. *6.1969:* Entered round the world service from San Diego. *10.2.1976:* Laid up at Hong Kong. *2.4.1976:* Arrived at Kaohsiung and delivered on the 13th to the I Shing Steel & Iron Works Co. Ltd who began demolition on 21.6.1976.

Bridge and quartermaster, RANGITANE — *(VHY/NZA)*

RUAHINE at Auckland — *(IJF)*

## 91. RUAHINE (1951—1966)

Official Number: 184417
Tonnages: 17,851 gross, 10,123 net, 12,380 deadweight. Dimensions: 563.5 (584.5 overall) x 75.2 x 43.5 feet. Draft: 29.6 feet.
Twin screw, two x 6 cyl. 2 S.C.S.A. Doxford diesels by the shipbuilders, 14,200 bhp, 17 knots.
Passengers: 267 one class. 1968: 229 1st class.
Refrigerated space: 425,000 cu.ft.

*11.12.1950:* Launched by John Brown & Co. Ltd, Clydebank, (Yard No. 658), and delivered to NZS on 3.5.1951. *22.5.1951:* Sailed from London on her first New Zealand voyage to Auckland. *7.9.1954:* Broke a piston in her starboard engine shortly before reaching Balboa, bound Wellington to Southampton. Delayed 5 days for repairs. *1965:* Mainmast removed. *28.12.1966:* Transferred to the Federal S.N. Co. Ltd, (NZS, managers). *19.6.1968:* Left Auckland on her final sailing. *3.9.1968:* Sold for £352,083 to International Export Lines Ltd, Nassau, (Island Navigation Corp., managers), and renamed ORIENTAL RIO. *10.1968—1.1969:* Rebuilt at Hong Kong and transferred to the Chinese Maritime Trust Ltd, Keelung. *16.2.1969:* Entered round the world service from San Diego. *11.1.1974:* Arrived at Kaohsiung and sold on the 15th to the Nan Feng Steel Enterprise Co. Ltd which began demolition on 18.2.1974.

# Chapter 7: Towards Containers and Absorption

The 1950's in the New Zealand trade were years of general prosperity fuelled in the early stages by the Korean War boom but tailing off towards the end as for the first time people began to wonder whether the traditional ships and methods were the answer for the future. It was a time of slow turn round in New Zealand ports with operations governed by the cost plus mentality underpinned by the stranglehold of the ''Conference Lines''—Shaw Savill, NZS/Federal, Port and Blue Star—on the trade. Incentive for major change was minimal, and this was reflected in the ships built for the Company at the time which incorporated incremental rather than radical changes; an officer or seaman familiar with the layout of the OTAIO of 1930 would have had little difficulty with the PIAKO of 1962.

The fourth OTAKI in 1953 introduced one change in being the first major cargo ship in the Company for over 25 years other than war-built tonnage to be driven by a single screw though she still had two main engines geared to the shaft in the manner pioneered in the Federal fleet 2 years earlier. The OTAIO of 1958 reverted to the twin screw arrangement, but the PIAKO in 1962, the last ship to be built with the traditional yellow funnel, was given both a single screw and a single main engine.

Subsidiary services were subject to changes in the 1950's. The first came in 1954 when it was decided to establish a separate company, the Avenue Shipping Company Ltd, under the management of Trinder, Anderson & Company to operate the smaller non-refrigerated ships in a back up capacity to the main fleet or for charter out as required. The 5 KAI ships were transferred to the new company and to replace them in the North American trades the 3 WH class ships WHAKATANE, WHANGAROA and WHARANUI were commissioned in 1954/56.

Launch of the WHARANUI (96) at Clydebank. Note that the forecastle has yet to be built on    (NZA)

The other initiative was one taken in conjunction with the other three Conference lines. New Zealand was seeking to diversify its export markets from their heavy reliance on the United Kingdom trade and, fearful that an outsider might attempt to cater for this need, the Conference lines in 1957 established the Crusader Shipping Company Ltd, principally to serve the trade to Japan, but later extended to the Caribbean. Each of the four lines had a 25% interest in the new company, but it was under the management of Shaw Savill with NZS/Federal having no direct part in its operation. The TURAKINA was built for Crusader service in 1960.

TURAKINA (98) in Crusader colours

(NZA)

The 1960's saw the first major re-thinking of new tonnage for over 30 years with the ordering of the T class. Delivered as the TAUPO, TEKOA and TONGARIRO in 1966/67, they introduced a completely new profile with a more compact amidships structure, Hallen derricks for the handling of cargo and a much higher service speed of 20 knots. Cosmetic changes were even more radical with the introduction of a light green hull with darker green boot-topping which had first appeared on the Avenue Company's ARMAGH in 1958 and the replacement of the yellow funnel by the Federal pattern. The new design was carried a stage further with the delivery of the Japanese built MATAURA and MANAPOURI in 1968 which were conceived with an eye for world wide trading with refrigerated cargoes as well as the New Zealand service. Neither of them was actually owned by NZS, but they were the last of the traditional cargo liners to carry the traditional Maori names.

The rest of the NZS fleet had also adopted the Federal funnel over the earlier months of 1966 and at the end of that year nearly all of the ships passed into Federal ownership. The move was explained on the basis of taxation advantages requiring a U.K. company ownership whereas NZS was still New Zealand registered. But it had all the hallmarks of the beginning of the end.

Moves in that direction had already begun with the announcement in 1965 of the formation of Overseas Containers Ltd to conduct the container operations of the P&O, Ocean (Blue Funnel), Furness Withy and British & Commonwealth Groups. The first to be tackled was the Australian trade in 1969, the same year that a decision was made after many months of negotiation with the New Zealand Producer Boards for the containerisation of the New Zealand trade by the ordering of the 4 largest refrigerated container ships to date. But the whole project came to a sudden end in May 1971 when rapidly rising costs brought a decision to cancel the orders. One of the ships was too far advanced at that stage to be aborted and was eventually completed for P&O in 1973 with the traditional NZS name of REMUERA though never owned by the Company. Containerisation of the New Zealand trade finally came in 1972, beyond the scope of this story.    While containers would eventually have brought about the end of NZS in its traditional form, it was other factors which were immediately responsible. The passenger service was becoming more and more uneconomic with increasing jet aircraft competition and the unrewarding employment of large hotel crews during lengthy turn rounds in New Zealand. Some minor changes were made such as the introduction of summer cruises around New Zealand and to the Pacific Islands, and the adding of further calls at Tahiti and Florida or Bermuda on the main line service, but these were only a postponement of the inevitable. A major miscalculation was the attempt to replace the original RANGIs with the former Cunard PARTHIA in 1962. Despite a costly refit before commissioning as the REMUERA, she remained essentially a North Atlantic ship whose enclosed decks were ill adapted for the warmer waters across the Pacific. Her turbine machinery was also uneconomic on the long hauls and she was moved on after only 3 years. The final sailing from Auckland by the RANGITOTO in July 1969 ended 96 years of continuous involvement with the New Zealand passenger trade.

The end of the Line. RANGITOTO (89) leaves Auckland on the last NZS passenger sailing                    *(WAL)*

The actual trigger for the removal of NZS from the shipping scene was the commissioning by the P&O Group of a firm of management consultants, McKinsey & Co., to make recommendations on the future of the entire Group operations. The principal proposal was the abandonment of all the separate Group shipping companies and the transfer of their functions to five new operating divisions, the NZS being allocated to that labelled General Cargo Division. The NZS specialised refrigerated cargo operations fitted rather uncomfortably alongside some of the more general cargo services of other Group companies, and many who had spent a lifetime with the Company felt that its needs tended to be swamped beneath the greater number of such ships and operators.

The proposals were adopted by the main P&O Board and brought into effect from 1st October 1971. Thus only 15 months short of its centenary, NZS disappeared from the shipping scene though the corporate entity continued in being as P&O (NZ) Ltd as the principal New Zealand based subsidiary of the P&O Group. It remains in existence today with its name slightly altered since 1989 to P&O New Zealand Ltd.

## Ships 92 to 105: OTAKI—MANAPOURI

OTAKI at Auckland

*(C. W. Hawkins)*

## 92. OTAKI (1953—1966)

Official Number: 185886
Tonnages: 10,934 gross, 6,240 net, 12,520 deadweight. Dimensions: 505.0 (525.9 overall) x 70.2 x 31.9 feet. Draft: 30.6 feet. Two 12 cyl. 2 S.C.S.A. Sulzer diesels by the shipbuilders, driving a single shaft through single reduction gearing and electromagnetic couplings, 11,500 bhp, 16 knots. Refrigerated space: 476,300 cu.ft.

*24.10.1952:* Launched by John Brown & Co. (Clydebank) Ltd, Clydebank, (Yard No. 671), ran trials on 29.4.1953 and delivered to NZS on 1.5.1953. *28.12.1966:* Transferred to the Federal S.N. Co. Ltd, (NZS, managers). *1.9.1969:* Rescued the crew of the steamer AGHIA ANASTASIA (5,288g, 1956) 365 miles north-west of Amsterdam Island, when bound Liverpool to Geelong. *1.10.1971:* Management transferred to P&O General Cargo Division. *19.4.1973:* Transferred to The Peninsular and Oriental

S.N. Co. *10.12.1975:* Sold to the World Sea Shipping Co. Ltd, Limassol, (Roussos Bros, managers), and renamed MAHMOUD. *5.1.1976:* Arrived at Perama and laid up. *28.1.1976:* Suffered a fire at Perama while refitting and declared a constructive total loss. *1979:* Sold at auction to Gisserlis Brokerage Ltd, Panama, renamed NATALIA, but remained laid up at Perama. *25.2.1984:* Arrived at Aliaga in tow for demolition by Ucler Gemi Bozmacilar Ticaret ve Sirketi.

HAURAKI at Port Chalmers

*(Bain-Wright Collection)*

## 93. HAURAKI (1953—1966) See NORFOLK (No. F.50)

WHAKATANE at Auckland                                                                 (RCP)

## 94. WHAKATANE (1954—1964)

Official Number: 186058
Tonnages: 8,726 gross, 4,907 net, 10,400 deadweight. Dimensions: 439.4 (471.7 overall) x 62.9 x 39.5 feet. Draft: 30.5 feet.
6 cyl. 2 S.C.S.A. Doxford diesel by the shipbuilders, 7,200 bhp, 15.5 knots.
Passengers: 8 1st class.
Refrigerated space: 94,900 cu.ft.

*6.1.1954:* Launched by A. Stephen & Sons Ltd, Glasgow, (Yard No. 640), and delivered to NZS on 20.5.1954. *5.5.1964:* Sold to the Union Steam Ship Company of New Zealand Ltd, Wellington, (still registered at London) and renamed WAITAKI. *1970:* Sold to the Cia Maritima Ta Teh S.A., Panama, (Tung Lee Navigation Co. Ltd, managers), and renamed SUCCESSFUL ENTERPRISE. *1.1973:* Sold to the Wan Lung Navigation Co. S.A., Panama, (Wan Tung Transportation Co. Ltd, managers), and renamed WAN YU. *2.1977:* Transferred to the Truthful Shipping Co. S.A., Panama, (Wan Tung Transportation Co. Ltd, managers), and renamed TRUTHFUL. *10.5.1977:* Laid up at Kaohsiung. *25.7.1977:* Damaged in collision during Typhoon Thelma. *11.1.1979:* Demolition commenced at Kaohsiung by the An Sung Iron & Steel Co.

WHANGAROA at Dunedin                                                                 (IJF)

## 95. WHANGAROA (1955—1965)

Official Number: 186307
Tonnages: 8,701 gross, 4,907 net, 10,028 deadweight. Dimensions: 439.4 (471.9 overall) x 62.9 x 39.5 feet. Draft: 30.5 feet.
6 cyl. 2 S.C.S.A. Doxford diesel by the shipbuilders, 7,200 bhp, 16 knots.
Passengers: 8 1st class.
Refrigerated space: 92,150 cu.ft.

*21.6.1955:* Launched by John Brown & Co. (Clydebank) Ltd, Clydebank, (Yard No. 684), and delivered to NZS on 15.10.1955. *16.3.1956:* Collided with a dock wall at Philadelphia, bound Auckland to Saint John, N.B. *10.9.1965:* Sold for £850,000 to the Union Steam Ship Company of New Zealand Ltd, Wellington, (still registered at London), and renamed WAINUI. *10.3.1966:* Suffered a fire in her cargo at Wellington; 40 bales of jute destroyed. *31.3.1970:* Sold to the British India Steam Navigation Co. Ltd, London, and renamed WARINA. *17.4.1971:* Sold to the Admiti Shipping Co. Ltd, Famagusta, (Kardamylian Development Corp., managers), and renamed GAROUFALIA. *10.1972:* Sold to the Ganadera Sudamericana S.A., Famagusta, (N. & J. Vlassopulos, managers), renamed DROMEUS and registered at Chios. *3.1973:* Resold to the Admiti Shipping Co. Ltd, Famagusta, (Kardamylian Development Corp., managers), and renamed GAROUFALIA. *19.3.1974:* Arrived at Kaohsiung and 22.3.1974 delivered to the Tai Kien Industry Co. Ltd who commenced demolition on 28.6.1974.

WHARANUI at Auckland    (RCP)

## 96. WHARANUI (1956–1966)

Official Number: 187456
Tonnages: 8,706 gross, 4,914 net, 10,248 deadweight. Dimensions: 439.4 (471.8 overall) x 62.9 x 39.5 feet. Draft: 30.5 feet.
6 cyl. 2 S.C.S.A. Doxford diesel by the shipbuilders, 7,200 bhp, 16 knots.
Passengers: 8 1st class.
Refrigerated space: 102,000 cu.ft.

*11.5.1956:* Launched by John Brown & Co. (Clydebank) Ltd, Clydebank, (Yard No. 685), and delivered to NZS 28.9.1956. *28.12.1966:* Transferred to the Federal S.N. Co. Ltd, (NZS, managers). *20.10.1969:* Sold to the British India Steam Navigation Co. Ltd, London, and renamed WAIPARA. *7.7.1971:* Sold to Guan Guan Shipping Pte Ltd, Singapore, and renamed GOLDEN LION. *13.4.1979:* Delivered at Kaohsiung to the Yi Ho Steel Enterprise Corporation who began demolition on 9.5.1979.

WHARANUI as GOLDEN LION in a steep sea off Sydney Heads    (JYF)

OTAIO at Auckland    (RCP)

## 97. OTAIO (1958–1966)

Official Number: 187758
Tonnages: 13,314 gross, 6,875 net, 13,725 deadweight. Dimensions: 490.5 (526.2 overall) x 73.3 x 43.0 feet. Draft: 32.0 feet.
Twin screw, two 6 cyl. 2 S.C.S.A. Doxford diesels by the shipbuilders, 12,400 bhp, 17 knots.
Cadets: 40 deck and 30 engineer.
Refrigerated space: 429,300 cu.ft.

*9.12.1957:* Launched by John Brown & Co. (Clydebank) Ltd, Clydebank, (Yard No. 709), and delivered to NZS 10.4.1958 at a cost of £2,750,000. *18.2.1965:* Suffered a fire in the refrigeration installations while berthed in King George V Dock,

*Continued overleaf*

**97. OTAIO** — *continued*

London. *28.12.1966:* Transferred to the Federal S.N. Co. Ltd (NZS, managers). *1.10.1971:* Management transferred to P&O General Cargo Division. *19.4.1973:* Transferred to The Peninsular and Oriental S.N. Co. *21.7.1976:* Sold to the Laggan Bay Shipping Co. Ltd, Monrovia, (Gulf Shipping Lines Ltd, managers), and renamed EASTERN ACADEMY. *1977:* Managers became World

Shipmanagement Services Pte Ltd, Singapore. *1978:* Managers became Gulfeast Ship Management Ltd, Hong Kong. *1981:* Transferred to the Arabian Maritime Transport Co. Ltd, Jeddah, (Gulfeast Ship Management Ltd, managers). *18.12.1981:* Arrived at Karachi and laid up. *20.7.1982:* Beached at Gadani Beach where demolition by Geofman Pharmaceuticals Ltd began on 11.10.1982.

TURAKINA at Auckland (RCP)

## 98. TURAKINA (1960—1966)

Official Number: 301224
Tonnages: 7,707 gross, 3,973 net, 8,600 deadweight. Dimensions: 425.0 (454.9 overall) x 62.2 x 38.0 feet. Draft: 28.8 feet.
8 cyl. 2 S.C.S.A. Sulzer diesel by George Clark (Sunderland) Ltd, 10,400 bhp, 16 knots.
Refrigerated space: 334,900 cu.ft.

*26.2.1960:* Launched by Bartram & Sons Ltd, Sunderland, (Yard No. 384), and delivered to NZS on 3.9.1960 for Crusader Line service from New Zealand to Japan. *28.12.1966:* Transferred to the Federal S.N. Co. Ltd, (NZS, managers). *12.2.1967:* Suffered a fire in No. 4 tween deck in 18°23'S-161°49'E, bound Kobe to Auckland. She put into Noumea on the 13th where the fire was extinguished. *1.10.1971:* Management transferred to P&O General Cargo Division. *19.4.1973:* Transferred to The Peninsular and Oriental S.N. Co.. *24.9.1973:* Suffered a fire in No.

3 hold at Mount Maunganui. *22.8.1977:* Sold to Uiterwijk Line (Reefer) Inc., Monrovia, (Uiterwijk Corp., managers), and renamed PATRICIA U. *1979:* Sold to the Sparta Shipping Co. S.A., Piraeus, (Kallimassias Maritime Ltd, managers). *1982:* Transferred to the Armadora Cia Frigorifica S.A., Piraeus, (Kallimassias Maritime Ltd, managers), and renamed GULF REEFER. *20.6.1983—13.11.1985:* Laid up at Astakos. *1985:* Sold to the Lisboa Shipping Co. Ltd, Valletta, and renamed SINES. *21.1.1986:* Arrived at Huangpu for demolition.

REMUERA at Auckland in original rig (MP/WAL)

REMUERA with later dome top to funnel at Lyttelton                                    (NJK)

## 99. REMUERA (1961—1966)

Official Number: 182417
Tonnages: 13,362 gross, 7,393 net, 11,485 deadweight. 1962: 13,619 gross, 7,424 net. Dimensions: 500.0 (534.0 overall) x 70.3 x 46.0 feet. Draft: 30.2 feet.
Twin screw, two sets of high and low pressure turbines double reduction geared, by the shipbuilders, 15,000 shp, 17 knots.
Passengers: 250 1st class. 1962: 350 one class.
Refrigerated space: 62,169 cu.ft. 1962: 30,419 cu.ft.

*25.2.1947:* Launched by Harland & Wolff Ltd, Belfast, (Yard No. 1331) and completed 4.1948 for Cunard White Star Ltd, Liverpool, as PARTHIA. *1949:* Transferred to the Cunard Steam-Ship Co. Ltd. *1953:* Fitted with Denny-Brown stabilisers. *1.11.1961:* Sold to NZS for £705,000. She was refitted at Glasgow by A. Stephen & Sons Ltd at a cost of £392,750 and renamed REMUERA on 12.4.1962. The refit was delayed by an accommodation fire on 5.1.1962. *1.6.1962:* Sailed from London on her first New Zealand voyage to Wellington. *3.-8.1963, 4.1964:* Made trans-Tasman voyages, Wellington to Sydney and return, between her United Kingdom—New Zealand runs.

*18.2.1964:* Rescued 360 people from the earthquake stricken island of Sao Jorge, Azores and landed them at Terceira the next day. *12.1.1965:* Demise chartered to the Eastern & Australian Steam Ship Co. Ltd, London. She left Auckland on 12.1964 on her final NZS voyage to Hong Kong and was handed over there and renamed ARAMAC. *28.12.1966:* Transferred to the Federal S.N. Co. Ltd. *9.8.1968:* Sold to the Eastern & Australian Steam Ship Co. Ltd., London for £676,700. *22.11.1969:* Delivered at Kaohsiung to the Chin Ho Fa Steel & Iron Co. Ltd who began demolition on 5.3.1970.

PIAKO at Auckland                                                                      (DNB)

## 100. PIAKO (1962—1966)

Official Number: 302884
Tonnages: 7,596 gross, 4,050 net, 10,290 deadweight. Dimensions: 460.0 (488.3 overall) x 66.3 x 41.3 feet. Draft: 28.2 feet.
8 cyl. 2 S.C.S.A. Sulzer diesel by the shipbuilders, 10,400 bhp, 16.5 knots, (18.5 knots on trials).
Refrigerated space: 450,800 cu.ft.

*10.10.1961:* Launched by A. Stephen & Sons Ltd, Glasgow, (Yard No. 676), and delivered to NZS on 11.1.1962 at a cost of £1,500,000. *17.10.1965:* Rescued 23 of the crew of the steamer MARLIN (2,547g, 1944) which foundered off the North Carolina coast in 34°38'N-75°32'W, and landed them at Savannah. *28.12.1966:* Transferred to the Federal S.N. Co. Ltd, (NZS, managers). *1.10.1971:* Management transferred to P&O General Cargo Division. *19.4.1973:* Transferred to The Peninsular

and Oriental S.N. Co. *21.1.1978:* Suffered fire damage to her cargo while berthed at Lyttelton. *28.9.1978:* Laid up at Birkenhead. *31.1.1979:* Sold to the Blue Ocean Cia Maritima S.A., Piraeus, (Eureka Shipping Co. S.A., managers), registered at Panama and renamed REEFER QUEEN. *1982:* Sold to Coronado Shipping Inc., Piraeus, (Arvaship Inc., managers), still registered at Panama. *12.8.1984:* Arrived at Shanghai for demolition.

TAUPO at Auckland                                                                                                (MP)

## 101. TAUPO (1966–1969)

Official Number: 308044
Tonnages: 8,219/10,983 gross, 4,474/6,126 net, 11,325/11,866 deadweight. Dimensions: 490.1 (527.6 overall) x 71.3 x 44.5 feet. Draft: 29.7/30.4 feet.
8 cyl. 2 S.C.S.A. Sulzer diesel by George Clark & N.E.M. Ltd, Sunderland, 17,600 bhp, 20 knots.
Refrigerated space: 483,100 cu.ft.

*27.8.1965:* Launched by Bartram & Sons Ltd, Sunderland, (Yard No. 401), and delivered to NZS on 18.3.1966. *12.3.1967:* Grounded on arriving at Nelson. Refloated undamaged after 10 hours. *6.1969:* Transferred to the Federal S.N. Co. Ltd, (NZS, managers). *1.10.1971:* Management transferred to P&O General Cargo Division. *19.4.1973:* Transferred to The Peninsular and Oriental S.N. Co. *10.1.1975:* Put back to Gisborne 50 miles out, bound for the United Kingdom, after developing cracks in a turbo blower. Delayed for 3 days. *21.4.1977:* Transferred to Strick Line Ltd, London. *19.6.1980:* Sold to Austasia Line (Pte) Ltd, Singapore, delivered that day and renamed MANDAMA. *28.5.1984:* Anchored off Chittagong for demolition. *8.6.1984:* N.Z.N. Shipbreaking Co. commenced work.

TEKOA                                                                                                          (WAL)

## 102. TEKOA (1966–1969)

Official Number: 309760
Tonnages: 8,226/10,975 gross, 4,478/6,151 net, 11,325/11,866 deadweight. Dimensions: 490.1 (527.6 overall) x 71.3 x 44.5 feet. Draft: 29.7/30.4 feet.
8 cyl. 2 S.C.S.A. Sulzer diesel by George Clark & N.E.M. Ltd, Sunderland, 17,600 bhp, 20 knots.
Refrigerated space: 483,100 cu.ft.

*8.3.1966:* Launched by Bartram & Sons Ltd, Sunderland, (Yard No. 402), and delivered to NZS on 20.10.1966 at a cost of £2,004,000. *6.1969:* Transferred to the Federal S.N. Co. Ltd, (NZS, managers). *2.1970:* Dropped a propeller blade, bound Panama to Sydney and reached port on the remaining blades on 6.2.1970. *1.10.1971:* Management transferred to P&O General Cargo Division. *19.4.1973:* Transferred to The Peninsular and Oriental S.N. Co. *18.9.1978:* Transferred to Strick Line Ltd, London. *21.7.1980:* Sold to the Austasia Line (Pte) Ltd, Singapore, delivered that day and renamed MAHSURI. *27.1.1984:* Arrived at Kaohsiung where demolition by the Chin Tai Steel Enterprise Co. Ltd began on 16.2.1984.

TONGARIRO at Lyttelton

(NJK)

## 103. TONGARIRO (1967—1969)

Official Number: 309960

Tonnages: 8,233 gross, 4,483 net, 11,866 deadweight. Dimensions: 490.1 (527.6 overall) x 71.3 x 44.5 feet. Draft: 30.4 feet. 8 cyl. 2 S.C.S.A. Sulzer diesel by George Clark & N.E.M. Ltd, Sunderland, 17,600 bhp, 20 knots. Refrigerated space: 483,100 cu.ft.

*14.10.1966:* Launched by Bartram & Sons Ltd, Sunderland, (Yard No. 403). She had been named the previous day but bad weather delayed the launching. Delivered to NZS on 4.5.1967 at a cost of £2,004,000. *6.1969:* Transferred to the Federal S.N. Co. Ltd, (NZS, managers). *1.10.1971:* Management transferred to P&O General Cargo Division. *19.4.1973:* Transferred to The Peninsular and Oriental S.N. Co. *7.5.1978:* Lost a propeller blade shortly after leaving Singapore for Auckland, but completed the voyage on the remaining blades on 29.5.1978. She was docked

at Wellington for repairs on 10.6.1978. *18.9.1978:* Transferred to Strick Line Ltd. *30.11.1979:* Sold to Seaspeed Maritime Inc., Piraeus, (Arvaship Inc., managers), and renamed REEFER PRINCESS. *2.1982:* Sold to the Platana Maritime Co. S.A., Piraeus, (Diana Shipping Agencies S.A., managers), and renamed CAPETAN LEONIDAS. *8.9.1983:* Laid up at Piraeus. *10.9.1985:* Delivered at Karachi to the M. Nasir Trading Co. and beached at Gadani Beach on the 15th. Demolition began that day.

MATAURA at Auckland

(DNB)

## 104. MATAURA (1968—1971)

Official Number: 335736

Tonnages: 9,504 gross, 4,454 net, 11,731 deadweight. Dimensions: 505.0 (540.0 overall) x 74.8 x 46.2 feet. Draft: 30.2 feet. 9 cyl. 2 S.C.S.A. B & W diesel by the shipbuilders, 20,700 bhp, 21 knots. Refrigerated space: 546,250 cu.ft. 1977: 633,800 cu.ft.

*18.12.1967:* Launched by Mitsui Zosen, Tamano, (Yard No. 786), and delivered 15.5.1968 into the ownership of The Peninsular and Oriental S.N. Co., (NZS, managers). *1.10.1971:* Management transferred to P&O General Cargo Division. *23.3.1977:* Transferred to the Federal S.N. Co. Ltd. *30.8.1977:* Renamed WILD MALLARD for service with Lauritzen Peninsular Reefers A/S, and refrigerated capacity enhanced at Sandefjord from 5—9.1977. *2.10.1981:* Sold to the Hampton Shipping Corp., Piraeus, (Comninos Bros Shipping Co. S.A., managers), with a

charter back and renamed MACEDONIAN REEFER. *28.5.1985:* Laid up at Setubal. *9.1987:* Transferred to the National Renewal Cia Nav. S.A., Piraeus, (Comninos Bros Shipping Co. S.A., managers), registered at Panama and renamed MARACAIBO REEFER. *1988:* Sold to the Meadway Navigation Co. Ltd, Panama, (International Reefer Services S.A., managers) and renamed BOLERO REEFER. *1996:* Renamed CORRADO I. Still in service.

MANAPOURI at Lyttelton

(NJK)

## 105. MANAPOURI (1968—1971)

Official Number: 335896
Tonnages: 9,505 gross, 4,457 net, 11,705 deadweight. Dimensions: 505.0 (540.0 overall) x 74.8 x 46.3 feet. Draft: 30.2 feet.
9 cyl. 2 S.C.S.A. B & W diesel by the shipbuilders, 20,700 bhp, 21 knots.
Refrigerated space: 546,248 cu.ft. 1977: 633,800 cu.ft.

*26.3.1968:* Launched by Mitsui Zosen, Tamano, (Yard No. 787), and delivered 28.8.1968 into the ownership of the Federal S.N. Co. Ltd, (NZS, managers). *1.10.1971:* Management transferred to P&O General Cargo Division. *2.11.1977:* Renamed WILD MARLIN for service with Lauritzen Peninsular Reefers A/S, and refrigerated capacity enhanced at Sandefjord from 8—11.1977. *8.2.1982:* Sold to the Lex Maritime Corp., Piraeus, (Comninos Bros Shipping Co. S.A., managers), delivered that day with charter back and renamed MARATHON REEFER. *20.6.1985:* Laid up at Setubal. *12.1987:* Sold to Naval Link S.A., Piraeus, (Transcontinental Maritime & Trading S.A., managers), and renamed CORFU REEFER. *1990:* Sold to the Tritonis Maritime Corp., Panama, and renamed TRITON K. *1990:* Sold to Continental Success S.A., Piraeus, (PMT Shipping S.A., managers), and renamed LIMON TRADER. *1992:* Managers became Target Marine S.A., Piraeus. *1996:* Sold to Seastone Maritime Ltd, Valletta. Still in service.

The following ship, although never owned by NZS, is included as she had an NZS name, was designed for an NZS service, was commanded by the former NZS Commodore on her maiden voyage and, had matters turned out otherwise, would probably have finished up in NZS ownership.

REMUERA at Sydney on ACT charter

(JYF)

## (106). REMUERA

Official Number: 360840
Tonnages: 42,007 gross, 24,806 net, 32,753 deadweight. Dimensions: 774.3 (826.8 overall) x 105.4 x 68.0 feet. Draft: 36.2 feet.
Twin screw, two sets of high and low pressure turbines double reduction geared, by GEC Turbine Generators Ltd, Manchester, 48,660 shp, 23 knots, (25 knots on trials). 1983: Single screw, 9 cyl. 2 S.C.S.A. Sulzer diesel by Mitsubishi Heavy Industries Ltd, Kobe, 29,610 bhp, 21 knots.
Refrigerated capacity: 1,151 TEU containers below deck, plus 50 maximum on deck.

*12.6.1972:* Launched by Swan Hunter Shipbuilders Ltd, Walker, (Yard No. 40), and delivered 13.12.1973 into the ownership of The Peninsular and Oriental S.N. Co., London. (see Chronology). Chartered on completion to Associated Container Transportation (Australia) Ltd. *22.1.1975:* Suffered boiler trouble, bound London to Wellington. She put into Monrovia for repairs (twice) and then returned to Zeebrugge where she arrived on 21.3.1975. She was under repair at the shipbuilders for 3 months. *30.5.1975:* Container Fleets Ltd became the managers. *1.9.1975:* Put into Las Palmas with defective steering gear, bound London to Wellington. *13.6.1977:* Renamed REMUERA BAY and chartered to Overseas Containers Ltd., London. *6.10.1977:* Suffered a minor engineroom fire at Hamburg. *12.11.1980:* Arrived at Wellington from London on one screw following a breakdown of one turbine set. Repaired at Wellington. *1981:* Overseas Containers Ltd became the managers. *21.2.1983:* Sold to Headwest Ltd, London. *1983:* Transferred to Lombard Charterhire Ltd, London. *18.8.1983—1.1984:* Re-engined at Chita by Ishikawajima-Harima Heavy Industries Ltd. *1985:* Sold to Overseas Containers Ltd, London. *1.1.1987:* Owners renamed P&O Containers Ltd, following full acquisition by P&O on 28.5.1986. *18.3.1991:* Sold to Abbey National March Leasing (1) Ltd, London, and leased back. *1.1994:* Renamed BERLIN EXPRESS and painted in Hapag-Lloyd colours as part of the new space sharing arrangements in the Australian and New Zealand trade. *18.12.1996:* Reverted to P&O Containers Ltd. *31.12.1996:* Owners renamed P&O Nedlloyd Ltd. Still in service.

# VESSELS IN NOMINAL NZS OWNERSHIP BUT MANNED AND MANAGED BY OTHER P&O GROUP COMPANIES

## G.1 QUILOA (1960—1966) Tanker

Official Number: 301108
Tonnages: 13,113 gross, 7,341 net, 19,026 deadweight. Dimensions: 535.0 (560.0 overall) x 72.0 x 39.6 feet. Draft: 30.2 feet.
High and low pressure turbines double reduction geared, by the shipbuilders, 8,800 shp, 16.09 knots on trials.

*3.11.1959:* Launched by Scotts' Shipbuilding & Engineering Co. Ltd, Greenock, (Yard No. 678), and delivered 24.3.1960 to NZS, (British India Steam Navigation Co. Ltd, managers). *18.6.1963:* Managers became Trident Tankers Ltd. *26.3.1966:* Transferred to the British India Steam Navigation Co. Ltd, London, (Trident Tankers Ltd continuing as managers). *1.10.1969:* Transferred to Trident Tankers Ltd, London. *16.8.1971:* Managers became P&O Bulk Shipping Division. *7.3.1972:* Sold to the Pandora Shipping Co. S.A., Famagusta, (JOC Tankers, managers), and renamed MICHIEL. *1.1974:* Sold to the Kai Sun Shipping Co. S.A., Panama, (Seashine Navigation Corp. Ltd, Hong Kong, managers) and renamed GREAT JUSTICE. *12.2.1977:* Arrived at Kaohsiung for demolition.

QUILOA in Trident colours                          *(A. Duncan)*

## G.2 KOHINUR (1963—1968)

Official Number: 304468
Tonnages: 10,039 gross, 5,852 net, 14,515 deadweight. Dimensions: 470.0 (508.3 overall) x 65.3 x 40.0 feet. Draft: 30.1 feet.
5 cyl. 2 S.C.S.A. Sulzer diesel by Barclay, Curle & Co. Ltd, Glasgow, 7,500 bhp, 14.5 knots.

*28.12.1962:* Launched by C. Connell & Co. Ltd, Glasgow, (Yard No. 500), and delivered 12.3.1963 to NZS, (Asiatic Steam Navigation Co. Ltd, managers). *17.2.1964:* Managers became Hain-Nourse Management Ltd. *30.9.1968:* Transferred to Hain-Nourse Ltd, London. *1.10.1971:* Managers became P&O General Cargo Division. *11.5.1972:* Transferred to The Peninsular and Oriental S.N. Co. *17.4.1975:* Renamed STRATHNAIRN. *24.11.1977:* Sold to the British Bay Shipping Co. Ltd, Singapore, (Zodiac Maritime Agencies Ltd, managers), and renamed SILVERGATE. *6.1979:* Renamed ANTILLA. *7.1984:* Managers became Soc. Anon. Monegasque d'Administration Maritime et Aerienne, Monte Carlo. *22.3.1986:* Arrived at Kaohsiung for demolition by the Gwo Feng Steel Enterprise Co. Ltd. Work began on the 27th.

KOHINUR at Auckland in Hain-Nourse colours                *(WAL)*

NURJEHAN                                            (A. Duncan)

## G.3 NURJEHAN (1963—1968)

Official Number: 304514

Tonnages: 8,380 gross, 4,731 net, 12,087 deadweight. Dimensions: 450.5 (481.8 overall) 62.5 x 37.9 feet. Draft: 29.7 feet.
5 cyl. 2 S.C.S.A. B & W diesel by J.G. Kincaid & Co. Ltd, Greenock, 8,120 bhp, 14.5 knots.

*29.1.1963:* Launched by Lithgows Ltd, Port Glasgow, (Yard No. 1122), and delivered 30.4.1963 to NZS, (Asiatic Steam Navigation Co. Ltd, managers). *17.2.1964:* Managers became Hain-Nourse Management Ltd. *30.9.1968:* Transferred to Hain-Nourse Ltd, London. *2.1971:* Renamed ADVOCATE for duration of a time charter to the Charente Steam Ship Co. Ltd, Liverpool, (T & J Harrison Ltd, managers). *1.10.1971:* Owners' managers became P&O General Cargo Division. *11.5.1972:* Transferred to The Peninsular and Oriental S. N. Co. *30.1.1973:* Renamed NURJEHAN on completion of the time charter. *28.8.1975:* Renamed STRATHNEVIS. *9.12.1977:* Sold to Unimed Shipping Inc., Piraeus, (Thenamaris Maritime Inc., managers), and renamed IOANNIS. *1980:* Managers became Labora Maritime Inc. *1981:* Managers became the Shipping & Commercial Corp. *1982:* Sold to the Dafnopotamos Maritime Corp., Piraeus, (Loutra Shipping & General Enterprises Ltd, managers), and renamed DIMITRIOS P. PAPASTRATIS. *12.1984:* Eastern Shipbreakers commenced demolition at Chittagong.

TRENEGLOS at Cape Town                              (NJK)

## G.4 TRENEGLOS (1963—1968)

Official Number: 304673

Tonnages: 9,976 gross, 5,793 net, 14,457 deadweight. Dimensions: 470.0 (505.3 overall) x 65.3 x 40.0 feet. Draft: 27.1 feet.
5 cyl. 2 S.C.S.A. Sulzer diesel by Fairfield-Rowan Ltd, Glasgow, 7,500 bhp, 15 knots.

*28.3.1963:* Launched by Wm Hamilton & Co. Ltd, Port Glasgow, (Yard No. 527), and delivered 8.1963 to NZS, (Hain Steamship Co. Ltd, managers). *17.2.1964:* Managers became Hain-Nourse Management Ltd. *12.11.1964:* Grounded on Patiti Reef 1 mile south of Timaru, bound Timaru to Dunedin. Refloated on the 16th with severe bottom damage and returned to Timaru. Left in tow for Wellington on 22.11.1964, temporarily repaired there and permanently repaired at Hong Kong. *4.1966:* Collided at Beira with the tanker IOANNA V (12,920g, 1956). *30.9.1968:* Transferred to Hain-Nourse Ltd, London. *1.10.1971:* Managers became P&O General Cargo Division. *11.5.1972:* Transferred to The Peninsular and Oriental S.N. Co. *28.11.1974:* Renamed STRATHTRUIM. *27.1.1978:* Sold to Torenia Maritime Inc., Singapore, (Zodiac Maritime Agencies Ltd, managers), and renamed SIAM BAY. *1980:* Sold to Chrysalis Compania Navigation S.A., Piraeus, (Family Shipping Co. S.A., managers), and renamed FAMILY ANGEL. *1984:* Transferred to Temple S.A., Panama, same managers, and renamed DOMAN. *2.8.1985:* Arrived at Nantong for demolition.

# VESSELS MANAGED FOR H.M. GOVERNMENT
## FIRST WORLD WAR

### M.1 WAR CHARON (1918—1919)

Official Number: 142772
Tonnages: 7,900 gross, 4880 net, 10,800 deadweight. Dimensions: 450.0 x 58.5 x 37.1 feet. Draft: 29.3 feet.
Twin screw, two T.3 cyl. by the shipbuilders, 7,000 ihp, 13 knots.
Refrigerated space: 428,119 cu.ft.

*22.11.1918:* Launched by Workman, Clark & Co. Ltd, Belfast, (Yard No. 438), for The Shipping Controller, (NZS, managers), a G class standard ship. *25.1.1919:* Ran trials as ROYALSTAR having been sold while fitting out to the Royalstar Steamship Co. Ltd, London, (Blue Star Line Ltd, managers). *26.1.1919—17.7.1919:* Taken up under the Liner Requisition Scheme. *14.4.1920:* Transferred to the Union Cold Storage Co. Ltd, (Blue Star Line (1920) Ltd, managers). *2.9.1929:* Managers became Blue Star Line Ltd and renamed ROYAL STAR. *31.3.1940—20.4.1944:* Requisitioned for the Liner Division. *11.3.1941:* Damaged by air attack off Stonehaven. *20.4.1944:* Sunk by aircraft torpedo north-east of Algiers (37°02'N-03°41'E), bound Buenos Aires to Malta, Taranto and Alexandria with refrigerated cargo. 1 life lost.

WAR CHARON as ROYAL STAR at Liverpool *(IJF)*

LUCIE WOERMAN at Sydney in NZS colours

*(IJF)*

### M.2 LUCIE WOERMANN (1919—1920)

Official Number: 143075
Tonnages: 4,630 gross, 2,861 net. Dimensions: 366.5 x 47.1 x 25.1 feet.
T.3 cyl. by the shipbuilders, 2,600 ihp, 12.5 knots.
Passengers: 1919: 420 in troop conditions. 1922: 61 1st, 76 2nd, 42 3rd class.

*5.7.1902:* Launched by Blohm & Voss, Hamburg, (Yard No. 157), and delivered 13.9.1902 to the Woermann Linie Kom. Ges., Hamburg. *1913:* Owners became Woermann Linie A.G. *1915:* Requisitioned by the German Navy as an auxiliary and served in the Submarine School. *20.3.1919:* Surrendered to the British Government and registered in the name of The Shipping Controller, London, (NZS, managers). *28.3.1919:* Arrived at London and requisitioned as an Expeditionary Force Transport until *3.2.1920.* *16.7.1920:* NZS management ceased and chartered to a consortium of German sailing ship owners to take crews to South America. *29.1.1921:* Allocated to the French Government. *1.1922:* Transferred to the Societe des Services Contractuels des Messageries Maritimes, Marseilles, and renamed AVIATEUR ROLAND GARROS. *5.6.1931:* Arrived at Savona for demolition.

WINDHUK at Sydney in NZS colours                    (IJF)

## M.3 WINDHUK (1919—1920)

Official Number: 143111
Tonnages: 6,344 gross, 3,950 net, 7,380 deadweight. Dimensions: 410.4 x 50.7 x 28.6 feet.
Twin screw, two T.3 cyl. by the shipbuilders, 2,800 ihp, 12.5 knots.
Passengers: 100 1st and 260 3rd class. 1919: 96 1st, 62 2nd and 80 3rd class. 1928: 340.

*8.11.1905:* Launched by Blohm & Voss, Hamburg, (Yard No. 181), and delivered 25.1.1906 to the Woermann Linie Kom. Ges., Hamburg, as GERTRUD WOERMANN. *14.4.1907:* Collided with the barque WANDERER (2,813g, 1891) in the Elbe. The barque sank on the 16th. *25.4.1907:* Sold to the Hamburg-Amerikanische Packetfahrt A.G., Hamburg, and renamed WINDHUK. *4.8.1914:* Laid up as a depot ship at Hamburg. *28.3.1919:* Arrived at London, surrendered 1.4.1919 to the British Government and registered in the name of The Shipping Controller, London, (NZS, managers). *1.4.1919—15.12.1919:*

Requisitioned as an Expeditionary Force Transport. *3.1.1920:* Management transferred to Elder Dempster & Co. Ltd. *29.12.1920:* Sold to Ellerman Lines Ltd, Liverpool, (H.H. McAllester, manager), and renamed CITY OF GENOA. *1926:* W.T. Murray became manager. *3.7.1928:* Sold for £40,000 to the Cia Colonial de Navegacao, Lisbon, registered at Loanda and renamed JOAO BELO. *5.7.1950:* Sold to BISCO and allocated to the Stockton Shipbreaking & Salvage Co. Ltd who began demolition at Stockton on 25.7.1950.

## M.4 LA PLATA (1919—1919)

Official Number: 143209
Tonnages: 4,004 gross, 2,544 net, 4,280 deadweight. Dimensions: 361.3 x 44.8 x 25.7 feet.
T.3 cyl. by the Reiherstieg Maschinenfabrik, Hamburg, 2,000 ihp, 11.5 knots.
Passengers: 54 1st class, 330 steerage.

15.6.1898: Launched by the Reiherstieg Schiffswerft, Hamburg, (Yard No. 401), and delivered 20.8.1898 to the Hamburg-Sudamerikanische Dampfs. Ges., Hamburg, as PELOTAS. *27.2.1901:* Renamed LA PLATA. *24.5.1904:* Sold to the Hamburg-Amerikanische Packetfahrt A.G., Hamburg. *26.3.1919:* Surrendered to the British Government and registered in the name of The Shipping Controller, London, (NZS, managers from 1.5.1919). *3.4.1919—23.2.1921:* Requisitioned as an Expeditionary Force Transport. *1.7.1919:* Management transferred to Ellerman's Wilson Line Ltd. *1921:* Sold to H.H. Schmidt, Hamburg. *1923:* Sold to the Cia Colonial de Navegacao, Lisbon, (Soc. Agricola da Ganda, managers to 1925), registered at Loanda and renamed GUINE. *22.8.1930:* Went ashore at Areia Branca, Bolama, (11°N—15°W) bound Luanda to Lisbon with passengers and general. She was finally abandoned on the 28th, but most of the cargo was salved.

LA PLATA in Ellerman's Wilson colours         (WAL)

SWAKOPMUND as ARAFURA       *(IJF)*

## M.5 SWAKOPMUND (1919—1921)

Official Number: 143182
Tonnages: 5,631 gross, 3,544 net. Dimensions: 403.0 x 49.2 x 27.1 feet.
T.3 cyl. by the shipbuilders, 2,500 ihp, 11 knots.
Passengers: 44 1st, 20 2nd, 32 3rd class and 638 steerage. 1921: 30 saloon.
Refrigerated space (from 1922): 21,400 cu.ft.

*28.11.1903:* Launched by the Bremer Vulkan, Schiffbau & Maschinenfabrik, Vegesack, (Yard No. 453), and ran trials on 16.1.1904 for the Dampfs. Ges. Argo, Bremen, as FLORIDA. *15.10.1904:* Sold to the Woermann Linie Kom. Ges., Hamburg, and renamed PROFESSOR WOERMANN. *11.5.1907:* Sold to the Hamburg-Amerikanische Packetfahrt A.G., Hamburg, and renamed SWAKOPMUND. *6.4.1919:* Surrendered to the British Government and registered in the name of The Shipping Controller, London, (NZS, managers from 10.4.1919). *7.4.1919—5.10.1919* and *27.1.1920—5.2.1921:* Requisitioned as an Expeditionary Force Transport. *27.11.1919:* Suffered a fire in No. 3 hold in Victoria Dock, London. *4.2.1921:* Sold to the Eastern & Australian Steam Ship Co. Ltd, London, and renamed ARAFURA. *24.2.1929:* Lost a propeller blade 10 miles off North Reef, bound Townsville to Brisbane. As a cyclone was expected, the tug CORINGA (294g, 1914) was despatched and took her in tow on the 26th. The weather worsened and the tug FORCEFUL (288g, 1925) was also sent out. After passing through the eye of the cyclone, ARAFURA's engines broke down completely on 2.3.1929 and she finally reached Brisbane in tow on the 3rd. *23.8.1929:* Sold to the Osaka Kaiji K.K., Osaka. *3.1930:* Broken up in Japan.

## M.6 TASMANIA (1920—1921) See TASMANIA (No. 64)

# SECOND WORLD WAR

EMPIRE AVOCET as COTATI
*(National Maritime Museum, San Francisco/NZA)*

## M.7 EMPIRE AVOCET (1941—1942)

Official Number: 168289
Tonnages: 6,015 gross, 4,315 net. Dimensions: 402.6 (416.5 overall) x 53.0 x 32.0 feet.
High and low pressure turbines, double reduction geared to a single shaft, by W. & A. Fletcher Co., Hoboken, 637 nhp, 11 knots.
Refrigerated space: 307,900 cu.ft. (Laid down as a dry cargo ship, but converted to refrigerated while under construction).

*30.3.1919:* Launched by the Moore Shipbuilding Co., Oakland, (Yard No. 1019), and delivered 26.8.1919 to the United States Shipping Board, San Francisco, as COTATI. *28.10.1936:* Transferred to the United States Maritime Commission. *23.1.1941:* Sold to the Ministry of Shipping, later Ministry of War Transport, London, (NZS, managers). *26.9.1941:* Delivered at Baltimore, having been requisitioned for the Ship Management Division on 14.7.1941. *1942:* Renamed EMPIRE AVOCET. *29.9.1942:* Sunk by torpedo and gunfire from U 125 300 miles south of Freetown (04°05'N-13°23'W), bound Buenos Aires and Rio Grande to Freetown and Britain with refrigerated and general cargo. 2 lives lost and 2 taken prisoner by the submarine.

EMPIRE MERGANSER                                          (Mariners Museum/NZA)

## M.8 EMPIRE MERGANSER (1941—1947)

Official Number: 168292
Tonnages: 6,187 gross, 4,453 net. Dimensions: 402.6 (416.5 overall) x 53.0 x 32.0 feet.
High and low pressure turbines, double reduction geared to a single shaft, by the Westinghouse Electric & Manufacturing
Co., East Pittsburgh, 652 nhp, 11 knots.
Refrigerated space: 291,500 cu.ft. (Laid down as a dry cargo ship, but converted to refrigerated while under construction).

*4.7.1918:* Launched by the Moore Shipbuilding Co., Oakland, (Yard No. 148), and delivered 7.6.1919 to the United States Shipping Board, San Francisco, as GUIMBA. *26.10.1936:* Transferred to the United States Maritime Commission. *23.1.1941:* Sold to the Ministry of Shipping, later Ministry of War Transport, London, (NZS, managers). *28.12.1941:* Delivered at Baltimore, having been requisitioned for the Liner Division from 14.7.1941—20.6.1947. She spent from 22.7.1944—7.12.1944 as a military store ship and from 8.12.1944—8.1.1946 as a

refrigerated store ship. *1942:* Renamed EMPIRE MERGANSER. *17.3.1943:* Suffered a fire in coal in No. 4 hold at Bahia. The fire was put out on the 23rd and she sailed on the 30th. *20.6.1947:* Sold to United Whalers Ltd, London, (N.R. Bugge, manager), and renamed KETOS on 23.10.1947. *1949:* Transferred to Hector Whaling Ltd, London. *2.4.1951:* Suffered an engineroom explosion and sank on the 3rd 650 miles north-east of Ceara, Brazil (02°25'N-30°30'W).

EMPIRE WHIMBREL                                          (Mariners Museum/NZA)

## M.9 EMPIRE WHIMBREL (1941—1943)

Official Number: 168242
Tonnages: 5,983 gross, 3,663 net. Dimensions: 402.6 (416.5 overall) x 53.0 x 32.0 feet.
High and low pressure turbines, double reduction geared to a single shaft, by the Midwest Engine Co., Indianapolis, 637 nhp, 11 knots.
Refrigerated space: 291,540 cu.ft. (Laid down as a dry cargo ship but completed as a refrigerated vessel).

*21.12.1918:* Launched by the Moore Shipbuilding Co., Oakland, (Yard No. 1017), and ran trials 12.7.1919 for the United States Shipping Board, San Francisco, as MONASSES. *26.10.1936:* Transferred to the United States Maritime Commission. *23.1.1941:* Sold to the Ministry of Shipping, later Ministry of War Transport, London, (NZS, managers). *25.10.1941:* Delivered at

Baltimore, having been requisitioned for the Liner Division on 14.7.1941. *1941:* Renamed EMPIRE WHIMBREL. *11.4.1943:* Torpedoed and sunk off West Africa (02°31'N-15°55'W) by U 181, bound Buenos Aires and Rio Grande to Freetown and Britain with refrigerated and general cargo. No loss of life.

EMPIRE FLAG as Donaldson's CARMIA
*(Mariners Museum/NZA)*

## M.10 EMPIRE FLAG (1943—1946)

Official Number: 169169
Tonnages: 7,024 gross, 4,734 net, 9,655 deadweight. Dimensions: 430.9 (446.3 overall) x 56.2 x 35.2 feet. Draft: 26.8 feet.
T.3 cyl. by the North Eastern Marine Engineering Co. (1938) Ltd, Wallsend, 2,500 ihp, 11 knots.
Refrigerated space: 253,380 cu.ft.

*2.6.1943:* Launched by Armstrong, Whitworth & Co. (Shipbuilders) Ltd, Newcastle, (Yard No. 4), and delivered 29.10.1943 to the Ministry of War Transport, London, (registered at Newcastle), (NZS, managers), as EMPIRE FLAG. *29.10.1943—16.4.1946:* Requisitioned for the Liner Division. *16.4.1946:* Sold to the Donaldson Line Ltd, Glasgow, (Donaldson Bros & Black Ltd, managers). *1946:* Transferred to the Donaldson Atlantic Line Ltd, Glasgow, (Donaldson Bros & Black Ltd, managers) and renamed CARMIA. *14.4.1949:* Transferred to the Donaldson Line Ltd, Glasgow, (Donaldson Bros & Black Ltd, managers). *3.5.1954:* Sold to the Blue Star Line Ltd, London, and renamed VICTORIA STAR on 8.10.1954. *26.11.1955:* Sold to the Douglas Steam Ship Co. Ltd, Hong Kong, (Douglas Lapraik & Co., managers), and renamed INCHEARN on 30.11.1955. *26.8.1966:* Arrived at Osaka for demolition which began at Izumi-Ohtsu in 10.1966.

SAMSIP
*(Mariners Museum/NZA)*

## M.11 SAMSIP (1943—1944)

Official Number: 169743
Tonnages: 7,219 gross, 4,380 net, 10,865 deadweight. Dimensions: 422.8 (441.5 overall) x 57.0 x 34.8 feet. Draft: 27.8 feet.
T.3 cyl. by the General Machinery Corp., Hamilton, 2,500 ihp, 11 knots.

*1.11.1943:* Launched by the Bethlehem-Fairfield Shipyard Inc., Baltimore, (Yard No. 2264), for the United States War Shipping Administration as EDWIN A. ROBINSON. Delivered under "Lend-Lease" 9.11.1943 to the Ministry of War Transport, London, (NZS, managers), and renamed SAMSIP. *9.11.1943:* Allocated to the Ship Management Division, then to the Liner Division from 2.1944 and served as a mechanical transport ship from 24.5.1944. *7.12.1944:* Mined off the Scheldt 5 miles north-west of Blankenberghe (51°23'N-03°03'E), bound Antwerp to the Thames, with the loss of 7 lives.. The wreck was sunk by gunfire.

SAMKEY at Auckland

(MP/WAL)

## M.12 SAMKEY (1943–1948)

Official Number: 169788
Tonnages: 7,219 gross, 4,380 net, 10,865 deadweight. Dimensions: 422.8 (441.5 overall) x 57.0 x 34.8 feet. Draft: 27.8 feet.
T.3 cyl. by the Ellicott Machinery Co., Baltimore, 2,500 ihp, 11 knots.

*17.12.1943:* Launched by the Bethlehem-Fairfield Shipyard Inc., Baltimore, (Yard No. 2295), for the United States War Shipping Administration as CARL THUSGAARD. Delivered under ''Lend Lease'' 24.12.1943 to the Ministry of War Transport, London, (NZS, managers) and renamed SAMKEY. *24.12.1943:* Allocated to the Ship Management Division, but spent 5–7.1944,

1–4.1945, 12.1945–5.1947 and 10.1947–1.1948 with the Liner Division. *24.1.1948:* Left London for Santiago, Cuba, in ballast and last reported on 31.1.1948 in 41°48′N-34°00′W. Presumed to have foundered shortly afterwards when her ballast shifted in rough weather.

## M.13 SAMESK (1944–1947) See LEICESTER (No. F.51)

SAMINGOY at Auckland

(NJK)

## M.14 SAMINGOY (1944–1947) See STAFFORD (No. F.52)

EMPIRE CYPRUS as NORTH BRITAIN at Dunedin *(IJF)*

## M.15 EMPIRE CYPRUS (1945—1945)

Official Number: 169523
Tonnages: 7,200 gross, 4,945 net, 9,660 deadweight. Dimensions: 432.7 (447.8 overall) x 56.2 x 34.4 feet. Draft: 26.2 feet. T.3 cyl. by Duncan Stewart & Co. Ltd, Glasgow, 2,500 ihp, 11 knots.

*18.4.1945:* Launched by Lithgows Ltd, Port Glasgow, (Yard No. 1005), for the Ministry of War Transport, London, (NZS, managers), but completed 18.6.1945 with Charlton, McAllum & Co. Ltd, Newcastle, appointed managers. Registered at Greenock. *18.6.1945—19.10.1946:* Requisitioned for the Liner Division, but spent from 13.10.1945 to 5.5.1946 as a military transport ship. *19.10.1946—19.1.1948:* Chartered to the North Shipping Co. Ltd, Newcastle, (Hugh Roberts & Son, managers).

*20.1.1948:* Sold to the North Shipping Co. Ltd, Newcastle, (Hugh Roberts & Son, managers), and renamed NORTH BRITAIN. *28.1.1952:* Broke her moorings and driven into the wharf at Suva during a hurricane. *1962:* Sold to the Kinabatangan Shipping Co. Ltd, Hong Kong, (United China Shipping Co., managers), and renamed JESSELTON BAY, still registered at Newcastle. *2.4.1968:* Arrived at Kaohsiung for demolition.

EMPIRE ABERCORN on trials                                                                 *(NJK)*

## M.16 EMPIRE ABERCORN (1945—1946) See RAKAIA (No. 85)

EMPIRE WINDRUSH                                                                                     (NJK)

## M.17 EMPIRE WINDRUSH (1945—1954)

Official Number: 181561
Tonnages: 13,882 gross, 7,788 net, 8,530 deadweight. 1947: 14,414 gross, 8,193 net. 1950: 14,651 gross, 8,305 net.
Dimensions: 500.3 (523.0 overall) x 65.7 x 37.8 feet.
Twin screw, four 6 cyl. 4 S.C.S.A. M.A.N. diesels by the shipbuilders, single reduction geared, 6,880 bhp, 14.5 knots.
Passengers: 1,372 tourist class and 1,036 steerage. 1950: 450 cabin and 834 troops.

*4.12.1930:* Launched by Blohm & Voss, Hamburg, (Yard No. 492), and delivered 3.1931 to the Hamburg-Sudamerikanische Dampfs. Ges., Hamburg, as MONTE ROSA. *21.3.1931:* Left Hamburg on her first voyage to Buenos Aires. *11.1.1940:* Requisitioned as a barracks ship at Stettin. *1942/43:* In trooping service to Norway and Denmark. *10.1943:* Served as an accommodation and workshop ship at Altenfjord. *3.1944:* Returned to trooping service and c.*8.1944* mined in the Baltic, bound Norway to Swinemunde. *15.1.1945:* Following repairs entered service as a hospital ship. *16.2.1945:* Struck a mine off Hela, East Prussia, towed to Gydnia, then after temporary repairs to Copenhagen with refugees. *24.6.1945:* Arrived at Kiel in tow from Copenhagen and laid up. *31.8.1945:* Surrendered to the British Government and allocated to the Ministry of War Transport (Sea Transport Division) for use as a troopship. NZS became managers on 8.11.1945. *1.4.1946:* Owners became the Ministry of Transport. *22.6.1946—18.3.1947:* Refitted as a troopship by A. Stephen & Sons Ltd, Glasgow. Suffered a fire in 12.1946 and renamed EMPIRE WINDRUSH on 21.1.1947. *5.1949:* Boiler room fire in the Mediterranean. Put into Gibraltar for repairs. *1950:* Accommodation upgraded and engines converted from blast to solid injection at Southampton. *28.3.1954:* Suffered an engineroom fire 32 miles north-west of Cape Caxine (37°05'N-02°25'E), bound Kure to Southampton. She was taken in tow by the destroyer HMS SAINTES (2,315 tons, 1946), but sank at 00.30 on the 30th in 37°00'N-02°11'E. 4 members of the crew were lost.

# HULKS

From the advent of its first steamer, NZS relied largely on the bunkering services and hulks of other enterprises until those tasks were assumed by the Blackball Coal Company from 1892. It therefore owned only two hulks in its own name, both of which were based in its then home port of Lyttelton.

## H.1 DERWENT (1883—1898) Wood brig

Official Number: 9334
Tonnage: 221 gross. Dimensions: 87.5 x 24.0 x 16.0 feet.

*11.1.1834:* Launched by Scott Peile, Workington, for Robert and Henry Jefferson, Whitehaven. *1839:* Rebuilt. *1841:* Sold to James McMinn and others, Whitehaven. *1849:* Sold to M. B. Walker, Whitehaven. *1851:* Sold to Henry Jefferson the elder and Henry Jefferson the younger, Whitehaven. *1863:* Sold to H.R. Fuller, Adelaide. *1865:* Sold to H.D. Dale and others, Adelaide. *1866:* Sold to G. W. Allen, Sydney. *1867:* Sold to H. Currie, Sydney. *1867:* Sold to W. G. Laidley, Sydney. *1872:* Sold to Thomas Rossiter, Sydney. *1872:* Sold to G. Middleton, Sydney. *1872:* Sold to R.J. Hardy, Sydney. *1872:* Sold to George Holdship, Auckland. *1873:* Sold to Joseph Howard and J.W. Waller, Auckland. *1875:* Sold to J.W. Waller, G.W. Binney, J.M. Clark & T. Morrin, Auckland. *1875:* Sold to C.W. Turner, Christchurch. *3.1879:* Converted to a hulk at Lyttelton. *1883:* Sold to NZS. *9.4.1890:* Registry transferred to Lyttelton. *1898:* Sold for £10 and dismantled in Rhodes Bay, Lyttelton harbour.

## H.2 BLACKWALL (1883—1908) Wood Ship

Official Number: 50120
Tonnage: 1,190 gross. Dimensions: 175.2 x 36.8 x 23.5 feet.

*1858:* Completed by Trufant & Drummond, Bath, Maine, to their own account as the full rigged ship NATIONAL. *1863:* Transferred to W. & J. Drummond, Bath. *1864:* Transferred to British registry at London and renamed BLACKHEATH. *1866:* Transferred to G.C. Trufant, London, and renamed BLACKWALL. *1880:* Sold to G. Croshaw, London. *1881:* Sold to J. Randall, London. *1882:* Sold to C. West, London. *16.6.1882:* Towed into Waratah Bay by the steamer GAZELLE (79g, 1852) after dismasting off the Victorian coast, bound Burrard's Inlet to Melbourne. *1.1883:* Sold at Melbourne to Captain Robert Power on behalf of NZS. *20.2.1883:* Transferred to NZS, and on 24.4.1883 arrived at Lyttelton where she was converted to a hulk. (The transfer was not registered until 15.1.1890). *5.4.1907:* Sank at her moorings, but raised on 17.10.1907 and refitted. *15.9.1908:* Left Lyttelton in tow of the tug CANTERBURY (292g, 1907) for Wellington for service at that port. *1908:* Transferred to the Blackball Coal Company Ltd. *1.4.1922:* Sold to the Union Steam Ship Company of New Zealand Ltd, Wellington. *5.11.1923:* Having been condemned for further service, sold to T. Eckford & Co., Blenheim, and left Wellington in tow to be used as a breakwater at the mouth of the Wairau River. They sheltered in Port Underwood where she went ashore the same day and was abandoned, being later burnt to recover her fastenings.

BLACKWALL being refloated after sinking at Lyttelton in 1907 *(C. Amodeo)*

---

# LIVERY

**HOUSEFLAG:** First adopted in June 1874. A red St George's cross on a white ground with ''N'', ''Z'', ''S'' and ''Co.'' in blue in each quarter. In power driven ships this was surmounted by a ''steam cornet'', a vertically divided red, white and blue pennant, until it was dropped from 1965.

**HULL: Sailing ships:** A black hull with a broad white band with black squares, commonly described as ''painted ports''.

    **Steamers:** Black hull with red boot-topping, separated from 1891 by a white line. Vessels built after 1965: Pale eau de nil with darker green boot-topping.

**UPPERWORKS:** White.

**MASTS:** Dark brown.

**DERRICK POSTS & DERRICKS:** Dark brown to 1939; white from 1945.

**FUNNELS:** Pale yellow. From 1965 the Federal funnel colours were adopted.

RANGITIKI (69) — sailing day 1929          (IJF)

**R. M. S.  R A N G I T O T O**

*Captain J. D. GUYLER*

Saturday 21st October, 1967

# DINNER

*Chefs Suggestion*

Grilled Dover Sole, Lemon Segments

Tenderloin Steak, Alresienne

Club Savoury

Coupe St. Jacques

*Suggested Wines*

St. Emilion 1962 (de Tenet & de Georges)

Chablis (Lindeman's) Kirkton

Hors d'Oeuvres

Cold : Consomme Palesto          Cream Crecy

Grilled Dover Sole, Lemon Segments

Nut and Vegetable Cutlets, Spice Sauce

Roast Goose, Anglaise

Braised Corned Pork, Bretonne

*TO ORDER*
Tenderloin Steak, Arlesienne

Duchesse and Browned Potatoes

Garden Peas          Baked Parsnips

*COLD BUFFET*
Blanquette of Veal          Roast Quarter of Mutton

Salad :  Lorette

Peach Mascott

Coupe St. Jacques

Savoury Club

Fruits          Figs

Coffee will be served in the Dining Saloon

Smoking is permitted

**Clocks will be RETARDED 30 MINUTES at Midnight**

RANGITOTO (89) Dinner Menu 21st October 1967

# FEDERAL STEAM NAVIGATION COMPANY LTD

## Chronology

*28 July 1892* The Meteor Steam Navigation Company Ltd was formed in London by Allan Hughes of Allport & Hughes (founded in 1888 as Green, Allport & Co.), brokers to Money Wigram & Sons Ltd, with an authorised capital of £150,000. The directors were: J.G.S. and J.R Anderson, Charles Bethell, Allan Hughes, T.B. Robinson and A. Tait (died 1896).

*1894* The assets of Money Wigram & Sons Ltd (mainly the name, flag and goodwill) were purchased from the liquidators by Allan Hughes for Meteor.

*1894* The Australian agency was established as J.H. Geddes, Birt & Co. Ltd. From 1899 it became Birt & Co. Ltd, and from 1937 Birt & Co. Pty Ltd.

*12 December 1894* It was resolved to change the name of the Meteor Company to the King Steam Navigation Company Ltd with effect from 1 January 1895. The change was registered on 15 January 1895. The existing directors continued in office.

*1895* Allport & Hughes joined with J. Gavin Birt & Co. and John Potter & Co. to form the partnership of Birt, Potter & Hughes. It was incorporated as Birt, Potter & Hughes Ltd on 25.2.1898.

*24 April 1895* It was resolved to further change the name of the King Company to the Federal Steam Navigation Company Ltd. The change was registered on 28 May 1895 and Allan Hughes was elected chairman on 25 July 1895.

*13 September 1902* On the third calling of tenders by the New Zealand Government for a service to South Africa (for the first two callings of tenders, see the NZS chronology) and offering a subsidy of £30,000 per annum, Federal and Gulf Line Ltd submitted tenders and Federal were successful with a 1 year contract and an option for a 2 year extension.

*11 October 1902* The New Zealand & African Steam Shipping Company Ltd was registered with a nominal capital of £250,000 in £10 shares, but only 8 shares were issued, held 1 each by K.S. Anderson, Allan Hughes, William Milburn, Charles Bethell, O.J. Trinder, A.F. Houlder, T.B. Robinson and Thomas L. Devitt. Hughes and Houlder were appointed joint managers and the board met annually for formal business until 1911.

*6 January 1903* An agreement was concluded with Houlder Bros & Co. Ltd for a pooling of services between New Zealand and South Africa, and an associated South Africa—River Plate service was begun.

*27 October 1903* A majority interest in Birt, Potter & Hughes Ltd was purchased for £250,000.

*November 1903* Negotiations began and a formal agreement was concluded in August 1904 with Houlder Bros & Co. and Turnbull, Martin & Co. to form the Federal-Houlder-Shire Line serving Britain/South Africa/Australia/New Zealand. The New Zealand connection was discontinued in 1910 in which year The Clan Line Steamers Ltd acquired a controlling interest in Turnbull, Martin & Co, forming the Scottish Shire Line Ltd. In December 1911 (fully effective from April 1912) Houlder Bros withdrew from the Australasian trades, their share being taken successively by NZS and then the Union Steam Ship Company of New Zealand Ltd. The service was renamed the Federal Shire Line and the New Zealand connection restored.

*December 1903* The New Zealand Government invited tenders for a service from New Zealand to the west coast of the United Kingdom. NZS, Federal, and Shaw Savill submitted tenders and that of Federal was accepted. The service was run in conjunction with the New Zealand—South Africa service and when the contract for the latter expired, Federal began to send ships back via Cape Horn in July 1905 and to London from 1906. The London service raised direct competition with NZS and Shaw Savill who began a west coast service in retaliation. In November 1906 both parties agreed to return to their original spheres.

*1907* In conjunction with Trinder, Anderson & Co. and Bethell, Gwyn & Co., Federal purchased the Liverpool business of James Dowie & Co. NZS acquired the Trinder, Anderson and Bethell, Gwyn interests in 1922 and the business was amalgamated with Marwood & Robertson in 1962 to form Dowie & Marwood Ltd.

New Zealand House, 17 Water Street, Liverpool, the offices of Dowie & Marwood
*(P&O)*

113

The battered wreck of ESSEX (F.43) at Malta in 1943

(Michael Cassar)

*17 March 1911* The nominal capital of the Federal Steam Navigation Company Ltd was £600,000 and the issued capital £487,900.

*29 January 1912* NZS purchased 43,116 £10 Federal shares for 27,818 NZS shares valued at £20 each. NZS thus became the majority and controlling shareholder in Federal.

*21 July 1914* An interest was purchased in R. & H. Green & Silley, Weir Ltd.

*1914—1918* The First World War. Federal lost 4 ships out of 11 owned in 1914.

*23 June 1915* The nominal capital was increased to £900,000.

*7 September 1916* NZS and Federal were acquired by The Peninsular and Oriental Steam Navigation Company. Federal continued as an independent entity in the NZS Group, but the manning of the ships was completely integrated with officers and crew serving in the ships regardless of the nominal owner and funnel colour.

*30 May 1918* Cox & Co. (Engineers) Ltd acquired.

*26 June 1918* Falmouth Docks Co. Ltd acquired.

*1937* The former interest, amounting to 20%, of the West Australian Steam Navigation Co. Ltd (which was in course of being wound up) in the Australind Steam Shipping Company Ltd was purchased. The interest was increased in 1961 following the purchase of Bethell, Gwyn & Co. Ltd, but never exceeded 38%.

*1939—1945* The Second World War. Federal lost 10 ships out of 17 owned in 1939 plus 1 delivered during the conflict.

*1951* John Mill & Co. Ltd, Dunedin, purchased from the Union Steam Ship Co. of New Zealand Ltd. It was wound up in 1953.

*29 December 1958* The first tanker owned by the NZS/Federal Group, LINCOLN, was delivered.

*December 1961* Bethell, Gwyn & Co. Ltd acquired.

*1 January 1966* Federal Tankers Ltd formed.

*28 December 1966* Federal became the registered owners of most of the NZS fleet although NZS remained the managers.

*January 1971* The "Wild" project was announced, as a world wide refrigerated service to be operated by Federal. The first ship, WILD AUK, was launched on 22 July 1971.

*1 October 1971* Management of the Federal ships passed to P&O General Cargo Division.

*23 December 1971* Lauritzen Peninsular Reefers A/S formed in Copenhagen to operate the "Wild" ships in conjunction with the refrigerated fleet of Lauritzen's Rederiet Ocean A/S.

*19 April 1973* Ownership of the remaining Federal ships, other than the "Wild" ships, passed to The Peninsular and Oriental Steam Navigation Company.

*February 1983* P&O announced that it would withdraw with effect from 23 May 1983 from Lauritzen Peninsular Reefers; the remaining Federal ships were sold and Federal ceased to be a shipowner.

*7 November 1991* Federal Steam Navigation Company Ltd placed in liquidation.

WILD AVOCET (F.90) with Lauritzen funnel colours at Auckland

(DNB)

# Chapter 1:   The Founding Years

The Federal Line was first registered on 28th July 1892 as the Meteor Steam Navigation Company Ltd to enter the Australian refrigerated and general cargo trade. It was the brainchild of Allan Hughes, a partner in the London shipbrokers, Allport & Hughes, who had been extensively involved in those trades with chartered tonnage over the previous 10 years. Two other London shipbroking firms were also involved, Anderson, Anderson & Company who saw a cargo service as a useful complement to their jointly managed Orient Line passenger fleet, and Charles Bethell & Company who were managers and major shareholders in the West Australian Steam Navigation Company Ltd operating out of Fremantle. Other shareholders were The Peninsular and Oriental Steam Navigation Company, Trinder Anderson & Company with their extensive West Australian links, and the Australian shipowners McIlwraith McEacharn & Company who provided an important entry to the Queensland frozen meat trade.

Initially the new company continued with chartered ships, not acquiring its first owned vessels until January 1894 when the CELTIC KING and MAORI KING were acquired from W. Ross & Company from whom they had been on charter. Two changes later that year reflected past associations. In recent times Allport & Hughes had acted as brokers for the long established firm of Money Wigram & Sons Ltd. It had mistakenly placed its faith in auxiliary steamers when making the switch from sail to steam, and had moved to fully powered vessels too late to retrieve its fortunes in the face of competition from better equipped rivals. When it was finally placed in liquidation in 1893, Hughes purchased from the receivers its Australian goodwill and the right to use its historic houseflag first flown in 1824; this remained the Federal flag to the end of its career. The other change was the decision in December to rename the Meteor Steam Navigation Company the King Steam Navigation Company Ltd in keeping with the names of the two purchased ships, to take effect from January 1895.

The favourable results from the first two years trading of owned ships encouraged the placing of the King Steam Navigation Company on a firmer basis. By this stage Hughes had made the decision to adopt not only the Money Wigram flag but also its system of naming its vessels after English counties. This was to be introduced with the first newbuildings for the Company, and the recently adopted King name was therefore changed again in May 1895 to the Federal Steam Navigation Company Ltd, reflecting the combination of interests involved in its ownership. Capital was increased to fund the new construction, and Hughes' own firm also underwent change in that year when it combined with J. Gavin Birt & Company and John Potter & Company to form Birt, Potter & Hughes. The Sydney based subsidiary of the first named, known simply as Birt & Co. Ltd. from 1899, was to be Federal's principal agent in Australia for nearly 80 years.

The first ships to bear the county names were the CORNWALL and DEVON which were acquired while in the course of construction from William Milburn & Company, whose Anglo-Australasian Steam Navigation Company was another Australian trader. Although launched under their Federal names, they were not formally acquired and paid for until after their trials. Given the background of the new Line's principal shareholders, little emphasis was placed on passengers, there being permanent accommodation for only 12 first class but with provision for large numbers of emigrants in the tween decks on outward voyages as required. 6 similar but slightly larger ships followed in rapid order over the 12 month period 1899/1900, but only 4 of these saw any lengthy Federal service. The first SUSSEX was sold on the stocks to Shaw Savill and completed as the KARAMEA while the first SUFFOLK was wrecked near Port Elizabeth in September 1900 when less than a year old. All 6 differed from the initial pair in being rigged with 4 masts rather than 2; multi-masts were to be a Federal feature until after the First World War.

The Federal routes out and back from Australia were the traditional sailing ship ones via the Cape of Good Hope and Cape Horn with calls at South African and South American ports as required. It was therefore not surprising that Federal ships were prominently involved in the movement of troops, horses and supplies for the Boer War over

NORFOLK (F.10) leaving Lyttelton with troops to the Boer War                                                                                       *(WAL)*

1899/1902. This included both Australia and New Zealand, bringing the ships to the latter country for the first time. Vessels involved directly as troopships were the MAORI KING, CORNWALL, DEVON, KENT, SURREY, NORFOLK and SUSSEX, while the SUFFOLK was bringing horses from the Adriatic when she was lost.

With the benefit of this experience, Federal was the successful bidder in 1902 when, after two abortive attempts, the New Zealand Government finally found a firm willing to perform a New Zealand-South Africa service on a permanent basis. The contract was actually awarded to the New Zealand & African Steam Shipping Company Ltd in which Hughes also obtained the involvement of Milburns, Trinder, Anderson, Houlders and Devitt & Moore, and the link with Houlders was strengthened the following year when the service was extended to the River Plate.

A much more important step came in November 1903 when the formation of the Federal-Houlder-Shire Line to trade between Britain, South Africa, Australia and New Zealand was announced. This was followed by Federal winning a New Zealand Government contract for a service from U.K. west coast ports to New Zealand against competing bids from NZS and Shaw Savill. The South African contract had proved marginal, and on its expiry in 1905 the Federal ships resumed their previous homeward sailings via Cape Horn. In contrast, the Federal-Houlder-Shire service prospered, though an attempt to extend it to London brought strenuous opposition from NZS and Shaw Savill and finally resulted in an agreement for all parties to stick to their previous spheres of interest.

Meanwhile the Federal fleet had almost doubled in size with 4 larger 4-masted ships delivered to the Company's own design from the John Brown yard at Clydebank in 1902/03. They introduced twin screws to the fleet and were followed by the smaller DURHAM bought on the stocks from Milburns in 1904. After this burst of activity, there was a period of consolidation until the wave of emigration in the years immediately prior to the First World War prompted the building of the independent Federal Line's largest and finest steamers for the Federal-Houlder-Shire service. Although the two Federal units bore county names, the SHROPSHIRE and WILTSHIRE were the only members of the fleet to include "shire" in their names, presumably to conform to their sister, the ARGYLLSHIRE which was owned by Turnbull Martin's Scottish Shire Line. Their 10,300 tons gross and 14 knots speed put them clearly in the liner class, and although primarily emigrant carriers, their original provision for 130 1st class passengers marked the Federal Line's only entry into major passenger traffic. Their principal external feature was no less than 5 masts, 3 before and 2 aft of the central structure. To finance such expensive ships, the Federal issued capital was again increased in March 1911 to just under £500,000.

The corporate manoeuvrings of 1910 to 1912 leading to the fusion of interests with NZS have already been described in NZS Chapter 4.

DEVON (F.5) wrecked at Pencarrow Head, 1913                                                                                                (NZA)

---

**CHAIRMEN**

From 1919 when the Federal Chairman, Allan Hughes, assumed the chairmanship of NZS, the Chairman of both companies was always the same person. (see P.19 for details)

# Ships F.1 to F.18   CELTIC KING — WILTSHIRE

CELTIC KING as CELTIC in U.S. naval service at Sydney
*(IJF)*

## F.1 CELTIC KING (1894—1898)

Official Number: 98196
Tonnages   3,738 gross, 2,429 net. Dimensions   371.8 x 44.2 x 27.2 feet.
T.3 cyl. by J. & J. Thomson, Glasgow, 350 nhp, 9 knots.
Refrigerated space: 120,000 cu.ft.

*1.11.1890:* Launched by Workman, Clark & Co. Ltd, Belfast, (Yard No. 73), and ran trials 27.12.1890 for W. Ross & Co., London. First registered on 24.1.1891. *1891:* Chartered to G.D. Tyser & Co., London. *19.1.1894:* Sold to Allan Hughes & J.R. Anderson, London, and placed in the Meteor Australian service. *27.8.1894:* Collided with the steamer NEMESIS (1,393g, 1880) in Darling harbour, Sydney. Damage minor. *28.8.1895:* Transferred with MAORI KING (No. F.2) to Federal for £76,500 the two. *24.9.1895:* Suffered a fire and explosion in the coal in the forehold at South West India Dock, London. 2 injured. *22.12.1897:* Collided with the steamer LUBRA (467g, 1874) at Newcastle, N.S.W. *14.5.1898:* Sold via her master, Captain G.B.

Hayward, to the United States Navy and became the supply ship CELTIC. She was employed first in Florida and Cuban waters, then moved to the Philippines until 1903. *10—11.1908:* Carried relief supplies to Messina, Sicily, after the earthquake there. *16.6.1914-24.7.1915:* Lay at anchor off Vera Cruz during the Mexican Civil War. *1.7.1918:* Allocated to the Naval Overseas Transportation Service. *3.1921:* Became a station ship (AF-2) at Apra, Guam. *23.6.1922:* Decommissioned by the United States Navy and stricken from the Navy List on 17.1.1923. *23.1.1923:* Sold to the Robert Dollar Co., San Francisco. *4.1923-5.1928:* Laid up at San Francisco. *8.8.1929:* Left Kobe for demolition at Osaka.

MAORI KING at Brisbane embarking troops to the Boer War   *(John Oxley Library)*

## F.2 MAORI KING (1894—1904)

Official Number: 96689
Tonnages: 3,807 gross, 2,476 net. Dimensions: 365.0 x 44.2 x 19.4 feet.
T.3 cyl. by the shipbuilders, 390 nhp 9 knots.
Refrigerated space: 124,000 cu.ft.

*23.11.1889:* Launched by Wm Doxford & Sons, Sunderland, (Yard No. 192), and first registered 13.1.1890 to W. Ross & Co., London. *1890:* Chartered to G.D. Tyser & Co., London. *10.12.1890:* Grounded in the Brisbane River on arrival from Sydney. *26.4.1894:* Sold to Allan Hughes & J.R. Anderson and placed in the Meteor Australian service. *29.8.1895:* Transferred with CELTIC KING (No. F.1) to Federal for £76,500 the pair. *13.1.1900:* Sailed from Brisbane with the Second Queensland Mounted Infantry Contingent to the Boer War. Arrived in Table Bay on 22.1.1900 and the troops disembarked on the 24th. She subsequently made 2 voyages from the River Plate with mules to South Africa and later served as a refrigerated store ship at Durban. *10.1904:*

Sold to C.H. Collet, Havre, (allegedly on behalf of the Russian Government) and renamed ESPERANCE (sometimes spelt ESPERANZA). *25.10.1904:* Discovered to be in a sinking condition at Barry through a sea-cock being left open. *28.3.1906:* Transferred to J.M. Dow, Shanghai, (British flag), and renamed MAORI KING. *4.12.1907:* Arrested by order of the British Court at Shanghai for wrongly adopting the British flag, Dow being an employee of the Russian firm, M. Ginsburg & Co. *23.4.1908:* Forfeited to the Crown by order of the Court. *15.6.1908:* Returned to M. Ginsburg & Co., Shanghai, (Russian flag), against a bond of £10,000. *17.9.1909:* Struck a rock off Ningpo and foundered, bound Taku to Hong Kong with coal.

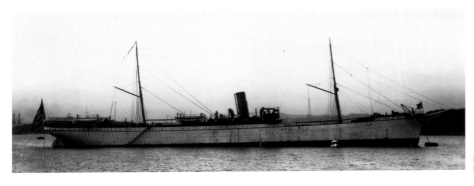

PORT CHALMERS as GLACIER in U.S. naval service at
Sydney                                                    (IJF)

## F.3 PORT CHALMERS (1896—1898)

Official Number: 98973
Tonnages: 4,154 gross, 2,667 net. Dimensions: 371.0 x 46.1 x 27.7 feet.
T.3 cyl. by J. Dickinson, Sunderland, 600˙nhp, 11 knots.
Refrigerated space: 91,100 cu.ft.

*22.7.1891:* Launched by J.L. Thompson & Sons, Sunderland, (Yard No. 277), and first registered at London 29.8.1891 for J.D. Milburn, Newcastle, for operation by the Anglo-Australasian Steam Navigation Co. Ltd. *16.1.1892:* Transferred to Wm Milburn, Newcastle; still registered at London. There followed various transfers of shares within the Milburn family through to 16.7.1893. *27.7.1895:* Seriously damaged by a collision with an iceberg in the South Indian Ocean, bound London to Sydney. The bowsprit and figurehead were lost and the bow plating smashed in for 20 feet. *30.5.1896:* Sold to Federal for £46,750 and delivered 15.6.1896. *5.7.1898:* Sold via her master, Captain G.B. Hayward, to the United States Navy and commissioned 6.7.1898 as the supply ship DELMONICO . *12.7.1898:* Renamed GLACIER. Served in the Philippines, 7.1899—4.1903, in the Pacific Fleet 1.1909—3.1918, and in the Naval Overseas Transportation Service from 4.1918 (AF-4 from 1920). *17.8.1922:*

Sold for $22,000 to the Barde Steel & Machinery Co., Seattle. *27.1.1925:* Sold to Northern Fisheries Inc., San Francisco. *18.1.1938:* Sold to the Alaska Salmon Co., San Francisco. *3.1941:* Sold for $110,000 to the Carbella Steam Ship Co., Panama, and renamed CARBELLA. *1.1945:* Sold to the Cia Continental de Navegacion S.A., Mexico City, registered at Vera Cruz, and renamed PRESIDENTE JUAREZ. *1955:* Sold to the Cia Continental de Exportacion y Importacion Mexicana S.A. de C.V., Mexico City, still registered at Vera Cruz. *28.11.1955:* Arrived at Bermuda in tow of the tug TYNE, (384g, 1944) with a list while bound Hampton Roads to Rotterdam with coal, and beached at Flatt's Inlet. *3.12.1955:* Refloated and 7.3.1956 left for Rotterdam, still in tow of the TYNE. *22.4.1956:* Arrived in tow of the tug RODE ZEE (500g, 1949) at Inverkeithing for demolition by T.W. Ward Ltd.

PORT CHALMERS as PRESIDENTE JUAREZ under the
Mexican flag                      (Mariners Museum/NJK)

## F.4 CORNWALL (1896—1913)

Official Number: 105897
Tonnages: 5,490 gross, 3,554 net, 9,450 deadweight. Dimensions: 420.0 x 54.0 x 28.7 feet.
T.3 cyl. by the shipbuilders, 4,000 ihp, 11 knots.
Passengers: 12 1st and 156 3rd class.
Refrigerated space: 230,000 cu.ft.

*23.9.1896:* Launched by R. & W. Hawthorn, Leslie & Co. Ltd, Hebburn, (Yard No. 339), and first registered at London 14.11.1896 to Wm Milburn, Jnr. *24.12.1896:* Transferred with DEVON (No. F.5) to Federal for £136,500 the pair. *1.11.1899:* Sailed from Brisbane with the first Contingent of the Queensland Mounted Infantry to the Boer War. She arrived in Table Bay on 12.12.1899 and the troops disembarked on the 13th. She subsequently made a second voyage with horses. *30.3.1900:* Sailed from London with Boer War troops and supplies. *30.1.1901:* Sailed from Auckland with the 6th New Zealand

Contingent to the Boer War. *8.2.1902:* Sailed from Lyttelton with half the 8th New Zealand Contingent to the Boer War. *16.4.1904:* Returned to London with machinery damage following sailing for Buenos Aires. *10.3.1910:* Struck the wharf while berthing at Newcastle, N.S.W. *29.1.1913:* Sold to the Atlantide Soc. Italiana di Nav., Genoa, (Coe & Clerici, managers), and renamed ATLANTIDE. *1917:* Sold to the S.A. Ilva, Genoa. *9.2.1918:* Captured and scuttled by U 156 off Madeira, bound Genoa to New Orleans.

CORNWALL leaving Auckland with troops to the Boer War

*(WAL)*

# F.5 DEVON (1897—1913)

Official Number: 108171
Tonnages: 5,489 gross, 3,546 net, 9,450 deadweight. Dimensions: 420.0 x 54.0 x 28.7 feet.
T.3 cyl. by the shipbuilders, 4,000 ihp, 11 knots.
Passengers: 12 1st and 150 3rd class.
Refrigerated space: 230,000 cu.ft.

*20.11.1896:* Launched by R. & W. Hawthorn, Leslie & Co. Ltd, Hebburn, (Yard No. 340), and first registered at London 6.2.1897 to Wm Milburn, Jnr. *23.2.1897:* Transferred with CORNWALL (No. F.4) to Federal for £136,500 the pair. *6.3.1901:* Sailed from Fremantle with the 5th Australian Mounted Infantry Contingent for the Boer War, and arrived at Durban on the 28th. *19.3.1902:* Sailed from Auckland with half the 9th New Zealand Contingent to the Boer War. *29.7.1912:* Dumped by a heavy sea leaving Durban for Brisbane, buckling the pillars of the tween decks. *25.8.1913:* Wrecked on Pencarrow Head, Wellington, inward bound from Montreal via Sydney and Auckland. 300 tons of cargo were salved before the aft end of the ship disappeared in October and the remains of the bow finally disappeared in a gale in October 1916.

DEVON at Adelaide

*(IJF)*

KENT leaving Port Chalmers                                                                  (IJF)

## F.6 KENT (1899—1915)

Official Number: 110127
Tonnages: 5,464 gross, 3,505 net, 9,500 deadweight. Dimensions: 420.0 x 54.0 x 28.6 feet.
T.3 cyl. by the shipbuilders, 4,000 ihp, 11 knots.
Passengers: 12 1st and 150 3rd class.
Refrigerated space: 225,050 cu.ft.

*11.3.1899:* Launched by R. & W. Hawthorn, Leslie & Co. Ltd, Hebburn, (Yard No. 369), and first registered at London to Federal on 23.5.1899. *30.10.1899:* Sailed from Sydney with the 2nd draft of New South Wales Lancers for the Boer War, arriving at Cape Town on 2.12.1899. *17.1.1900:* Sailed from Sydney with the Service Squadron of the 1st Australian Horse for the Boer War, and arrived at Cape Town on 23.2.1900. *17.9.1900:* Sailed from Fiume with horses and supplies for the Boer War. *22.12.1901:* Sailed from Southampton with troops and supplies for the Boer War. *12.3.1902:* Sailed from Port Chalmers with half the 9th New Zealand Contingent to the Boer War. *20.12.1909:* Outward bound from Adelaide struck the sunken wreck of the barque NORMA (2,123g, 1891), off Wonga shoal, Semaphore anchorage. Damage to the bottom plates was minor and after return for inspection she was able to proceed. *1.10.1911:* Suffered a fire in No. 4 hold at Auckland. It was brought under control with the help of the fire brigade. *7.9.1912:* Collided with and sank the steamer TALBOT (549g, 1890) in the River Mersey, inward bound to Liverpool from New Zealand. *5.8.1913:* Fractured the main steam pipe soon after leaving Bluff for Brisbane and returned the next day for repairs. *14.10.1915:* Sold to the Brodlea Steamship Co. Ltd, London, (Blue Star Line Ltd, managers), and renamed BRODLEA. *26.6.1917—3.4.1919:* Served under the Liner Requisition Scheme. *14.4.1920:* Transferred to the Union Cold Storage Co. Ltd, (Blue Star Line (1920) Ltd, managers), and renamed SAXONSTAR on 11.11.1920. *7.7.1926:* Grounded, bound Zarate to Buenos Aires. *2.9.1929:* Transferred to the Blue Star Line Ltd and renamed SAXON STAR on 27.9.1929. *10.1.1930:* Suffered a fire in the bunkers and No. 3 hold off Panama, bound Seattle to Liverpool and put into Balboa. 2 of the crew were injured. *19.9.1932:* Suffered a bunker fire bound Boanamary, Madagascar, to U.K. *11.1933:* Laid up in the Tyne. *8.1934:* Sold for £8,000 to the Soc. Anon. Ricuperi Metallici and arrived at Savona on 17.9.1934 for demolition. 2 workers were injured in a fire on board on 10.11.1934

SURREY at Adelaide                                                                          (IJF)

## F.7 SURREY (1899—1915)

Official Number: 110184
Tonnages: 5,455 gross, 3,498 net, 9,500 deadweight. Dimensions: 420.4 x 54.0 x 28.6 feet.
T.3 cyl. by the shipbuilders, 4,000 ihp, 11 knots.
Passengers: 12 1st and 150 3rd class.
Refrigerated space: 225,050 cu.ft.

*8.7.1899:* Launched by R. & W. Hawthorn, Leslie & Co. Ltd, Hebburn, (Yard No. 370), and first registered at London to Federal on 9.9.1899. *26.1.1900:* Sailed from Adelaide with the 2nd South Australian Mounted Rifles Contingent to the Boer War and from Fremantle with the 2nd West Australian Mounted Infantry Contingent on 3.2.1900. She arrived at Cape Town on 24.2.1900. and the troops disembarked on the 25th. *4.4.1900* and *19.5.1900:* Sailed from Buenos Aires with horses and supplies for the Boer War. *15.3.1901:* Grounded on leaving Brisbane, but refloated undamaged. *16.7.1901:* Sailed from Southampton with troops and supplies for the Boer War. *1.2.1902:* Sailed from Auckland with half the 9th New Zealand Contingent to the Boer War. *14.10.1909:* Suffered a fire in the bunkers, bound Sydney to Melbourne. Hatches were battened down, holes cut to let the water in and she was put on a sandbank on arrival at Melbourne. She was refloated on the 17th. *17.8.1911:* Struck the quay on arrival at Hobart, bound Liverpool to Auckland. *29.10.1912:* In collision with NGATORO (No. B.6) at Wellington. *6.6.1914:* Suffered a fire in the cargo at Avonmouth. *25.2.1915:* Mined off Dunkirk, inward bound from Liverpool with coal and refrigerated cargo. Beached at North Deal the following day, refloated on 28.5.1915, but beached again on Mucking Flats on the 29th. *20.6.1915:* Refloated and arrived at Tilbury where, following examination, she was abandoned as a constructive total loss. *6.8.1915:* Sold to the Brodstream Steamship Co. Ltd, London, (Blue Star Line Ltd, managers). *9.8.1915:* The owning company was renamed the Brodfield Steamship Co. Ltd. She was repaired at Tilbury and renamed BRODFIELD on 15.12.1915. *13.11.1916:* Wrecked at Blue Carn, St Mary's, Isles of Scilly, in fog, bound Le Havre to Barry in ballast.

## F.8 SUFFOLK (1899—1900)

Official Number: 112617
Tonnages: 5,364 gross, 3,442 net. Dimensions: 420.7 x 54.0 x 28.8 feet.
T.3 cyl. by the North Eastern Marine Engineering Co. Ltd, Wallsend, 4,000 ihp, 11 knots.
Passengers: 12 1st and 150 3rd class.
Refrigerated space: 225,000 cu.ft.

*25.7.1899:* Launched by the Sunderland Shipbuilding Co. Ltd, Sunderland, (Yard No. 201), and first registered at London on 1.11.1899 in the names of F.B. Birt, O.J. Trinder & C. Bethell for Federal service. *24.9.1900:* Grounded on Klippin Point, near Port Elizabeth, bound Fiume to Cape Town with horses. Towed off by the steamer LAKE ERIE (7,550g, 1900) the same day but sank 12 hours later. All saved, but 800 horses lost.

## (F.9) SUSSEX

Official Number: 110264
Tonnages: 5,564 gross, 3,553 net. Dimensions: 420.0 x 54.0 x 28.6 feet.
T.3 cyl. by the shipbuilders, 4,000 ihp, 12 knots.
Passengers: 24 1st and 200 3rd class.
Refrigerated space: 225,050 cu.ft.

Laid down for Federal, but sold on the stocks and *22.8.1899:* Launched by R. & W. Hawthorn, Leslie & Co. Ltd, Hebburn, (Yard No. 371), for the Shaw Savill & Albion Co. Ltd, London as KARAMEA. Registered at Southampton, and delivered 11.1899. *30.8.1912:* Collided in Bugsby's Reach, River Thames with the steamer MARIE GARTZ (922g, 1901). *1917—1919:* Taken up
*Continued overleaf*

*(F.9) SUSSEX — continued*

SUSSEX as completed for Shaw Savill & Albion as
KARAMEA, at Lyttelton *(IJF)*

under the Liner Requisition Scheme. *12.2.1919:* Outward bound
from Montevideo, collided with the steamer HAUGLAND
(3,167g, 1896) off the Whistling buoy. *18.7.1919:* Suffered a fire
in the starboard bunker which lasted 3 days, bound London to
Cape Town. *1925:* Sold for £30,000 to the Soc. Anon. Nav.
Alta Italia, Genoa, and renamed MONGIOIA. *16.4.1929:* Sold for
demolition at Genoa.

A fourth member of this class was sold, before laying down, to NZS and was launched as the 2-masted WHAKATANE (No. 38).

NORFOLK at New York *(IJF)*

## F.10 NORFOLK (1900—1914)
Official Number: 112685
Tonnages: 5,310 gross, 3,405 net. Dimensions: 420.7 x 54.1 x 28.8 feet.
T.3 cyl. by the North Eastern Marine Engineering Co. Ltd, Wallsend, 4,000 ihp, 11 knots
Passengers: 12 1st and 150 3rd class.
Refrigerated space: 266,300 cu.ft.

*18.12.1899:* Launched by the Sunderland Shipbuilding Co. Ltd,
Sunderland, (Yard No. 202), completed 7.4.1900 and registered
at London 4.1900 in the names of F.B. Birt, O.G. Trinder & C.
Bethell for Federal service. *19.4.1900:* Sailed from Gibraltar for

NORFOLK arriving at Fremantle under jury rig, 1906 *(IJF)*

South Africa with horses and mules. *20.6.1900:* Sailed from Buenos Aires with horses and supplies for the Boer War. *12.1.1901:* Sailed from London with troops and supplies for the Boer War. *15.9.1901:* Sailed from Southampton with troops and supplies for the Boer War. *19.4.1902:* Sailed from Lyttelton with half the 10th New Zealand Contingent to the Boer War. *10.6.1906:* Broke her shaft in the South Indian Ocean (36°20′S-99°47′E), bound Durban to Albany in ballast. Sailed

with improvised rig 1,000 miles to Rottnest Island where she arrived on the 21st and was brought into Fremantle by tugs. *6.4.1911:* Ownership transferred to J.W. Potter, O.J. Trinder & W.J. Gwyn. *28.7.1914:* O.J. Trinder's interest transferred to A.A. Trinder. *8.11.1914:* Caught fire in 38°27′S-147°06′E the day after leaving Melbourne for Sydney. Beached on Ninety Mile Beach, Victorian coast, on the 9th and abandoned on the 18th. She was reported to be in 3 pieces by the 28th.

SUSSEX at Sydney

*(NZA)*

## F.11 SUSSEX (1900—1923)

Official Number: 112686
Tonnages: 5,474 gross, 3,505 net, 9,770 deadweight. Dimensions: 420.0 x 54.0 x 28.7 feet.
T.3 cyl. by the shipbuilders, 4,000 ihp, 11 knots.
Passengers: 12 1st and 52 2nd class. Also 100 emigrants until 1919.
Refrigerated space: 239,100 cu.ft.

*16.1.1900:* Launched by R. & W. Hawthorn, Leslie & Co. Ltd, Hebburn, (Yard No. 373), and first registered at London to Federal on 28.3.1900. *16.5.1900:* Sailed from Fiume with horses, mules and supplies for the Boer War. *22.7.1900:* Sailed from Buenos Aires with horses, mules and supplies for the Boer War. *1.2.1901:* Sailed from Fiume with horses, mules and supplies for the Boer War. *20.12.1903:* Collided with the anchored steamer GLADESTRY (2,360g, 1890) in fog 1 mile south-half-east of the Mersey Bar lightship while in charge of the pilot, bound Liverpool to London. *22.11.1910:* Collided with the steamer NEWSTEAD (2,836g, 1894) at Las Palmas, bound Liverpool to Wellington. The SUSSEX's bows were badly damaged and the forepeak flooded. She was delayed 8 days for repairs. *19.4.1913:* Grounded in Kinellan Reach, Brisbane River, but refloated undamaged in half an hour. *29.1.1916:* Arrived at London after collision in the Thames with the steamer PONTOPOROS (4,049g, 1913). *29.4.1916:* Attacked by gunfire from UC 45 100 miles west of Ushant, but escaped. *31.12.1916:* Struck a mine laid by UC 1 4 miles north of Gravelines, bound Sydney to

Dunkirk with refrigerated and general cargo. Beached 4 miles east of Dunkirk on 1.1.1917. Refloated and repaired. *14.3.1917—24.3.1919:* Taken up under the Liner Requisition Scheme. *23.12.1920:* Grounded leaving Saint John, N.B., but refloated undamaged. *25.1.1921:* Ran onto the breakwater at Colon, arriving from New York. Refloated and drydocked at Balboa on 1.2.1921 for repairs and finally sailed on 10.3.1921 for Auckland. *10.1923:* Sold for £12,000 to the Union Steam Ship Company of New Zealand Ltd, Wellington, for the Calcutta—New Zealand trade but remained registered in nominal Federal ownership to enable the employment of an Indian crew. *16.4.1929:* Sold for £17,000 to Summers & Co., Tokyo, for demolition. *26.4.1929:* On her final voyage, bound Calcutta to Auckland, suffered a fire in No. 4 hold and beached at Semarang. Refloated on the 29th and minimal repairs carried out at Sourabaya. *11.7.1929:* Arrived at Osaka and delivered on the 15th to the Osaka Marine Co. Ltd who began demolition the following month.

## F.12 SUFFOLK (1902—1927)

Official Number: 115859
Tonnages: 7,083 gross, 4,521 net, 10,000 deadweight. Dimensions: 460.0 x 58.2 x 31.2 feet.
Twin screw, two T.3 cyl. by the shipbuilders, 918 nhp, 13 knots.
Passengers: 12 1st class and 200 emigrants.
Refrigerated capacity: 300,000 cu.ft.

*23.5.1902:* Launched by John Brown & Co. Ltd, Clydebank, (Yard No. 349), and first registered at London on 14.7.1902 to F.B. Birt, O.J. Trinder and C. Bethell for Federal service. *10.1904:* Became the first ocean going twin screw vessel to transit the Manchester Ship Canal. *15.10.1904:* Left Liverpool on the first Federal-Houlder-Shire Line voyage. *6.4.1911:* Transferred to J.W. Potter, O.J. Trinder and W.J. Gwyn. *28.7.1914:* A.A. Trinder took over

O.J. Trinder's interest. *4.9.1914—30.8.1917:* Requisitioned as the Australian Expeditionary Force transport A 23 with accommodation for 36 officers and 1,000 troops. She left Sydney on 18.10.1914 with the 2nd A.I.F. battalion for Alexandria. *26.12.1916:* Mined 6 miles south-east of the Owers Light Vessel, bound London to Devonport with stores and put into Portsmouth for repairs. *14.6.1917:* Collided with the steamer ULYSSES

*Continued overleaf*

SUFFOLK at Adelaide                                                     (IJF)

(14,499g, 1913) at Durban. *31.8.1917—25.6.1919:* Taken up under the Liner Requisition Scheme. *1.7.1920:* Transferred to Federal (not registered until 11.9.1922). *27.2.1922:* Arrived at Glasgow after colliding in the Clyde with the steamer VANCOUVER (4,415g, 1905). *8.6.1923:* Struck by the steamer NALPA (685g, 1918) while berthed at Adelaide. *17.8.1925:* Suffered an engineroom fire at Glasgow. *5.1.1927:* Sold with the DORSET (No. F.14) for £28,500 the pair to P. & W. MacLellan Ltd and broken up at Bo'ness.

ESSEX at Adelaide                                                       (IJF)

## F.13 ESSEX (1902—1927)

Official Number: 115939 Tonnages: 7,016 gross, 4,481 net, 10,340 deadweight. Dimensions: 460.4 x 58.2 x 31.2 feet.
Twin screw, two T.3 cyl. by the shipbuilders, 918 nhp, 13 knots.
Passengers: 24 1st class and 200 3rd class (to 1919).
Refrigerated space: 300,000 cu.ft.

*1.11.1902:* Launched by John Brown & Co. Ltd, Clydebank, (Yard No. 354), and first registered at London on 16.12.1902 to Federal. She cost £106,000 and had been ordered originally in the name of Trinder, Anderson & Co. *22.6.1903:* Delayed at Sydney with leaks in the seams of her plating, bound New Zealand to South Africa. Her cargo had to be discharged before repairs could be made. *17.10.1910:* Collided with and sank the hopper barge PUMBA (450g, 1887) in the Brisbane river. *29.9.1917—7.6.1919:* Taken up under the Liner Requisition Scheme. *9.6.1918:* Missed by a torpedo from U 96 in St George's Channel. *1920:* Began service as a cadet ship for 20 cadets. *25.10.1927:* Sold for £20,000 to the Cie. Internationale de Commerce & d'Armement, Antwerp, (M. Gumuchdjian, manager), and renamed VAN. *2.4.1932:* Laid up at Antwerp. *27.12.1932:* Sold for £5,500 to P. & W. MacLellan Ltd and arrived at Bo'ness on 18.1.1933 for demolition.

DORSET at Sydney

(IJF)

# F.14 DORSET (1903—1927)

Official Number: 118256
Tonnages: 6,990 gross, 4,469 net, 10,490 deadweight. Dimensions: 460.0 x 58.2 x 31.0 feet.
Twin screw, two T.3 cyl. by the shipbuilders, 918 nhp, 13 knots.
Passengers: 12 1st class and 200 3rd class passengers.
Refrigerated space: 300,000 cu.ft.

14.2.1903: Launched by John Brown & Co. Ltd, Clydebank, (Yard No. 357), and first registered at London on 8.4.1903 to F.B. Birt, O.J. Trinder & C. Bethell for Federal service. 17.10.1904: Suffered a fire in the bunkers at Fremantle shortly after arriving from New York. The insulation between the bunkers and the hold was burnt through. 12.7.1909: Struck an uncharted pinnacle of rock 1.5 miles south-west of North Reef, and east of Cape Capricorn, bound Townsville to Brisbane. She reached Brisbane on the 13th leaking slightly in No. 1 ballast tank. 6.4.1911: Transferred to J.W. Potter, O.J. Trinder and W.J. Gwyn. 10.1.1912: Suffered damage to her bottom plates at London. 23.12.1912: Suffered a fire at

Liverpool. 28.7.1914: A.A. Trinder took over O.J. Trinder's interest. 11.12.1915: Struck the quay wall leaving Le Havre and returned for repairs. 8.3.1917—10.3.1919: Taken up under the Liner Requisition Scheme. 10.12.1918: Grounded off Ward Island, Wellington, on arrival from London. Refloated undamaged on the 16th. 11.9.1922: Transferred to Federal. 19.3.1924: Suffered a fire in No. 4 hold at Glasgow when about to sail for Liverpool. The fire was out by the next day and she sailed on the 23rd. 5.1.1927: Sold with the SUFFOLK (No. F.12) for £28,250 the pair to P. & W. MacLellan Ltd and broken up at Bo'ness.

SOMERSET at Sydney

(Dufty/WAL)

# F.15 SOMERSET (1903—1917)

Official Number: 118292
Tonnages: 7,110 gross, 4,481 net, 11,300 deadweight. Dimensions: 460.5 x 58.2 x 31.0 feet.
Twin screw, two T.3 cyl. by the shipbuilders, 918 nhp, 13 knots.
Passengers: 12 1st and 200 3rd class. Refrigerated space: 300,000 cu.ft.

25.4.1903: Launched by John Brown & Co. Ltd, Clydebank, (Yard No. 358), and first registered at London to Federal on 10.6.1903. 30.11.1903: Ran aground in the Port River, Adelaide. Refloated on 1.12.1903. 22.4.1909: Collided with the steamer MOOLTAN

(9,621g, 1905) at Suez. 11.5.1917: Taken up under the Liner Requisition Scheme. 26.7.1917: Torpedoed and sunk by U 54 230 miles south-west of Ushant (46°09'N-09°32'W), bound Buenos Aires to Le Havre with refrigerated cargo.

DURHAM at Wellington

(WAL)

## F.16 DURHAM (1904—1924)

Official Number: 118499
Tonnages: 5,561 gross, 3,550 net, 9,400 deadweight. Dimensions: 420.7 (434.5 overall) x 54.0 x 28.6 feet.
T.3 cyl. by the North Eastern Marine Engineering Co. Ltd, Wallsend, 518 nhp, 11 knots.
Passengers: 12 1st class.
Refrigerated space: 310,600 cu.ft.

*18.2.1904:* Launched by R. & W. Hawthorn, Leslie & Co. Ltd, Hebburn, (Yard No. 392), and first registered at London on 3.10.1904 to A. Hughes & Wm Milburn for Federal service. She was delivered on 9.12.1904 and had been ordered originally as the PORT PHILLIP by Wm Milburn & Co. *10.3.1906:* Collided with the steamer INDIAN, (9,121g, 1900) off Bardsey Island, outward bound from Liverpool and put into Holyhead on the 11th for repairs. *1.1907—7.1913:* The shares in the ship were progressively transferred to Federal via members of the Hughes and Milburn families. *30.11.1912:* Suffered a fire at Brisbane.

Minor damage only. *10.8.1917—22.4.1919:* Taken up under the Liner Requisition Scheme. *12.10.1923:* Grounded in Sandon Basin, Liverpool. *15.7.1924:* Sold for £35,000 to A. Zanchi fu G., Genoa, and renamed AUGUSTA. *10.6.1940:* Interned at Bahia and seized by the Brazilian Government in 12.1941. *1942:* Transferred to the Lloyd Brasiliero Patrimonio Nacional, Rio de Janeiro, and renamed MINASLOIDE. *1949:* Returned to Ditta A. Zanchi and renamed AUGUSTA. *15.5.1950:* Arrived in tow at Spezia where demolition by S.A. Cantieri di Portovenere began on 6.8.1950.

SHROPSHIRE at Adelaide

(IJF)

## F.17 SHROPSHIRE (1911—1923)

Official Number: 132607
Tonnages: 10,374 gross, 6,586 net. 1923: 12,112 gross, 7,705 net. Dimensions: 526.4 (544.0 overall) x 61.4 x 33.3 feet.
Twin screw, two Q.4 cyl. by the shipbuilders, 6,500 ihp, 14 knots. 2,700 tons of coal fuel. 1923: Converted to oil firing.
Passengers: 130 1st class and 270 emigrants. 1912: 66 1st class. 1923: 131 1st and 270 3rd class. 1933: 400 tourist class.
Refrigerated space: 358,600 cu.ft.

*27.4.1911:* Launched by John Brown & Co. Ltd, Clydebank, (Yard No. 400), and first registered at London to Federal on 19.9.1911. *24.8.1914—5.8.1917:* Requisitioned as the Australian Expeditionary Force transport A 9 (57 officers, 878 troops and 461 horses) and sailed 1.11.1914 in the first convoy from Albany to Alexandria. *21.11.1914:* Collided with the steamer ASCANIUS (10,048g, 1910) in convoy between Colombo and Aden. *6.8.1917—2.7.1919:* Taken up under the Liner Requisition Scheme. *13.10.1919:* Suffered a hold fire at Glasgow. *24.6.1920:* Suffered a fire in the bunkers, bound Manchester to Adelaide and returned to Liverpool. *27.10.1921:* Suffered a fire in the air trunks of Nos. 1, 2, 3 and 4 holds whilst repairing at Falmouth. 1 life lost. The fire was out on the 29th, but the ship remained

laid up at Falmouth, suffering another fire on 11.11.1921. *5.12.1921—12.3.1923:* Given an extensive conversion at Falmouth to a passenger ship, renamed ROTORUA on 19.3.1923 and entered NZS service on sailing from Southampton for Wellington on 29.3.1923. *2.9.1927:* Struck the quay while berthing at Southampton from London and delayed for 1 day. *1934:* Mainmast top demolished by a crane at Wellington and never replaced. *1.10.1936:* Formally transferred to NZS ownership for £7,850, and re-registered at Plymouth on 2.3.1937. *9.2.1940:* Requisitioned for the Liner Division. *11.12.1940:* Torpedoed and sunk by U 96 110 miles west of St Kilda (58°56'N-11°20'W) with the loss of 21 lives. She was bound Lyttelton to Avonmouth in Convoy HX 92 with refrigerated and general cargo.

WILTSHIRE at Liverpool

*(NZA)*

## F.18 WILTSHIRE (1912—1922)

Official Number: 132675
Tonnages: 10,390 gross, 6,598 net. Dimensions: 526.5 (544.0 overall) x 61.4 x 33.3 feet.
Twin screw, two Q.4 cyl. by the shipbuilders, 6,500 ihp, 14 knots.
Passengers: 130 1st class and 270 emigrants. 1912: 66 1st class.
Refrigerated space: 375,000 cu.ft.

*19.12.1911:* Launched by John Brown & Co. Ltd, Clydebank, (Yard No. 401), and first registered at London to Federal on 15.2.1912. *7.9.1914—27.12.1917:* Requisitioned as the Australian Expeditionary Force transport A 18 (36 officers, 720 troops and 505 horses), and sailed 1.11.1914 in the first convoy from Albany to Alexandria. *28.12.1917—5.9.1919:* Taken up under the Liner

Requisition Scheme. *2.10.1920:* Collided with the tug HEROIC (268g, 1909) at Sydney. *31.5.1922:* Wrecked in Rosalie Bay, Great Barrier Island, bound Liverpool to Auckland. She broke in two on 1.6.1922 but all the crew were rescued over the following 2 days.

WILTSHIRE with her back broken on Great Barrier Island

*(DNB)*

# Chapter 2: The First World War and Between the Wars

Following the merger, Federal Steam Navigation Company as an English registered company tended to be the vehicle for the acquisition of English subsidiaries of the Group, while NZS was used for New Zealand interests. Federal had already acquired a majority interest in the capital of Birt, Potter & Hughes in 1903, and in 1914 it moved to protect the Group interests by purchasing a major holding in the London shiprepairing firm of R & H Green & Silley, Weir Ltd. This was followed in 1918 by the acquisition of the Falmouth firms in the same trade, Cox & Company and Falmouth Docks. At the end of 1913 the NZS/Federal Group caused a furore in British shipping circles by ordering 3 major cargo liners from a French yard at a time when it was unheard of for leading British liner companies to build abroad. The reason lay in the early delivery dates promised at a time of full order books in British yards plus the benefit of subsidies granted by the French Government to its shipbuilders. In the event, the DEVON of 1915 was the only one of the 3 to enter the Federal fleet, though two similar ships, the CUMBERLAND and WESTMORELAND, were delivered from British yards in 1915 and 1917. While the French ship had conventional reciprocating engines, the British deliveries introduced the geared turbine to the Federal fleet, a type of prime mover to which it was to remain dedicated until the delivery of the first motorships nearly 20 years later.

Also delivered during the war years was the NORTHUMBERLAND which at 12,160 tons gross was to remain the largest dry cargo ship ever to wear Federal colours. All of them introduced a new profile to the fleet with a cruiser stern and a long centrecastle running from the main mast to the mizzen and available for migrants or cargo as required. Federal made a major contribution to the Australian war effort from the start, with the SHROPSHIRE, WILTSHIRE and SUFFOLK being part of the initial 1914 troop convoy. 3 of the fleet were lost to torpedo and mine while 4 others reached port after damage or attack. The first of a new class developed from the war time deliveries, but of single screw design, was completed as the KENT during 1918 to be followed by 3 sisters and the slightly larger twin screw CORNWALL in 1919/20.

Then from 1921 Federal became the somewhat less than willing recipient of a number of ex-German ships taken over as war reparations. The first group of 5 ships, all over 10,000 tons gross, were high class twin screw liner tonnage originally built for the Hamburg Amerika Linie, but they were coal burning general cargo ships for which the Company had little use. They spent a good deal of time laid up in the River Fal until over 1923/25 they were successively fitted with refrigerated capacity and converted to oil fuel after which they became very useful members of the the fleet though their German design features always marked them out from the purpose built ships of the Company. In the early 1930's their speed or economy as required was given a boost by the fitting of exhaust turbines on each shaft.

The second group of 5 ships was a much more mixed bag of 3 8,000 and 2 7,000 ton single screw cargo ships which had first been allocated to a fellow P&O subsidiary, the Hain Steamship Company. As ex-liner tonnage they were really too good for the Hain tramp operations, but they were ill matched to Federal requirements. As part of their lack of identity, they were given NZS names although owned and managed by Federal, and a plain black funnel relating to neither. They never really fitted in, and there was little sorrow when they were sold for demolition during the 1930's.

DORSET (F.42) on the ways at Belfast ready for launching *(A.J. Smythe)*

The first newbuildings for the Federal flag for 14 years and the first motorships in the fleet were delivered in 1934 as the DURHAM and DORSET. Developments of the NZS O class, they were flush deckers rather than having the 3 island hull of the O's, while their 16 knot speed introduced new standards in the Federal fleet. They were followed in 1936/37 by the even larger ESSEX and SUSSEX which although technically owned by the parent P&O remained under Federal colours and management. With the wholly owned SUFFOLK which was about to be handed over by the builders when war broke out in September 1939, they were among the finest and fastest refrigerated cargo liners afloat with a capacity in excess of 500,000 cu.ft.

## Ships F.19 to F.45: MIDDLESEX — SUFFOLK

MIDDLESEX at Sydney                     (IJF)

### F.19 MIDDLESEX (1914—1917)

Official Number: 135569
Tonnages: 7,264 gross, 4,639 net. Dimensions: 470.0 x 58.0 x 32.0 feet.
T.3 cyl. by D. Rowan & Co., Glasgow, 557 nhp, 12 knots.
Refrigerated space: 322,700 cu.ft. (installed November 1914).

*12.2.1914:* Launched by C. Connell & Co. Ltd, Glasgow, (Yard No. 357), for the Knight Steam Ship Company Ltd, Liverpool, (Greenshields, Cowie & Company, managers), and first registered 6.4.1914 as KNIGHT BACHELOR. *20.8.1914:* Sold to Federal and renamed MIDDLESEX on 20.11.1914, remaining registered at Liverpool. *10.4.1917:* Taken up under the Liner Requisition Scheme. *16.5.1917:* Torpedoed and sunk by U 30 150 miles north-west of Tory Island (56°03′N-12°30′W), bound Manchester to Australia with general cargo.

DEVON at Adelaide                       (IJF)

### F.20 DEVON (1915—1934)

Official Number: 139098
Tonnages: 9,661 gross, 6,147 net, 11,300 deadweight. Dimensions: 473.3 (495.0 overall) x 59.9 x 36.7 feet. Draft: 30.3 feet.
Twin screw, two T.3 cyl. by the shipbuilders, 5,000 ihp, 13 knots.
Passengers: 300 emigrants.
Refrigerated space: 440,000 cu.ft.

*12.1914:* Launched by Ateliers & Chantiers de France, Dunkirk, (Yard No. 98), for Federal as DEVON, having been laid down originally as CORNWALL. She left the yard in tow on 2.6.1915 and on 4.6.1915 arrived at London where she was completed
*Continued overleaf*

*F.20 DEVON — continued*

by Silley, Weir & Co. Ltd. First registered at London on 1.11.1915. *14.11.1916:* Collided with the steamer A1 (127g, 1895) in the Bristol Channel. *13.12.1916 — 4.7.1917:* Requisitioned as an Expeditionary Force transport. *5.7.1917 — 24.3.1919:* Taken up under the Liner Requisition Scheme. *29.5.1922:* Suffered a bunker fire at Lyttelton. *15.3.1924:* Arrived at Napier after having lost half her rudder and proceeded to Auckland for docking. *18.5.1926:* Towed the disabled steamer EASTERN MOON (5,116g, 1919) 440 miles from off Elizabeth Reef to Sydney where they arrived on 25.5.1926. *13.1.1927:* While lying in the stream at Wellington, the hulk ARAWATA (1,096g, 1875) coming

alongside to bunker her, bumped heavily on the DEVON and had to be beached in a sinking condition. *1927 — 1933:* Served as a cadet ship for 20 cadets. *7.5.1929:* Suffered a fire in the bunkers at Port Chalmers. *8.1933 — 3.1934:* Laid up at Truro. *28.8.1934:* Sold for £10,000 to the British India Steam Navigation Co. Ltd, London. *9.1934 — 8.1939:* Served as a cadet ship for 38 cadets. *2.4.1940:* Requisitioned for the Liner Division. *19.8.1941:* Sunk by the raider KOMET (3,287g, 1937) 200 miles south-west of the Galapagos Islands (04°08'S-92°23'W), bound Newcastle to New Zealand. All on board taken prisoner.

As well as DEVON (No. F.20), two further sister ships were also ordered from the yard of Ateliers & Chantiers de France at Dunkirk for Federal-Shire service. Both were requisitioned by the French authorities under war conditions, Yard No. 99 (originally to have been ABERDEENSHIRE) being completed in November 1916 as LA PEROUSE and Yard No. 100 (originally to have been DEVON and then CORNWALL) being completed as JACQUES CARTIER in October 1918.

NORTHUMBERLAND in original rig with 4 topmasts at Auckland *(WAL)*

## F.21 NORTHUMBERLAND (1916 — 1951)

Official Number: 139112

Tonnages: 12,160 gross, 7,834 net, 13,821 deadweight. Dimensions: 530.5 (550.5 overall) x 63.0 x 31.9 feet. Draft: 31.8 feet.

Twin screw, two sets of high and low pressure turbines single reduction geared, by the Wallsend Slipway & Engineering Co. Ltd, Wallsend, 1,923nhp, 14 knots. 14.66 knots on trials. Converted to oil fuel in 1926.

Refrigerated space: 466,300 cu.ft.

*6.2.1915:* Launched by Swan, Hunter & Wigham Richardson Ltd, Wallsend, (Yard No. 955), completed in 11.1915, but laid up until 8.2.1916. First registered to Federal on 27.1.1916 and ran trials on 15.2.1916. Cost £201,604. *13.4.1917:* In collision at Norfolk, Va. *7.5.1917 — 7.3.1919:* Taken up under the Liner Requisition

Scheme. *11 — 26.9.1917:* Grounded in Platypus Channel, Townsville. *1924 — 1934:* Served as a cadet ship for 42 cadets. *15.9.1924:* Suffered a fire in the bunkers and in No. 4 hold in the Indian Ocean, outward bound from Liverpool. She arrived at Fremantle on the 19th and the fire was out by the 27th.

NORTHUMBERLAND at Adelaide in later rig with fore and jigger topmasts removed *(IJF)*

*17.11.1924:* Grounded off the mouth of the Patuxent River, Maryland, inward bound to Baltimore from Swansea. *25.1.1927:* Struck a submerged object between Gable End Foreland and Tuahine Point 14 miles north of Gisborne, bound Auckland to Napier. She anchored off Gisborne for temporary repairs, sailed on 2.2.1927, but had to return and finally left on the 9th. Permanent repairs in dock at Auckland took 6 weeks. *2.5.1928:* Suffered a fire in the cargo at Plymouth. *3—4.2.1931:* Assisted with earthquake relief while anchored in the roadstead at Napier. *26.9.1936:* Collided with the motor tanker ATHELREGENT (8,884g, 1930) at Falmouth. *8.2.1940—10.8.1946:* Requisitioned for the Liner Division, but spent the period from 8.1.1941—26.1.1942 as a personnel ship for 1,600 troops. *23.9.1940:* Collided with the tug HERO (161g, 1892) off Blue's Point, Sydney. The tug capsized and sank, but was later salvaged. *10.12.1944:* Collided with the KENT (No. F.24) at London. *13.1.1951:* Sold for £80,000 to BISCO, arrived at Rosyth on the 15th and demolition by T.W. Ward Ltd began at Inverkeithing on the 21st.

NORTHUMBERLAND undergoing repairs in Calliope Dock (showing the extension to the dockhead to accommodate her) after her mishap at Gisborne in 1927
*(WAL)*

CUMBERLAND on trials

*(IJF)*

## F.22 CUMBERLAND (1915—1917)

Official Number: 139102
Tonnages: 8,993 gross, 5,727 net. Dimensions: 474.0 x 60.0 x 36.7 feet.
Twin screw, two sets of high and low pressure turbines single reduction geared, by D. Rowan & Co. Ltd, Glasgow, 4,000 shp, 14 knots.
Refrigerated space: 386,000 cu.ft.

*6.3.1915:* Launched by Wm Hamilton & Co. Ltd, Port Glasgow, (Yard No. 298), first registered at London to Federal on 1.12.1915, and ran trials on 17.12.1915. *6.7.1917:* Struck a mine laid by the German raider WOLF (5,809g, 1913) 10 miles off Gabo Island, bound Sydney to Melbourne. She was beached on the 7th, refloated on 11.8.1917, but sank that day in tow 6 miles south east of Green Cape. 94% of her lead, copper and zinc cargo was salved by the salvage vessel FOREMOST 17 (601g, 1911) of Risdon, Beazley & Co. Ltd from 1.1952—1.1953.

## NORFOLK (1915) later HURUNUI (1920-1922) See No. 62

WESTMORELAND at Adelaide (IJF)

### F.23 WESTMORELAND (1917—1942)

Official Number: 140292
Tonnages: 9,512 gross, 6,099 net. Dimensions: 473.0 (494.5 overall) x 60.1 x 36.7 feet. Draft: 30.6 feet.
Twin screw, two sets of high and low pressure turbines, single reduction geared, by the Wallsend Slipway & Engineering
Co. Ltd, Wallsend, 4,000 shp, 14 knots. Converted to oil fuel in 12.1926.
Refrigerated space: 350,700 cu.ft.

*1916:* Launched by D. & W. Henderson & Co. Ltd, Glasgow, (Yard No. 492), and first registered at London to Federal on 27.4.1917. *8.5.1917—14.2.1919:* Taken up under the Liner Requisition Scheme. *12—24.9.1917:* Suffered a bunker fire at sea, outward bound for Auckland. *6.2.1918:* Torpedoed by UB 57 in the Irish Sea (54°20′N-03°30′W), bound Wellington to Liverpool with refrigerated cargo. Beached 2 miles west of Ravenglass and towed to Liverpool on 10.5.1918. 1 life lost. Repairs were not completed until 11.2.1919. *28.2.1919:* Struck by the tug as she left Liverpool denting a plate in the port bow. *21.5.1919:* Grounded leaving Bluff for Wellington. Refloated the following day and docked at Port Chalmers 26.5.1919 for repairs. *20.10.1919:* Grounded on Cockle Bank leaving dry dock at Port Chalmers and returned to dock for further repairs. *19.11.1919:* Suffered a fire at Timaru. *31.12.1919:* Struck the wharf heavily

when berthing at Sydney, C.B., bound Wellington to Liverpool. *1.5.1923:* Suffered a minor engineroom fire in the Royal Albert Dock, London. *6.9.1923:* Suffered a bunker fire at Auckland. *7.7.1925:* Grounded off Trieste, inward bound from Australia, but refloated the following day. *1927—1934:* Served as a cadet ship for 40 cadets. *8—12.1931:* Laid up at Falmouth. *19.2.1940:* Requisitioned for the Liner Division, but served from 28.1.1942—20.3.1942 as a mechanical transport ship. *29.1.1941:* Mined 3 cables from the Bar Lightship, inward bound from Glasgow to Liverpool with general cargo. She was abandoned, then beached and was brought in to Liverpool in tow on the 31st with the engine and boiler rooms flooded. *1.6.1942:* Sunk by gunfire and torpedoes from U 566 240 miles north of Bermuda (35°55′N-63°35′W), bound Wellington to Liverpool with wool and general cargo. 3 lives lost.

KENT at Lyttelton (WAL)

## F.24 KENT (1918—1955)

Official Number: 142611
Tonnages: 9,857 gross, 7,447 net. Dimensions: 460.6 x 62.8 x 34.9 feet.
High and low pressure turbines single reduction geared to one shaft, by the shipbuilders, 5,000 shp, 14 knots. 1924: Boilers converted to oil fuel.
Refrigerated space: 378,800 cu.ft.

14.12.1917: Launched by Palmers' Shipbuilding & Iron Co. Ltd, Jarrow, (Yard No. 867), and delivered to Federal on 8.8.1918. 8.8.1918—4.4.1919: Taken up under the Liner Requisition Scheme. 12.8.1918: Missed by a torpedo, probably from U 113, in the North Sea. 3.9.1925: Suffered a fire in No. 2 hold at Auckland. The hold was flooded and the fire extinguished on the 4th. 21.4.1926: Grounded at Suez. 9.10.1927: Collided with the breakwater at New Plymouth, damaging her bow. 29.6.1934: Grounded at Port Alma. 25.3.1936: Collided with the steamer AMBLE (1,162g, 1920) at Gravesend. 10.6.1936: Suffered an engine breakdown in Kandavu Passage, bound Liverpool to Dunedin. Drifted for 2 days close to Mbenga Reef before limping

into Suva. 14.6.1940—18.4.1946: Requisitioned for the Liner Division. 11.6.1942: Picked up 35 crew from the torpedoed steamer AMERICAN (4,846g, 1916) off Honduras. 21.9.1942: Collided with the motorship FERNWOOD (4,695g, 1930) while both ships were at anchor at New York. 10.7.1943: Suffered an engineroom fire at Melbourne. 2.12.1943: Collided with the steamer EMPIRE MOONRISE (6,854g, 1941) on leaving New York for Wellington. 10.12.1944: Collided with the NORTHUMBERLAND (No. F.21) at London. 16.1.1945: Mainmast collapsed and was replaced at London. 16.8.1955: Arrived at Blyth, having been sold to BISCO on the 12th and allocated to the Hughes Bolckow Shipbreaking Co. Ltd for demolition there.

SOMERSET at Sydney as built in dazzle paint *(NZA)*

## F.25 SOMERSET (1918—1941)

Official Number: 142696
Tonnages: 9,773 gross, 7,384 net. Dimensions: 460.6 x 62.8 x 34.6 feet.
High, intermediate and low pressure turbines double reduction geared to one shaft, by the shipbuilders, 5,000 shp, 14 knots. 10.1924: Boilers converted to oil fuel.
Refrigerated space: 360,000 cu.ft.

1918: Launched by Earle's Shipbuilding & Engineering Co. Ltd, Hull, (Yard No. 625), and delivered to Federal on 24.10.1918. 26.10.1918—3.6.1919: Taken up under the Liner Requisition Scheme. 1920—1927: Served as a cadet ship for 20 cadets. 11.1920: Arrived at Lyttelton from New York with a fire in the cargo in No. 3 hold. 4.10.1922: Grounded leaving Adelaide for London. 26.5.1929: Broke adrift in a gale at Fremantle and collided with the steamer BUTESHIRE (6,544g, 1912) and the

barge KALAROO (118g, 1912). 26.12.1929: Collided with the steamer STEEL TRADER (5,687g, 1920) at Balboa. 3.2.1939: Grounded at Newcastle, N.S.W. 6.8.1940: Requisitioned for the Liner Division. 11.5.1941: Heavily damaged by aircraft torpedo 200 miles west of Achill Head (54°54'N-16°20'W), bound Buenos Aires to Liverpool with refrigerated and general cargo. The crew were rescued without loss of life by the corvette HMS ALISMA (925 tons, 1941) which then sank the wreck by gunfire.

SOMERSET in Federal colours at Adelaide

*(IJF)*

SURREY at Adelaide                                                                                              *(IJF)*

## F.26 SURREY (1919–1942)

Official Number: 143352
Tonnages: 9,783 gross, 6,228 net, 11,550 deadweight. Dimensions: 460.4 (480.1 overall) x 62.8 x 34.9 feet.
High and low pressure turbines, single reduction geared to one shaft, by the shipbuilders, 5,000 shp, 14 knots. 1924:
Boilers converted to oil fuel.
Refrigerated space: 382,200 cu.ft.

*15.4.1919:* Launched by Palmers' Shipbuilding & Iron Co. Ltd, Jarrow, (Yard No. 868), and delivered to Federal 24.7.1919. *25.1.1925:* Collided with the steamer COOMA (3,839g, 1907) at Brisbane. *25.11.1925:* Collided with the sludge carrier J.H. HUNTER (1,500g, 1924) in the Thames, outward bound for Timaru. Her stem was damaged and she had to return, discharge 5,000 tons of cargo and be docked for repairs before resuming her voyage to Auckland. *1.3.1940:* Requisitioned for the Liner Division. *22.12.1941:* Damaged in collision with an unidentified small craft off Avonmouth, outward bound in ballast for Buenos Aires, and had to put into Milford Haven for repairs. *8.1.1942:*

Lost her rudder in the North Atlantic (51°02'N-36°42'W). She was taken in tow, first by the steamer CAVINA (6.907g, 1924) and then by the motor tug ROODE ZEE (468g, 1938) on the 26th and reached Bermuda on the 30th. She left Bermuda again in tow of the U.S. Navy tug OWL (1,009 tons, 1918) on 10.2.1942 and arrived at Baltimore for repairs on the 23rd. *10.6.1942:* Torpedoed and sunk by U 68 150 miles north of Cristobal (12°45'N-80°20'W) after leaving convoy the previous day, bound New York to Sydney with war supplies and general cargo. 10 crew and 2 gunners were lost.

MIDDLESEX at Wellington                                                                                      *(ATL/NZA)*

## F.27 MIDDLESEX (1920–1941)

Official Number: 145237
Tonnages: 8,569 gross, 5,436 net. Dimensions: 460.0 x 62.8 x 35.2 feet.
High and low pressure turbines, double reduction geared to one shaft, by the shipbuilders, 5,000 shp, 14 knots. 15.49
knots on trials. *4.1925:* Boilers converted to oil fuel.
Refrigerated space: 380,000 cu.ft.

*22.3.1920:* Launched by Swan, Hunter & Wigham Richardson Ltd, Wallsend, (Yard No. 1026), and completed 1920 but delivery delayed. Ran trials 16.6.1921 and delivered to Federal on 24.6.1921. *8.9.1923:* Collided with the steamer TYRA BRATT (1,301g, 1923) in King's Dock, Swansea, bound Manchester to

Brisbane. *13.12.1928:* Collided with the steamer CHIOS (1,731g, 1912) in the River Thames, inward bound from Antwerp. *1.3.1940:* Requisitioned for the Liner Division. *10.1.1941:* Mined and sunk off Flatholm, Bristol Channel, bound Cardiff to Fremantle with tinplate and general cargo. All saved.

CORNWALL at Adelaide

*(IJF)*

# F.28 CORNWALL (1920—1949)

Official Number: 145038
Tonnages: 10,669 gross, 6,781 net. Dimensions: 495.1 (508.1 overall) x 63.1 x 40.3 feet.
Twin screw, two sets of high and low pressure turbines, single reduction geared, by D. Rowan & Co. Ltd, Glasgow, 5,000 shp, 14 knots. 1.1928: Boilers converted to oil fuel.
Refrigerated space: 460,000 cu.ft.

*3.4.1920:* Launched by Wm Hamilton & Co. Ltd, Port Glasgow, (Yard No. 378), and delivered to Federal on 27.10.1920. *18.5.1929:* Struck a quay wall at Avonmouth. *3.3.1930:* Grounded at Curacao, bound Auckland to London. Refloated on the 15th and after temporary repairs, resumed her voyage on the 22nd. *6.1931—7.1934:* Served as a cadet ship. *25.9.1932:* Grounded on the north side of the channel just past the North Arm, Port Adelaide, when passing a moored dredge and the inward bound steamer KAREPO (2,563g, 1929) did not leave enough room. Refloated undamaged the next day.

*4.5.1940—26.4.1946:* Requisitioned for the Liner Division. *31.8.1940:* Damaged by bombs south of Crete (35°15'N-23°15'E), bound Rockhampton to U.K. with general cargo. 1 killed and 10 injured. She arrived at Malta on 2.9.1940 and left on 26.11.1940. *26.4.1942:* Collided with the steamer RICHARD HENRY LEE (7,191g, 1942). *12.1948:* Laid up at Avonmouth. *1.3.1949:* Sold to BISCO for £26,000 and arrived 15.3.1949 at Briton Ferry where demolition by T.W. Ward Ltd began on the 17th.

HERTFORD at Adelaide

*(IJF)*

# F.29 HERTFORD (1921—1942)

Official Number: 144656
Tonnages: 10,923 gross, 6,934 net, 15,173 deadweight. Dimensions: 520.7 (533.0 overall) x 64.2 x 38.1 feet. Draft: 31.8 feet.
Twin screw, two T.3 cyl. by the shipbuilders, 5,800 ihp, 13.5 knots. Low pressure turbines of 800 shp connected to shafts through double reduction gearing and Bauer-Wach couplings installed in 1929.
Refrigerated space: 426,500 cu.ft. (installed in 1923).

*1912:* Ordered by the Hamburg-Amerikanische Packetfahrt A.G., Hamburg from the Bremer Vulkan, Schiffbau & Maschinenfabrik, Vegesack, (Yard No. 577), as the cargo vessel FRIESLAND. The order was changed in 1913 to one for the
*Continued overleaf*

### F.29 HERTFORD — continued

passenger liner RHEINLAND, but the keel was not laid until 1916 by which time the order had changed back again to a cargo vessel. *13.10.1917:* Launched as the RHEINLAND, renamed FRIESLAND while fitting out in 1919 and ran trials 30.6.1920. *6.7.1920:* Arrived at Leith and surrendered to the Allied Control Commission. *18.11.1920:* Allocated to Britain and handed over to The Shipping Controller, London, (Glen Line Ltd, managers). *6.5.1921:* Sold to Federal while lying at Avonmouth and laid up at Falmouth until 9.5.1922 when recommissioned as HERTFORD. *3—11.1923:* Converted to oil fuel and refrigeration installed at Falmouth. *21.7.1927:* Collided with the tugs CARLGARTH (179g, 1922) and YORKGARTH (179g, 1922) at Liverpool. *5—7.1928:* Laid up at Falmouth. *12.1.1930:* Broke adrift at Avonmouth and collided with the LILLA VENN (58g, 1860) and BULL DOG (122g,

1884). *7—11.1931:* Laid up at Falmouth. *3.1.1938:* Collided with the motorship MOVERIA (4,867g, 1925) off Dumbarton Rock, River Clyde, inward bound from New Zealand. *1.7.1938:* Stood by and rescued the crew of the schooner ST CLAIR THERIAULT (331g, 1919). *10.4.1940:* Requisitioned for the Liner Division. *7.12.1940:* Struck a mine laid by the raider PINGUIN (7,760g, 1936) off the mouth of the Spencer Gulf (33°50'S-135°25'E), bound Liverpool to Brisbane with general cargo. She was towed to Spalding Cove, Port Lincoln on the 9th, arrived at Adelaide in tow on 1.4.1941 and at Sydney on 22.8.1941 where repairs were completed on 24.11.1941. *29.3.1942:* Torpedoed and sunk by U 571 150 miles south-east of New Bedford, Mass., (40°50'N-63°31'W), with the loss 4 lives, bound Colon to Halifax with refrigerated and general cargo.

CUMBERLAND at Lyttelton                                    *(IJF)*

## F.30 CUMBERLAND (1921—1940)

Official Number: 145052
Tonnages: 10,943 gross, 6,922 net, 15,115 deadweight. Dimensions: 520.0 x 64.2 x 29.0 feet. Draft: 31.8 feet.
Twin screw, two T.3 cyl. by the shipbuilders, 5,800 ihp, 13.5 knots. Low pressure turbines of 800 shp connected to shafts through double reduction gearing and Bauer-Wach couplings installed in 1931.
Refrigerated space: 442,900 cu.ft. (installed in 1924).

*8.11.1919:* Launched by the Bremer Vulkan, Schiffbau & Maschinenfabrik, Vegesack, (Yard No. 587), as WENDLAND for the Hamburg-Amerikanische Packetfahrt A.G., Hamburg, and ran trials on 30.8.1920. *7.9.1920:* Arrived at Leith and delivered to the Allied Control Commission. *18.11.1920:* Allocated to Britain and handed over to The Shipping Controller, London, (Furness, Withy & Co. Ltd, managers). *6.5.1921:* Sold to Federal, handed over at Devonport and laid up at Falmouth. Renamed CUMBERLAND and recommissioned in 1922. *7.12.1922:* Collided with the steamer HATARANA (7,922g, 1917) at Brisbane. *1924:* Converted to oil fuel and refrigeration installed. *30.10.1930:* Inward bound from Newcastle to Antwerp, collided with the steamer LLANSTEPHAN CASTLE, (11,293g, 1914) in the River Scheldt. Minor damage only. *9.2.1933:* Suffered a fire in the hemp cargo in No. 4 bridge deck at Lyttelton. *1.5.1936:* Torn from her moorings at New Plymouth in a cyclonic gale and had to put to sea until the next day. *20.6.1936:* Suffered a fire in No. 1 hold 700 miles south-west of the Bishop Rock, bound New Zealand to London. *2.4.1938:* Collided with and sank the tug FLYING SPRAY (217g, 1917) at Glasgow. *20.2.1940:* Requisitioned for the Liner Division. *23.8.1940:* Torpedoed by U 57 25 miles off Malin Head (55°44'N-07°32'W), bound

Liverpool to Port Chalmers in convoy OB 202 with general cargo. She sank the following day in 55°43'N-07°33'W with the loss of 4 lives.

CUMBERLAND on fire at Lyttelton, 1933                       *(DNB)*

CAMBRIDGE at Brisbane

*(VHY/NZA)*

## F.31 CAMBRIDGE (1921—1940)

Official Number: 144589
Tonnages: 10,964 gross, 6,919 net, 13,300 deadweight. Dimensions: 524.5 (544.5 overall) x 65.7 x 37.3 feet. Draft: 29.9 feet.
Twin screw, two T.3 cyl. by the shipbuilders, 5,200 ihp, 13.5 knots.
Refrigerated space: 418,700 cu.ft. (installed in 1925).

*9.12.1916:* Launched by J.C. Tecklenborg A.G., Geestemunde, (Yard No. 271), for the Hamburg-Amerikanische Packetfahrt A.G., Hamburg, as VOGTLAND and laid up. Ran trials on 27.11.1919. *14.5.1920:* Delivered at Leith to the Allied Control Commission. *18.11.1920:* Allocated to Britain and handed over to The Shipping Controller, London, (Glen Line Ltd, managers). *18.5.1921:* Sold to Federal, taken over at Tilbury and laid up at Falmouth. Renamed CAMBRIDGE and recommissioned on 12.9.1922. *9—11.1923:* Laid up at Falmouth. *15.12.1924:* Grounded in the Adelaide River. *1925:* Converted to oil fuel and refrigeration

installed. *26.4.1930:* Lost a propeller blade a week out from Panama, bound Liverpool to Auckland. *15.10.1930:* Suffered a fire in No. 3 hold in the Indian Ocean, bound Australia to U.K. *20.5.1933:* Collided with and sank the barge MAY (160g) in the English Channel off Portland Bill, bound London to Wanganui in ballast. *13.3.1939:* Suffered a fire at Tottenville, N.Y. *25.8.1940:* Requisitioned for the Liner Division. *7.11.1940:* Struck a mine laid by the German auxiliary PASSAT (8,998g, 1926) 6 miles east of Wilson's Promontory, bound Melbourne to Sydney, and sank on the 8th with the loss of 1 life.

NORFOLK at Brisbane

*(VHY/NZA)*

## F.32 NORFOLK (1921—1941)

Official Number: 144675
Tonnages: 10,946 gross, 6,889 net, 15,177 deadweight. Dimensions: 520.7 (533.0 overall) x 64.2 x 38.1 feet. Draft: 31.8 feet.
Twin screw, two T.3 cyl. by the shipbuilders, 5,800 ihp, 13.5 knots. Low pressure turbines of 800 shp connected to the shafts through double reduction gearing and Bauer-Wach couplings installed in 1931.
Refrigerated space: 427,450 cu.ft. (installed in 1924).

*1912:* Ordered by the Hamburg-Amerikanische Packetfahrt A.G., Hamburg from the Bremer Vulkan, Schiffbau &

Maschinenfabrik, Vegesack, (Yard No. 578), as the cargo vessel VOGTLAND. The order was changed in 1913 to a passenger liner
*Continued overleaf*

*F.32 NORFOLK — continued*

but the keel was not laid until 1916 by which time the order had been changed back to a cargo vessel. *24.5.1918:* Launched as SAUERLAND and ran trials on 17.7.1920. *1920:* Surrendered to the Allied Control Commission, allocated to Britain and handed over to The Shipping Controller, London, (Furness, Withy & Co. Ltd, managers), and laid up at Southampton. *18.4.1921:* Sold to Federal and laid up at Falmouth from 30.4.1921. Renamed NORFOLK and recommissioned on 28.4.1922. *5—10.1923:* Laid up at Falmouth. *1924:* Converted to oil fuel and refrigeration

installed. *4.4.1926:* Collided with the American schooner TRIGUENA, bound Colon to Curacao. *7—12.1931:* Laid up at Falmouth. *3.1.1933:* Grounded at Dakar. *16.9.1935:* Grounded at Falmouth. *9—11.1938:* Laid up at Falmouth. *30.5.1940:* Requisitioned for the Liner Division. *18.6.1941:* Torpedoed and sunk by U 552 150 miles north-west of Malin Head (57°17'N-11°14'W), bound Newport to New Zealand with general cargo. 1 life lost.

HUNTINGDON at Adelaide                                                  *(IJF)*

# F.33 HUNTINGDON (1921—1941)

Official Number: 145104

Tonnages: 10,951 gross, 6,299 net, 15,120 deadweight. Dimensions: 520.7 (533.0 overall) x 64.2 x 38.1 feet. Draft: 31.8 feet.

Twin screw, two T.3 cyl. by the shipbuilders, 5,800 ihp, 13.5 knots. Low pressure turbines of 800 shp connected to shafts through double reduction gearing and Bauer-Wach couplings installed in 1931.

Refrigerated space: 409,600 cu.ft. (installed in 1924).

*1918:* Laid down by the Bremer Vulkan, Schiffbau & Maschinenfabrik, Vegesack, (Yard No. 588), for the Hamburg-Amerikanische Packetfahrt A.G., Hamburg. *23.3.1920:* Launched as MUNSTERLAND and ran trials on 29.9.1920. *4.10.1920:* Surrendered at Leith to the Allied Control Commission. *18.11.1920:* Allocated to Britain and handed over to The Shipping Controller, London, (A. MacIntosh & Co., managers). *15.6.1921:* Sold to Federal and arrived Falmouth 21.6.1921 to lay up.

*29.1.1922:* Renamed HUNTINGDON and recommissioned. *1924:* Converted to oil fuel and refrigeration installed. *9.6.1940:* Requisitioned for the Liner Division. *24.2.1941:* Torpedoed and sunk by U 96 240 miles west-north-west of Rockall (58°25'N-20°23'W), bound Cardiff to Brisbane in Convoy OB 288 with general cargo. All on board were saved by the steamer PAPALEMOS (3,748g, 1910) and landed at Horta on 3.3.1941.

PAPANUI at Adelaide                                                  *(IJF)*

## F.34 PAPANUI (1924—1933)

Official Number: 144525
Tonnages: 8,046 gross, 5,075 net, 12,000 deadweight. Dimensions: 470.0 x 58.2 x 32.4 feet. Draft: 27.0 feet.
Q.4 cyl. by the shipbuilders, 3,700 ihp, 11 knots.

*25.8.1910:* Launched by John Brown & Co. Ltd, Clydebank, (Yard No. 417), for the Hamburg-Amerikanische Packetfahrt A.G., Hamburg, and ran trials 14.12.1910 as PREUSSEN. *8.1914:* Interned at Sabang. *22.9.1919:* Surrendered to the British Government, London, (British India Steam Navigation Company Ltd, managers). *19.9.1920:* Allocated to Britain. *13.12.1920:* Sold at Avonmouth for £160,000 to the Hain Steamship Company Ltd, St Ives, (E. Hain & Son, managers), and renamed TREVITHICK on 23.5.1921. *5.1921—6.1922:* Laid up at Falmouth.

*2.3.1923:* Collided with the steamer VECHTDIJK (6,869g, 1920), bound New York to Barry. *21.7.1924:* Sold to Federal, (NZS, managers), and registered at London. Renamed PAPANUI on 20.9.1924. *2.11.1930:* Collided with two tugs and a lighter at St Nazaire, bound Port Pirie to Bristol. *28.11.1930:* Struck by the steamer YORKSHIRE (10,184g, 1920) at Avonmouth. *1.1931—12.1933:* Laid up at Mylor. *11.1933:* Sold for £8,000 to Tamijo Okushaji, Osaka, and left Shimonoseki on 14.3.1934 for demolition at Kuchinotsu.

PAREORA at Adelaide                                      *(IJF)*

## F.35 PAREORA (1924—1933)

Official Number: 143074
Tonnages: 8,435 gross, 5,369 net, 12,253 deadweight. Dimensions: 479.7 x 62.1 x 33.0 feet. Draft: 27.6 feet.
Q.4 cyl. by the shipbuilders, 3,750 ihp,. 12 knots.

*10.7.1915:* Launched by A.G. Weser, Bremen, (Yard No. 208), for Deutsche D.G. Hansa, Bremen, and completed 11.1915 as FALKENFELS. *29.3.1919:* Surrendered to the Allied Control Commission. *1919:* Allocated to Britain and registered at London to The Shipping Controller, (James Chambers & Co., managers). *9.12.1920:* Sold for £190,000 to the Hain Steamship Company Ltd, St Ives, (E. Hain & Son, managers), and renamed TREDENHAM on 4.1.1921. *6.8.1924:* Sold to Federal, (NZS, managers), and registered at London 19.8.1924 as PAREORA. *10.11.1924:* Grounded in the Adelaide River. *20.9.1926:* Suffered

a fire at Avonmouth. *21—24.7.1929:* Suffered heavy weather damage, bound Whyalla to Rotterdam and had to put into Melbourne to discharge part of the iron ore cargo. *28.2.1930:* Collided with the steamer CITY OF ORAN (7,395g, 1915) at New York. *30.6.1930:* Struck a rock at Nukualofa. *9.1930—5.1931, 12.1931—8.1932* and *3—12.1933:* Laid up in the Fal. *11.1933:* Sold for £8,850 to the Mitsuwa Shoji K.K., Kobe, grounded at Newport on 21.12.1933 and arrived on 7.4.1934 at Tokuyama for demolition.

PAKIPAKI at Brisbane                                      *(VHY/NZA)*

## F.36 PAKIPAKI (1924—1933)

Official Number: 143291
Tonnages: 7,166 gross, 4,516 net, 11,410 deadweight. Dimensions: 472.0 x 60.8 x 28.6 feet. Draft: 26.3 feet.
T.3 cyl. by the shipbuilders, 686 nhp, 12 knots.

*16.5.1914:* Launched by the Flensburger S.G., Flensburg, (Yard No. 339), and ran trials 16.7.1914 for the Deutsche D.G. Kosmos,

Hamburg, as AMMON. *1915:* Served as an artillery transport in the Baltic. *9.1917:* Became a coastal craft depot ship. *10.6.1919:*
*Continued overleaf*

139

*F.36 PAKIPAKI— continued*

Surrendered to the Allied Control Commission and laid up at Hamburg. *20.9.1920:* Allocated to Britain and registered at London to The Shipping Controller, London, (Glover Bros, managers). *13.12.1920:* Sold for £160,000 to the Hain Steamship Company Ltd, St Ives, (E. Hain & Son, managers), and renamed TREWINNARD on 28.1.1921. *29.8.1924:* Sold to Federal, (NZS, managers), and registered at London 29.8.1924 as PAKIPAKI. *17.3.1926:* Suffered a fire, bound Sydney to Brisbane. *9.8.1928:* Struck a submerged object and damaged her propeller in

30°52'S-56°40'E, bound Port Pirie to Britain. *3.9.1928:* Stood by the steamer CLAN LAMONT (3,594g, 1900) which had taken a list in rough weather 46 miles south-west of East London and escorted her in to Port Elizabeth. *16.7.1929:* Suffered a fire in her forward store at New York when outward bound for Auckland. Nos. 1 & 2 holds were flooded to contain the blaze. *2—5.1930* and *1.1931—11.1933:* Laid up in the Fal. *3.11.1933:* Sold for £7,700 to Ditta L. Pittaluga Vapori, Genoa, and broken up in Italy in 1.1934.

PIPIRIKI at Lyttelton (IJF)

## F.37 PIPIRIKI (1924—1933)

Official Number: 143148
Tonnages: 6,704 gross, 4,276 net, 11,340 deadweight. Dimensions: 472.5 x 59.2 x 28.5 feet. Draft: 26.7 feet.
T.3 cyl. by the shipbuilders, 4,000 ihp, 12 knots.

*8.8.1914:* Launched by the Flensburger S.G., Flensburg, (Yard No. 341), and delivered 2.2.1915 to the Norddeutscher Lloyd, Bremen, as LIPPE. *2.4.1919:* Surrendered to the Allied Control Commission. Allocated to Britain and registered at London to The Shipping Controller, (Cairns, Noble and Company Ltd, managers). *1.2.1921:* Sold to the Hain Steamship Company Ltd, St Ives, (E. Hain & Son, managers), and renamed TRESITHNEY on 3.3.1921. *16.11.1922:* Collided with the steamer CARL O.

KJELLBERG (644g, 1883) on leaving Antwerp for Australia. *17.11.1924:* Sold to Federal, (NZS, managers), and registered at London 11.11.1924 as PIPIRIKI. *15.11.1929:* Grounded at Swansea on arriving from Port Pirie. *12.1929—7.1930* and *2.1931—11.1933:* Laid up in the Fal. *9.11.1933:* Sold for £7,300 to Ditta L. Pittaluga Vapori, Genoa, and arrived 3.12.1933 at Genoa where she was broken up in 1934.

PURIRI at Brisbane (VHY/NZA)

## F.38 PURIRI (1925—1933)

Official Number: 143094
Tonnages: 8,047 gross, 5,038 net, 12,015 deadweight. Dimensions: 475.5 x 60.8 x 33.0 feet. Draft: 28.0 feet.
T.3 cyl. by the shipbuilders, 4,400 ihp, 12 knots.

*22.1.1915:* Launched by the Flensburger S.G., Flensburg, (Yard No. 343), and delivered 5.2.1916 to the Norddeutscher Lloyd, Bremen, as AUGSBURG. Laid up at Kiel. *1.4.1919:* Surrendered to the Allied Control Commission and allocated to Britain. Registered at London to The Shipping Controller, (Watts, Watts & Company Ltd, managers). *9.12.1920:* Sold for £180,000 to the Hain Steamship Company Ltd, St Ives, (E. Hain & Son, managers), and renamed TREMERE on 13.1.1921. *28.1.1925:* Sold to Federal, (NZS, managers), and registered at London 30.1.1925 as PURIRI. *8.5.1930:* Suffered a fire in the forepeak at Falmouth. *7.1932—1.1934:* Laid up at Mylor. *10.1933:* Sold for £8,500 to the Mitsuwa Shoji K.K., Kobe, (registered at Osaka), and arrived in Japan in 5.1934 for demolition.

ARGYLLSHIRE at Adelaide

*(IJF)*

## F.39 ARGYLLSHIRE (1929—1932)

Official Number: 129581
Tonnages: 10,329 gross, 6,610 net. 1929: 11,916 gross, 7,487 net. 1933: 9,564 gross, 5,580 net. Dimensions: 526.2 x 61.4 x 33.3 feet.
Twin screw, two Q.4 cyl. by the shipbuilders, 6,500 ihp, 14 knots.
Passengers: 130 1st class and 270 emigrants. 1912: 66 1st class. 1920: 133 lst and 76 3rd class.
Refrigerated space: 442,850 cu.ft.

*27.2.1911:* Launched by John Brown & Co. Ltd, Clydebank, (Yard No. 399), and first registered 1.7.1911 to the Scottish Shire Line Ltd, Glasgow, (Turnbull, Martin & Co., managers). *18.8.1914—24.1.1918:* Requisitioned as the Australian Expeditionary Force Transport A 3, and sailed from Albany 1.11.1914 in the first convoy. *27.5.1915:* Reported being missed by 2 torpedoes off Le Havre. *5.2.1917:* Struck a mine laid by UC 46 3 miles south-west of Start Point, bound London to Barry. Put into Plymouth, then repaired at Falmouth. *25.1.1918—21.2.1919:* Taken up under the Liner Requisition Scheme. *1926—1927:* Laid up off Southend. *7.10.1929:* Sold to Federal, remaining registered at Glasgow. *10.1931:* Laid up in the Gareloch. *11.2.1932:* Grounded on Roseneath Point, Gareloch, bound for Glasgow for refitting. *15.11.1932:* Sold to The Clan Line Steamers Ltd, Glasgow, (Cayzer, Irvine & Company Ltd, managers), and renamed CLAN URQUHART on 5.12.1932. Refitted at Clydebank by John Brown & Co. Ltd and passenger accommodation removed. *7.1936:* Sold for £22,000 to T.W. Ward Ltd for demolition at Briton Ferry where she arrived 30.10.1936. *14.3.1937:* Caught fire while being broken up and scuttled in shallow water.

## F.40 RANGITATA (1929—1936) See No. 70

DURHAM at Wellington                                                                              (VHY/NZA)

## F.41 DURHAM (1934—1965)

Official Number: 163522
Tonnages: 10,893 gross, 6,261 net, 13,370 deadweight. Dimensions: 493.5 (513.0 overall) x 68.6 x 34.5 feet. Draft: 32.5 feet.
Twin screw, two x 8 cyl. 2 S.C.S.A. Sulzer diesels by the shipbuilders, 11,000 bhp, 16 knots.
Refrigerated space: 496,900 cu.ft.

*27.6.1934:* Launched by Workman, Clark (1928) Ltd, Belfast, (Yard No. 533), and delivered to Federal 21.9.1934 at a cost of £296,500. *1934—1939, 1946—1950* and *1955—1962:* Served as a cadet ship for 40 cadets. *9.8.1937:* Grounded at Townsville. *4.1.1939:* Struck the steamer WAIMARINO (3,341g, 1930) at Prince's Wharf, Auckland, as she left for Port Chalmers. *16.3.1940—26.6.1941* and *31.7.1943—5.6.1946:* Requisitioned for the Liner Division, serving as a military store ship from *27.6.1941—30.7.1943. 22.8.1941:* Mined west of Pantellaria, bound Malta to Gibraltar in ballast, and arrived at Gibraltar on the 24th. *20.9.1941:* Damaged by a limpet mine at Gibraltar and beached at La Linea. Refloated 16.12.1941 and left in tow of the motor tug BUSTLER (1,042g, 1942). She arrived at Falmouth on 3.9.1942 and remained under repair until 7.1943. *8.9.1943:* Suffered a fire in No. 5 shelter deck, bound New York to Australia. The fire was out the next day but she put into Papeete on the 12th and sailed again on the 24th. *8.1.1953:* Touched the bank in Culebra Cut, Panama Canal, bound London to New Zealand. Several plates were buckled and rivets sprung. *9.12.1957:* Arrived at Galveston with engine trouble, bound London and Liverpool to Wellington. The cargo was trans-shipped to the HAPARANGI (No. 86) and, after repairs at New York, she finally sailed again on 10.6.1958. *7—10.1960:* Laid up at Falmouth. *5.11.1965:* Sold for £140,000 to the Astroguarda Cia Nav. S.A., Panama, (Mavroleon Bros (Ship Management) Ltd, managers), and registered at Piraeus as RION. *26.3.1966:* Arrived at Kaohsiung for demolition which began on 5.4.1966.

The radio room in DURHAM                                                (WAL)

DORSET at Adelaide                                                                                      (IJF)

## F.42 DORSET (1934—1942)

Official Number: 163539
Tonnages: 10,624 gross, 6,298 net, 13,650 deadweight. Dimensions: 493.5 (513.0 overall) x 68.6 x 34.5 feet. Draft: 32.5 feet.
Twin screw, two x 8 cyl. 2 S.C.S.A. Sulzer diesels by Sulzer Bros, Winterthur, 11,000 bhp. 16 knots.
Refrigerated space: 496,700 cu.ft.

*28.7.1934:* Launched by Workman, Clark (1928) Ltd, Belfast, (Yard No. 534), and delivered to Federal 9.11.1934 at a cost of £296,500. *16.5.1940:* Requisitioned for the Liner Division, but served as a military store ship 5.9.1940—28.11.1940, as a mechanical transport ship 20.12.1941—22.4.1942 and again as a military store ship from 3.7.1942. *12* and *13.3.1941:* Suffered minor bomb damage at Liverpool. *18.3.1942:* Grounded at Port Said. *13.8.1942:* Bombed and sunk by aircraft south-east of Cape Bon (36°12'N-12°49'E), bound Gourock to Malta with military and general stores in convoy WS 21S (Operation Pedestal). No lives lost.

ESSEX at Sydney

*(NZA)*

## F.43 ESSEX (1936—1947)   NORFOLK (1955—1962)

Official Number: 165362
Tonnages: 11,063 gross, 6,521 net, 13,923 deadweight. Dimensions: 532.2 (551.3 overall) x 70.4 x 34.6 feet. Draft: 32.6 feet.
Twin screw, two x 5 cyl. 2 S.C.S.A. Doxford diesels by the shipbuilders, 13,250 bhp, 17 knots.
Refrigerated space: 516,700 cu.ft.

*19.9.1936:* Launched by John Brown & Co. Ltd, Clydebank, (Yard No. 545), ran trials 17.12.1936 and delivered 18.12.1936 to The Peninsular and Oriental Steam Navigation Co., (Federal S.N. Co., managers) at a cost of £356,500. She had been ordered originally by NZS as PAPANUI and the order was transferred to P&O on 25.5.1936. *11.8.1938:* Sank the tug TE AWHINA (220g, 1908) with her starboard screw while berthing at Auckland. *7.6.1940—30.5.1946:* Requisitioned for the Liner Division but spent the period 27.11.1940—27.11.1944 as a mechanical transport ship. *16.1.1941:* Struck by a bomb in the engineroom with the loss of 17 crew while berthed at Malta. The badly damaged vessel was towed to Frenchman's Creek. *7.3.1941:* Again damaged by bombing, the engineroom being flooded. She was then towed to Rinella Creek. *12.4.1942:* Received further damage and set on fire in an air attack and beached. *21.8.1943:* Left Malta in tow of the naval tug JAUNTY (1,045 tons, 1941) for Algiers where arrived on the 25th and left again on the 29th. *24.11.1943:* Left Gibraltar in tow of the motor tug ZWARTE ZEE (793g, 1933) and arrived on 11.12.1943 at Falmouth where she was under repair until 11.1944. *29.1.1947:* Transferred to P&O service and renamed PARINGA on 7.2.1947. *17.5.1955:* Returned to Federal management and renamed NORFOLK on 24.5.1955. *1.9.1962:* Sold for £127,000 to Toyo Menka K.K. who began demolition at Yokosuka the same day.

NORFOLK at Bluff

*(Maitland Downes)*

SUSSEX at Adelaide                                                      (IJF)

## F.44 SUSSEX (1937—1946)   CAMBRIDGE (1954—1962)

Official Number: 165389

Tonnages: 11,063 gross, 6,516 net, 14,067 deadweight. Dimensions: 532.2 (551.3 overall) x 70.4 x 34.6 feet. Draft: 32.6 feet. Twin screw, two x 5 cyl. 2 S.C.S.A. Doxford diesels by the shipbuilders, 13,250 bhp, 17 knots, (19.5 knots on trials). Refrigerated space: 516,700 cu.ft.

*17.11.1936:* Launched by John Brown & Co. Ltd, Clydebank, (Yard No. 546), ran trials 10.2.1937 and delivered 11.2.1937 to The Peninsular and Oriental Steam Navigation Co., (Federal S.N. Co., managers), at a cost of £356,500. She had been ordered originally by NZS as PAREORA, the order being transferred to P&O on 25.5.1936. *24.11.1939:* Struck a magnetic mine in the Thames off Southend when outward bound in ballast and returned to London for repairs. *16.5.1940—21.5.1946:* Requisitioned for the Liner Division, but spent the periods 30.10.1941—31.1.1942 and 15.4.1942—24.7.1942 as a mechanical transport ship. *30.9.1940:* Damaged and set on fire by aircraft bombing 350 miles west of Ireland (54°20'N-15°32'W), bound Townsville to Avonmouth with refrigerated and general cargo. She was bombed again in 53°07'N-17°37'W and then collided with a naval trawler on the way to the Clyde for repairs. *14.11.1946:* Transferred to P&O

service and renamed PALANA on 26.11.1946. *15.10.1948:* Arrived at Auckland after towing the motorship FERNMOOR (4,972g, 1936) 2,300 miles from mid-Pacific, 700 miles south-west of Pitcairn (29°44'S-144°42'W) in 23 days. *7.12.1948:* Suffered an engineroom fire in Victoria Dock, London. *3.1.1951:* Grounded on Pine Peak Island, 60 miles south-east of Mackay (21°30'S-150°17'E), bound Brisbane to Townsville in ballast. She was refloated the following day and abandoned. Reboarded on the 5th, she was then anchored off Mackay on the 19th and was beached there for temporary repairs on the 22nd. She arrived at Sydney on the 24th and was under repair at Cockatoo Dock until 7.1952. *13.8.1954:* Returned to Federal management and renamed CAMBRIDGE on 17.9.1954. *6.1960—1.1961:* Laid up at Falmouth. *5.11.1962:* Arrived at Niigita and sold for £142,000 on the 22nd to the Mitsubishi Shoji Kaisha who began demolition at Sakai on the 27th.

CAMBRIDGE at Auckland                                                   (RCP)

SUFFOLK at Wellington

*(WAL)*

# F.45 SUFFOLK (1939—1968)
Official Number: 167330
Tonnages: 11,145 gross, 6,566 net, 14,208 deadweight. Dimensions: 532.2 (551.3 overall) x 70.4 x 34.3 feet. Draft: 32.7 feet. Twin screw, two x 5 cyl. 2 S.C.S.A. Doxford diesels by the shipbuiders, 13,250 bhp, 17 knots.
Refrigerated space: 533,300 cu.ft.

*3.5.1939:* Launched by John Brown & Co. Ltd, Clydebank, (Yard No. 559), and delivered to Federal 11.9.1939 at a cost of £480,000. *29.9.1939:* Left the Clyde without running trials. *16.2.1940—2.3.1946:* Requisitioned for the Liner Division, but spent the periods 8—9.1940 as a military store ship, 17.7.1941—24.8.1941 as a mechanical transport ship and 11.1942—21.12.1942 as a military store ship. *8.1941:* In collision at Scapa Flow. Repaired at Glasgow, *24.2.1944:* Grounded off Hamilton Wharf, Brisbane River. *22.1.1947:* Collided with the dock wall while berthing at Newport. *5.11.1949—28.12.1949:* Served as a meat storage ship at Liverpool for the Ministry of Food. *12.1950:* Suffered an engine breakdown, bound U.K. to Australia and returned to Cape Town for repairs. She continued the voyage to New Zealand and back to the U.K. on the other engine, managing 11 knots. *9.11.1957:* Re-opened the port of Opua, closed since 1940. *30.4.1958:* Grounded on a sandbank in Otago harbour, outward bound from Port Chalmers to Lyttelton. Refloated the same day undamaged. *12.8.1963:* Suffered a fire in No. 6 hold at Auckland. The hold was flooded to extinguish the fire. *4.1967:* Suffered a major engine breakdown between Panama and New Zealand. Put into Papeete for repairs and reached Auckland 5.5.1967 three and a half weeks late. *3.10.1968:* Arrived at Kaohsiung and handed over on the 10th to the China Trade & Development Corp. for demolition. *1.1969:* Work began by Dah Nang Yung Steel Manufacturing Co. Ltd.

SUFFOLK at the re-opening of Opua, Bay of Islands, 1957

*(New Zealand Herald)*

145

S.S. "NORFOLK"

XMAS DAY 1939.

DINNER.

CREME OF TOMATO

FRIED FILLET OF PLAICE, MEUNIERE.

LAMB CUTLETS GREEN PEAS.

ASPARAGUS VINAIGETTE.

RST. TURKEY WITH SAUSAGE

BRAISED YORK HAM, MADERE.

XMAS PUDDING WITH HARD SCE,

MINCE PIES.

MACEDOINE OF FRUIT.

DESSERT. COFFEE.

Christmas Menu on board NORFOLK (F.32) 1939. The cargo ships fed well, too          *(J. S. Sinclair)*

# Chapter 3: The Second World War and Rebuilding

Federal losses in the Second World War tended to be less spectacular but more widespread than those of NZS. Two ships were lost by mining and 8 by torpedo, the SOMERSET by an aircraft rather than a submarine. Ironically the losses included all the five remaining ex-Hamburg Amerika ships from the First World War. The most notable loss was that of the DORSET which was bombed and sunk on her way to Malta in Operation Pedestal in August 1942. The ships that survived had equally strenuous careers, the SUSSEX being an early victim of a magnetic mine in the Thames in November 1939, the DURHAM being attacked in September 1941 by limpet mines laid from human torpedoes while lying damaged at Gibraltar from an earlier mining, and the ESSEX being crippled by a bomb in the engine room at Malta in January 1941. Both the latter were out of commission for 2 and 3 years respectively at a time when they could ill be spared.

Two smaller and only partly refrigerated ships, the GLOUCESTER and NOTTINGHAM, were added to the fleet in 1941, but the latter was lost with all hands in the North Atlantic on her maiden voyage. In the immediate post-war programme, Federal took delivery of 3 steamers, the DEVON and SOMERSET being basically repeats of the war-built NZS P class, while the DORSET, which was not delivered until 1949, was able to incorporate a number of refinements both in appearance and fittings. The NOTTINGHAM was largely a repeat of her lost namesake, while to fill the gaps pending the arrival of the new tonnage 2 Liberty ships were taken over in 1947 and introduced the new names of LEICESTER and STAFFORD. They fitted uneasily with the rest of the fleet and were disposed of after only 3 years.

The major post-war additions were the Federal members of the H class, originally 5 ships but reduced to 4 on the transfer of the NORFOLK to NZS as the HAURAKI in 1953. They were to remain the core of the Federal refrigerated fleet for the next 25 years. Federal had always been the major Group presence in Australia, a trade which tended to be more mixed than the New Zealand one, with less emphasis on wholly refrigerated tonnage. To cater for this, a series of 3 ships, each progressively larger than the previous one and with minimal refrigerated capacity, was commissioned in 1952 and 1953. The major change with the CORNWALL, SURREY and MIDDLESEX was in the machinery where 2 Sulzer diesels drove a single screw through hydraulic couplings in the first ship and electro-magnetic couplings in the others. This type of machinery was also chosen for the much larger and fully refrigerated ESSEX and NORTHUMBERLAND in 1954/55, but a single engine and screw was reverted to for the SOMERSET in 1962.

HERTFORD (F.29) in 1940 showing mine damage under repair    *(A.J. Smythe)*

A full house at Port Chalmers, showing ORARI (73), CUMBERLAND (F.54) and SUFFOLK (F.45), July 1952          *(Bain-Wright Collection/NZA)*

147

## Ships F.46 to F.63: GLOUCESTER — NORTHUMBERLAND and F.67: SOMERSET

GLOUCESTER at Adelaide *(JYF)*

### F.46 GLOUCESTER (1941—1966)

Official Number: 168192
Tonnages: 8,532 gross, 5,022 net, 9,333 deadweight. Dimensions: 457.5 (473.0 overall) x 60.3 x 35.6 feet.
Draft: 27.4 feet.
6 cyl. 2 S.C.S.A. Doxford diesel by Barclay, Curle & Co. Ltd, Glasgow, 6,000 bhp, 14 knots.
Refrigerated space: 268,100 cu.ft.

*3.3.1941:* Launched by A. Stephen & Sons Ltd, Glasgow, (Yard No. 575), and delivered to Federal 3.7.1941 at a cost of £278,250. *7.7.1941—30.5.1946:* Requisitioned for the Liner Division, but spent the period 11.11.1942—3.1.1943 as a military store ship. *30.9.1953:* Damaged by the steamer RIVER FITZROY (5,001g, 1944) which was blown against her while she was berthed at Newcastle, N.S.W. Minor damage to plating.

*15.3.1959:* Suffered a main engine failure off Ulladulla, 150 miles south of Sydney, bound Sydney to Hobart. Returned to Sydney under her own power for repairs. *22.6.1966:* Sold for £86,500 to the Embajada Cia Nav. S.A., Panama, (Rethymnis & Kulukundis & K. Stergiopoulos, managers), and registered at Piraeus as CONSULATE. *2.10.1966:* Arrived at Kaohsiung in tow from Hong Kong and demolition began on the 20th.

NOTTINGHAM in the Clyde *(NZA)*

### F.47 NOTTINGHAM (1941—1941)

Official Number: 168227
Tonnages: 8,592 gross, 5,028 net. Dimensions: 457.5 (473.0 overall) x 60.3 x 35.6 feet. Draft: 27.4 feet.
6 cyl. 2 S.C.S.A. Doxford diesel by Barclay, Curle & Co. Ltd, Glasgow, 6,000 bhp, 14 knots.
Refrigerated space: 270,000 cu.ft.

*12.8.1941:* Launched by A. Stephen & Sons Ltd, Glasgow, (Yard No. 576), and delivered to Federal 23.10.1941 at a cost of £275,250. *24.10.1941:* Requisitioned for the Liner Division. *7.11.1941:* Torpedoed and sunk by U 74 on her maiden voyage

with the loss of all 62 on board, 550 miles south-east of Cape Farewell (53°24′N-31°51′W). She was bound from Glasgow to New York with general cargo on account of the Anchor Line Ltd.

DEVON at Auckland

*(NJK)*

## F.48 DEVON (1946—1967) (1970—1971)

Official Number: 180799
Tonnages: 9,940 gross, 5,896 net, 10,320 deadweight. Dimensions: 477.0 (495.3 overall) x 64.8 x 39.0 feet. Draft: 27.3 feet.
High, intermediate and low pressure turbines, double reduction geared to a single shaft, by the shipbuilders, 8,000 shp, 15 knots.
Refrigerated space: 430,200 cu.ft.

*3.10.1945:* Launched by A. Stephen & Sons Ltd, Glasgow, (Yard No. 602), and delivered to Federal 18.2.1946. *18.2.1946—22.5.1946:* Requisitioned for the Liner Division. *8.1.1954:* Collided with the steamer ROTA (1,327g, 1923) at the mouth of the Humber, bound Hull to London. Slight damage only. *10.5.1954:* Struck a jetty when berthing at Bowen, bound Cairns to London. No damage to the ship, but considerable damage to the jetty. *3.6.—12.8.1960:* Laid up at Glasgow. *12.8.1966:* Struck a sandbank off Savannah, when outward bound for Auckland, damaging her rudder. *28.9.1967:* Sold for £145,000 to Overseas Containers Ltd, London, (Federal S.N. Co., managers). *28.9.1970:* Repurchased by Federal for £100,000. *16.7.1971:* Sold for $285,200 to the Leung Yau Shipbreaking Company and broken up at Hong Kong.

SOMERSET at Adelaide

*(JYF)*

## F.49 SOMERSET (1946—1954)

Official Number: 180927
Tonnages: 9,943 gross, 5,870 net, 10,530 deadweight. Dimensions: 477.0 (495.3 overall) x 64.8 x 39.0 feet. Draft: 27.4 feet.
High, intermediate and low pressure turbines, double reduction geared to a single shaft, by the shipbuilders, 8,000 shp, 15 knots.
Refrigerated space: 393,100 cu.ft.

*21.3.1946:* Launched by A. Stephen & Sons Ltd, Glasgow, (Yard No. 608), and delivered to Federal 11.9.1946 at a cost of £452,000. *4.12.1951:* Collided with the cruiser HMAS AUSTRALIA (9,870 tons, 1928) at Sydney, inward bound from Newport. *17.11.1954:* Transferred to the management of The Peninsular and Oriental Steam Navigation Company, having been renamed ADEN on 12.11.1954. *3.9.1963:* Her mainmast snapped at the base at Wynyard Wharf, Auckland, with the loss of the life of a waterside worker. *8.10.1967:* After a final MANZ Line round voyage, arrived at Kaohsiung and sold the following day for £105,575 to the Nan Tay Industries Company Ltd for demolition.

NORFOLK at Auckland

(DNB)

## F.50 NORFOLK (1947—1953) HAURAKI (1966—1973)

Official Number: 181558
Tonnages: 11,272 gross, 6,638 net, 14,350 deadweight. Dimensions: 541.3 (560.7 overall) x 70.2 x 34.7 feet. Draft: 32.6 feet.
Twin screw, two x 5 cyl. 2 S.C.S.A. Doxford diesels by the shipbuilders, 12,800 bhp, 16 knots.
Refrigerated space: 522,700 cu.ft.

*13.6.1946:* Launched by John Brown & Co. Ltd, Clydebank, (Yard No. 604), and delivered to Federal 15.2.1947 at a cost of £820,000. *17.7.1953:* Transferred to NZS for £529,100 and renamed HAURAKI on 20.7.1953. *17.5.1954:* Suffered an engineroom fire 150 miles west of Fremantle, bound Townsville to London. *4.2.1963:* Became the first vessel to work the new

mechanical meat loaders at Bluff. *28.12.1966:* Ownership transferred back to Federal, (NZS, managers). *1.10.1971:* Management transferred to P&O General Cargo Division. *19.4.1973:* Transferred to The Peninsular and Oriental S. N. Co. *22.12.1973:* Arrived at Kaohsiung where delivered on the 25th to the Chin Tai Steel Enterprise Co. Ltd for demolition.

LEICESTER at Auckland after rebuilding

(NZA)

## F.51 LEICESTER (1947—1950)

Official Number: 169824
Tonnages: 7,266 gross, 4,446 net, 10,712 deadweight. Dimensions: 423.9 (441.8 overall) x 57.0 x 34.8 feet. Draft: 27.8 feet.
T.3 cyl. by the Worthington Pump & Machinery Corp., Harrison, N.J., 2,500 ihp, 11 knots.

*22.1.1944:* Launched by the Bethlehem-Fairfield Shipyard Inc., Baltimore, (Yard No. 2314), and delivered 5.2.1944 to the Ministry of War Transport, London, (NZS, managers) as SAMESK. She had been ordered originally by the United States War Shipping Administration. *5.2.1944—25.4.1947:* Allocated to the Ship Management Division, but served with the Liner Division from 5.1944 to 8.1946 except for periods as a military transport ship from 7.1944—7.11.1944 and 15.6.1945—28.4.1946 and a reversion to the Ship·Management Division from 1.—4.1945. *25.4.1947:* Sold to Federal for £135,300 and renamed LEICESTER 30.7.1947. *16.9.1948:* Abandoned when her ballast shifted 400 miles south-west of Newfoundland, bound Tilbury to New York. 5 lives were lost. The remaining crew were picked up by the steamers TROPERO (7,667g, 1945) and CECIL N. BEAN, (7,176g 1944). She was taken in tow by the motor tug FOUNDATION JOSEPHINE (1,100g, 1942) on 27.9.1948 but both were driven ashore at the entrance to St George's harbour,

Bermuda on 7.10.1948. She was refloated on the 19th and brought into Hamilton. *24.10.1948:* Left in tow of the motor tug KEVIN MORAN (498g, 1943) for New York but diverted to Baltimore for repairs which were completed 14.12.1948. *15.9.1950:* Sold for £110,000 to the Nassau Maritime Company Ltd, London, (Ante Topic, manager), and renamed INAGUA. *1952:* Ricardo Arco became manager. *1958:* Register transferred to Nassau, Bahamas. *1958:* Transferred to the Cia Nav. Termar S.A., Monrovia, (Ante Topic, manager), and renamed SERAFIN TOPIC. *1962:* Renamed JELA TOPIC. *1965:* Sold to the Viking Shipping Company Ltd, Monrovia, (Pacific Steamship Agency Inc., managers), and renamed VIKING LIBERTY. *21.1.1966:* Grounded at Trinidad, bound Recife to New York. Arrived at New Orleans 1.2.1966 where repairs were found to be uneconomic. *2.1966:* Sold to Poul Christensen, Copenhagen, and resold to Spanish shipbreakers, arriving in tow at Santander 27.8.1966. Demolition began on the 30th.

LEICESTER on her beam ends after being towed into Bermuda, 1948

*(IJF)*

STAFFORD at Auckland

*(MP/NZA)*

# F.52 STAFFORD (1947—1950)

Official Number: 180548

Tonnages: 7,296 gross, 4,444 net, 10,712 deadweight. Dimensions: 422.8 (441.5 overall) x 57.0 x 34.8 feet. Draft: 27.8 feet. T.3 cyl. by the General Machinery Corp., Hamilton, Ohio, 2,500 ihp, 11 knots.

*30.4.1944:* Launched by the J.A. Jones Construction Company Inc., Brunswick, Ga., (Yard No. 142), and delivered 13.5.1944 to the Ministry of War Transport, London, (NZS, managers), as SAMINGOY. She had been ordered originally by the United States War Shipping Administration. *13.5.1944—20.6.1947:* Allocated to the Ship Management Division, but spent the periods 20.7.1944—17.3.1945 and 16.9.1945—2.12.1945 as a military transport ship and 4—8.1945 and 3.12.1945—6.1947 with the Liner Division. *7.10.1945:* Detonated a mine off Saigon and repairs at Bombay took 3 months. *20.6.1947:* Sold to Federal for £135,280 and renamed STAFFORD. *15.5.1950:* Sold for £110,000 to the Nassau Maritime Company Ltd, London, (Ante Topic, manager), and renamed BIMINI. *1952:* Ricardo Arco became manager. *1957:* Registry transferred to Nassau, Bahamas. *1959:* Transferred to the Bahamas Navigation Company Ltd, Nassau, Bahamas. *1961:* Sold to the Cia Auxiliar Maritima Ltda, Panama, and renamed HERNAN CORTES. *15.10.1966:* Grounded on Alacran Reef, Yucatan, bound Tampa to Montevideo with fertiliser. Abandoned on the 19th and later sacked by robbers. She was driven further onto the reef in a storm on 4.11.1966. *22.1.1967:* Refloated and towed to Coatzacoalcos where she arrived 11.2.1967. *27.5.1967:* Left Coatzacoalcos in tow for Veracruz where she was broken up 8.1967 by the Astilleros de Veracruz.

HUNTINGDON at Port Chalmers. Note the christmas tree on the foremast

*(IJF)*

## F.53 HUNTINGDON (1948—1973)

Official Number: 181898

Tonnages: 11,281 gross, 6,658 net, 14,800 deadweight. Dimensions: 541.3 (560.7 overall) x 70.2 x 34.7 feet. Draft: 32.7 feet. Twin screw, two x 5 cyl. 2 S.C.S.A. Doxford diesels by the shipbuilders, 12,800 bhp, 16 knots. Refrigerated space: 522,650 cu.ft.

*16.9.1947:* Launched by A. Stephen & Sons Ltd, Glasgow, (Yard No. 612), and delivered to Federal 2.5.1948 at a cost of £820,000. *1.10.1971:* Management transferred to P&O General Cargo Division. *19.4.1973:* Transferred to The Peninsular and Oriental S.N. Co. *8.8.1975:* Arrived at Hualien for demolition by Chou's Iron & Steel Co. Ltd.

CUMBERLAND at Auckland

*(RCP)*

## F.54 CUMBERLAND (1948—1973)

Official Number: 182901

Tonnages: 11,281 gross, 6,658 net, 14,350 deadweight. Dimensions: 541.3 (560.7 overall) x 70.2 x 34.7 feet. Draft: 32.7 feet. Twin screw, two x 5 cyl. 2 S.C.S.A. Doxford diesels by the shipbuilders, 12,800 bhp, 16 knots. Refrigerated space: 522,650 cu.ft.

*11.8.1948:* Launched by A. Stephen & Sons Ltd, Glasgow, (Yard No. 614), and delivered to Federal 12.12.1948 at a cost of £869,000. *12.1962:* Suffered a fire in the electrical switchboard at Wellington. *3.11.1967:* Suffered a cargo fire at Auckland. Extinguished without damage. *25.7.1971:* Suffered a fire in the wool cargo in No. 4 hold 30 miles from Auckland, inward bound from Port Chalmers. *1.10.1971:* Management transferred to P&O General Cargo Division. *19.4.1973:* Transferred to The Peninsular and Oriental S. N. Co. *4.2.1976:* Collided with the motor tug MAHIA (34g, 1970) when berthing at Napier. *21.12.1976:* Arrived at Kaohsiung and delivered on the 25th to the Nan Feng Steel Enterprise Co. Ltd for demolition. Work began on 10.3.1977.

HERTFORD at Auckland                                                                                    *(RCP)*

## F.55 HERTFORD (1948—1973)

Official Number: 182914
Tonnages: 11,276 gross, 6,640 net, 14,932 deadweight. Dimensions: 541.5 (560.8 overall) x 70.3 x 34.8 feet. Draft: 32.5 feet.
Twin screw, two x 5 cyl. 2 S.C.S.A. Doxford diesels by Vickers-Armstrongs Ltd, Barrow, 12,800 bhp, 16 knots.
Refrigerated space: 522,100 cu.ft.

*24.3.1948:* Launched by Vickers-Armstrongs Ltd, Newcastle, (Yard No. 106) and delivered to Federal 14.12.1948 at a cost of £780,000. *1.10.1971:* Management transferred to P&O General Cargo Division. *19.4.1973:* Transferred to The Peninsular and Oriental S. N. Co. *10.3.1976:* Sold to the Marevico Shipping Company, Limassol, (Roussos Bros, managers) and renamed THIA DESPINA. *9.7.1977:* Grounded off Port Said, bound Karachi to Livorno. Arrived at Piraeus on the 12th where declared a constructive total loss and laid up. *7.1978:* Transferred to the Netidi Shipping Company, Limassol, and renamed GEORGHIOS FRANGAKIS. *1.1985:* Sold to Cer Metal Sanayi ve Ticaret A.S. and beached at Aliaga 24.1.1985 for demolition by Nigdeliler Hurdacilik ve Ticaret A.S., having arrived from Piraeus in tow the previous day. *15.2.1985:* Work began.

HERTFORD Port engine control        *(Bain-Wright Collection)*

153

SUSSEX at Adelaide (JYF)

## F.56 SUSSEX (1949—1973)

Official Number: 183003
Tonnages: 11,272 gross, 6,642 net, 14,640 deadweight. Dimensions: 541.3 (560.7 overall) x 70.2 x 34.7 feet. Draft: 32.5 feet.
Twin screw, two x 5 cyl. 2 S.C.S.A. Doxford diesels by the shipbuilders, 12,800 bhp, 16 knots.
Refrigerated space: 522,700 cu.ft.

*7.10.1948:* Launched by John Brown & Co. Ltd, Clydebank, (Yard No. 643), and delivered to Federal 22.4.1949 at a cost of £975,000. *2.2.1954:* Collided in the Warp, River Thames, with the steamer FULHAM VI (1,552g, 1941), inward bound to London from Port Chalmers. Minor damage only. *3.9.1955:* Suffered a breakdown in the starboard engine, bound Townsville to Liverpool and completed the voyage on the port engine. *2.4.1964:* Suffered

an engine breakdown in Cook Strait, bound Picton to Britain and returned to Wellington the same day on the other engine for repairs. *1.10.1971:* Management transferred to P&O General Cargo Division. *19.4.1973:* Transferred to The Peninsular and Oriental S. N. Co. *11.12.1976:* Arrived at Hong Kong and delivered on the 15th to the Loy Kee Shipbreakers & Transportation Co., Hong Kong, for demolition there.

DORSET at Lyttelton (NJK)

## F.57 DORSET (1949—1972)

Official Number: 183140
Tonnages: 10,108 gross, 6,010 net, 11,090 deadweight. Dimensions: 477.0 (495.3 overall) x 64.8 x 39.0 feet. Draft: 28.8 feet.
High, intermediate and low pressure turbines, double reduction geared to a single shaft, by the shipbuilders, 8,000 shp, 16 knots.
Refrigerated space; 402,900 cu.ft.

*25.5.1949:* Launched by A. Stephen & Sons Ltd, Glasgow, (Yard No. 621), and delivered to Federal 26.11.1949 at a cost of £621,000. *1.1953:* Collided with the tanker CALTEX DUBLIN (10,643g, 1945) in the Brisbane River. *9.7.1955:* Struck a knuckle of the Duke Street bridge when moving from the East to the West Float, Birkenhead, outward bound for Port Kembla.

Delayed until the 31st for repairs. *1.10.1971:* Management transferred to P&O General Cargo Division. *9.6.1972:* Arrived at Hamburg and delivered on the 16th to Eckhardt & Co. Resold and arrived Istanbul in tow 5.8.1972. She was broken up at the Golden Horn by Mahmut Kizilkaya who began work on 4.9.1972.

NOTTINGHAM at Sydney                                                                                            *(JYF)*

## F.58 NOTTINGHAM (1950—1971)

Official Number: 183255
Tonnages: 6,689 gross, 3,701 net, 8,600 deadweight. Dimensions: 463.5 (480.3 overall) x 61.7 x 25.9 feet. Draft: 26.3 feet.
6 cyl. 2 S.C.S.A. Doxford diesel by the shipbuilders, 8,500 bhp, 16 knots.
Refrigerated space: 288,760 cu.ft.

*22.12.1949:* Launched by John Brown & Co. Ltd, Clydebank, (Yard No. 653), and delivered to Federal 12.6.1950 at a cost of £735,600. *21.10.1953:* Collided with an 80 ton floating crane while berthing at Fremantle, bound Liverpool to Adelaide. Some damage to the stem. *27.1.1955:* Put into Gibraltar after experiencing engine trouble on the 26th, bound Port Pirie to Liverpool. *11.8.1971:* Delivered to the Nantai Iron & Steel Co. for demolition at Kaohsiung. *6.11.1971:* Work began.

CORNWALL at Auckland                                                                                            *(RCP)*

## F.59 CORNWALL (1952—1967)

Official Number: 184554
Tonnages: 7,583 gross, 4,198 net, 9,417 deadweight. Dimensions: 472.5 (489.0 overall) x 62.6 x 26.0 feet. Draft: 26.8 feet.
Two 8 cyl. 2 S.C.S.A. Sulzer diesels by the shipbuilders, driving a single shaft through single reduction gearing and hydraulic couplings, 8,500 bhp, 15.5 knots, 18 knots on trials.
Refrigerated space: 65,750 cu.ft.

*21.6.1951:* Launched by A. Stephen & Sons Ltd, Glasgow, (Yard No. 627), and delivered to Federal 22.2.1952 at a cost of £758,500. *2.12.1954:* Suffered a major engine failure in the starboard engine off Smokey Cape, N.S.W., bound Melbourne to Brisbane. Temporary repairs were effected at Sydney and she returned to Britain on the port engine for permanent repairs by the shipbuilders. *4.1957:* Collided with 2 cranes on Powell wharf at Port Alfred. *25.8.1967:* Sold for £250,000 to the British India Steam Navigation Company Ltd, London, and renamed JUNA. *10.1967:* Suffered an engine failure 1 day out of Cochin, inward bound from Mombasa and reached port on the remaining engine. *8.4.1971:* Sold to the Great China Steel Enterprise Company Ltd. Demolition by the Chuang Kuo Steel & Iron Works began at Kaohsiung on 5.5.1971.

SURREY at Auckland

(MP)

## F.60 SURREY (1952—1969)

Official Number: 184624

Tonnages: 8,227 gross, 4,571 net, 10,270 deadweight. Dimensions: 482.7 (499.3 overall) x 64.7 x 27.0 feet. Draft: 27.3 feet. Two 9 cyl. 2 S.C.S.A. Sulzer diesels by the shipbuilders, driving a single shaft through single reduction gearing and electro-magnetic couplings, 9,000 bhp, 16 knots.

Refrigerated space: 82,300 cu.ft.

*17.10.1951:* Launched by A. Stephen & Sons Ltd., Glasgow, (Yard No. 630), and delivered to Federal 6.6.1952 at a cost of £850,000. *4.6.1953:* Arrived at Melbourne with failure in 2 cylinders of the starboard engine and returned to Britain on the port engine for repairs. *3.9.1969:* Sold to the British India Steam Navigation Company Ltd, London, delivered at Tilbury and

renamed JUWARA. *5.2.1970:* Suffered an engine explosion at Sydney which required return on the other engine alone to Britain for repairs. *1.10.1971:* Management transferred to P&O General Cargo Division. *9.5.1972:* Sold to Tung Cheng Steel Corp., Kaohsiung, where she had arrived on 5.5.1972 and where demolition began on 29.9.1972.

MIDDLESEX at Auckland

(DNB)

## F.61 MIDDLESEX (1953—1968)

Official Number: 185861

Tonnages: 8,284 gross, 4,609 net, 10,134 deadweight. Dimensions: 482.7 (499.3 overall) x 64.7 x 27.0 feet. Draft: 27.3 feet. Two 10 cyl. 2 S.C.S.A. Sulzer diesels, one by the shipbuilders and one by Sulzer Bros Ltd, Winterthur, driving a single shaft through single reduction gearing and electro-magnetic couplings, 9,000 bhp, 16 knots, 18.2 knots on trials.

Refrigerated space: 84,400 cu.ft.

*23.9.1952:* Launched by A. Stephen & Sons Ltd, Glasgow, (Yard No. 631), and delivered to Federal 9.4.1953 at a cost of £850,000. *11.10.1953:* Damaged the tugs REAGARTH (137g, 1921), ERNEST BROWN (54g, 1944) and JOHN PAYNE (145g, 1909) while berthing at Avonmouth. *28.7.1962:* Suffered an engineroom fire off the Casquets bound London to Port Chalmers. She arrived at Falmouth under her own power on the 30th for repair. *1.11.1968:* Sold to the British India Steam Navigation Company Ltd, London, delivered at Calcutta that day

and renamed JELUNGA. *24.3.1969:* Dragged her anchor in a storm at Abu Dhabi and collided with the motorship PHILIPPINE JASMIN (6,091g, 1945). *1.10.1971:* Management transferred to P&O General Cargo Division. *19.4.1973:* Transferred to The Peninsular and Oriental S. N. Co. *26.11.1975:* Renamed STRATHLEVEN. *26.10.1977:* Anchored off Karachi and sold 8.11.1977 for $617,500 to Pakistan Electrical & Mechanical Constructors Ltd who began demolition at Gadani Beach 1.1978.

ESSEX at Port Chalmers                                                                                (IJF)

## F.62 ESSEX (1954—1973)

Official Number: 186048
Tonnages: 10,936 gross, 6,090 net, 12,550 deadweight. Dimensions: 490.0 (535.8 overall) x 70.2 x 44.5 feet. Draft: 30.7 feet.
Two 12 cyl. 2 S.C.S.A. Sulzer diesels by the shipbuilders, driving a single shaft through single reduction gearing and electro-magnetic couplings, 11,500 bhp, 16 knots.
Refrigerated space: 475,900 cu.ft.

21.12.1953: Launched by John Brown & Co. (Clydebank) Ltd, Clydebank, (Yard No. 674), and delivered to Federal 30.4.1954. She had a minor collision with the steamer ARCADIA (29,734g, 1954) on launching. *4.10.1956:* Scraped her bottom along No. 1 Black Beacon off Goat Island, Otago harbour, outward bound from Dunedin to Timaru. Repaired in dock at Wellington and then at Falmouth. *26.4.1971:* Struck Butler's wall when leaving Gisborne, damaging her bow. Returned for repairs. *1.10.1971:* Management transferred to P&O General Cargo Division. *19.4.1973:* Transferred to The Peninsular and Oriental S. N. Co. *18.12.1975:* Sold for $650,000 to Guan Guan Shipping (Pte) Ltd, Singapore, and renamed GOLDEN GULF. *12.11.1977:* Arrived at Gadani Beach where demolition began the same month.

NORTHUMBERLAND at Auckland                                                                           (NZA)

## F.63 NORTHUMBERLAND (1955—1972)

Official Number: 186233
Tonnages: 10,335 gross, 5,698 net, 10,606 deadweight. Dimensions: 470.0 (499.3 overall) x 64.8 x 42.0 feet. Draft: 28.8 feet.
Two 10 cyl. 2 S.C.S.A. Sulzer diesels by the shipbuilders, driving a single shaft through single reduction gearing and electro-magnetic couplings, 9,000 bhp, 16 knots.
Refrigerated space: 343,800 cu.ft.

*7.2.1955:* Launched by John Brown & Co. (Clydebank) Ltd, Clydebank, (Yard No. 676), and delivered to Federal 12.5.1955. She had been ordered originally by NZS as TURAKINA. *7.3.1970:* Went ashore in Grand Harbour, Malta but refloated undamaged. *1.10.1971:* Management transferred to P&O General Cargo Division. *12.9.1972:* Sold to Navieros Progresivos S.A., Panama, (Gourdomichalis Maritime S.A., managers), and registered at Piraeus as KAVO ASTRAPI. *8.1973:* Sold to Guan Guan Shipping (Pte) Ltd, Singapore, and renamed GOLDEN CITY. *22.3.1978:* Arrived at Hong Kong where demolition by the Leung Yau Shipbreaking Company Ltd began 19.5.1978.

157

## CAMBRIDGE (1954—1962) see SUSSEX (No. F.44)

## NORFOLK (1955—1962) see ESSEX (No. F.43)

SOMERSET (Bain-Wright Collection/NZA)

### F.67 SOMERSET (1962—1973)

Official Number: 304382
Tonnages: 10,027 gross, 5,554 net, 10,256 deadweight. Dimensions: 460.0 (488.3 overall) x 66.3 x 41.0 feet. Draft: 28.2 feet.
8 cyl. 2 S.C.S.A. Sulzer diesel by the shipbuilders, 10,400 bhp, 16.5 knots.
Refrigerated space: 449,100 cu.ft.

30.7.1962: Launched by John Brown & Co. (Clydebank) Ltd, Clydebank, (Yard No. 717), and delivered to Federal 17.11.1962. 1.10.1971: Management transferred to P&O General Cargo Division. 19.4.1973: Transferred to The Peninsular and Oriental S. N. Co. 23.11.1979: Sold to the Damarika Shipping Corp., Piraeus, (Enias Shipping Company S.A., managers), and renamed AEGEAN SKY. 10.1984: Arrived at Chittagong prior to the 11th for breaking up by National Foundry & Engineering.

SOMERSET at Sydney (JYF)

# Chapter 4: Diversification

When the P&O Group as a whole decided to enter the field of tanker owning, the new tonnage was allocated around the existing shipping companies. Federal was selected as the NZS Group recipient of these vessels, and took delivery of 3 of them. As a new type of ship in the fleet, the first two ships, the 18,500 tons deadweight product carrier LINCOLN and the 48,800 tons crude oil carrier DERBY were given county names not previously used by the Company, but the DERBY's sister was given the traditional Federal name of KENT. They were delivered with grey rather than black hulls, and all were placed on charter to B.P. Experience soon showed that piecemeal management of the new vessels by companies with no tanker background was not efficient, and by the mid-1960's all 3 had passed to the management of the new Group company created for the purpose, Trident Tankers Ltd, though each kept her Federal name until sold out of the Group. The two larger vessels were also transferred during 1966 to the newly formed subsidiary, Federal Tankers Ltd, to overcome a crewing dispute.

In 1966 Federal commissioned the WESTMORLAND, its sole allocation from the NZS T class and the last conventional refrigerated meat and dairy produce ship built for it. She introduced to Federal the pale green hull which was to become standard for new ships. At the beginning of the following year, most of the remaining NZS ships assumed Federal colours and ownership, though management remained technically with NZS until 1969.

The second major diversification for Federal came in January 1971 with the announcement that the Company was to build a series of ships for world wide trading in all commodities requiring refrigerated carriage. Orders for 6 ships based on standard Norwegian high speed fruit carrier designs were placed with Norwegian and German yards for delivery over 1971 to 1974. Presumably at the behest of marketing/public relations experts, the time honoured county names were abandoned for the new ships, all of which received names beginning with WILD followed by that of a sea bird. The significance of the first word to Federal remains elusive; at least the bird names had some connection with an equally historic and soon to disappear P&O Group subsidiary, the General Steam Navigation Company.

WILD CORMORANT (F.91)                                                                                    (I.G.B. Lovie/NZA)

By the time the first ship, the WILD AUK, came into service, Federal had ceased to be an operating entity and management had passed to the newly established General Cargo Division of the P&O Group, though Federal remained owner of the vessels. Change came again only a week after the WILD AUK had been taken over with the news that GCD was forming Lauritzen Peninsular Reefers A/S with the Danish Lauritzen Lines to manage both reefer fleets on a common pooling basis. Control of the new operation was centred in the Lauritzen head office in Copenhagen, and Federal as such remained little more than nominal owner for both the initial 6 ships and 4 subsequent additions in 1977. The ships at first flew the Federal flag and carried its funnel markings, until these were replaced by the P&O blue funnel and flag in 1976. The Lauritzen partnership was terminated in 1983 when both groups went their separate ways. Regrettably, whereas Lauritzen continued as a major force in refrigerated transport, the remaining Federal ships were sold and its name disappeared from the list of shipowners.

## Ships F.64 to F.66: LINCOLN, DERBY and KENT

## Ships F.68 to F.98: WESTMORLAND — WILD GREBE

LINCOLN                                                                                          (NJK)

### F.64 LINCOLN (1958—1965) Tanker

Official Number: 300819
Tonnages: 12,780 gross, 7,021 net, 18,500 deadweight. Dimensions: 530.0 (558.3 overall) x 72.3 x 39.0 feet. Draft: 30.2 feet.
High and low pressure turbines, double reduction geared to a single shaft, by the shipbuilders, 7,750 shp, 14.5 knots.

*11.9.1958:* Launched by John Brown & Co. (Clydebank) Ltd, Clydebank, (Yard No. 707), and delivered to Federal 29.12.1958. *27.1.1964:* Management transferred to Trident Tankers Ltd, London. *1965:* Sold the Gaulic Shipping Corp. S.A., Port-au-Prince, Haiti, (Lyras Bros, managers), and renamed AMPHION. *1966:* Re-registered at Piraeus. *4.1971:* Sold to Philtankers Inc., Monrovia, (Phillips Petroleum Company, managers), and renamed PHILLIPS NEW JERSEY. *1978:* Sold through Walter Ritscher, Hamburg, to the Brownsville Steel & Salvage Yard Inc., who began demolition at Brownsville, Texas, on 10.3.1978. She had arrived there on 4.3.1978.

DERBY at Port Said                                                                               (VHY)

### F.65 DERBY (1960—1968) Tanker

Official Number: 301141
Tonnages: 31,791 gross, 19,028 net, 48,884 deadweight. Dimensions: 726.8 (759.2 overall) x 97.6 x 52.0 feet. Draft: 39.5 feet.
High and low pressure turbines, double reduction geared to a single shaft, by the shipbuilders, 18,000 shp, 16.5 knots.

*14.1.1960:* Launched by John Brown & Co. (Clydebank) Ltd, (Yard No. 706), and delivered 11.5.1960 to the Charter Shipping Company Ltd, Hamilton, Bermuda, (Federal S.N. Co., managers). *7.8.1966:* Transferred to Federal Tankers Ltd, London, (Trident Tankers Ltd, managers) *24.6.1968:* Sold for $2,400,000 to the Vira Cia Nav. S.A., Monrovia, (Lykiardopulo & Company, managers), and renamed OKEANIS. *27.1.1975:* Laid up at Piraeus. *7.8.1976:* Delivered at Kaohsiung to the Sing Chen Yung Iron & Steel Company Ltd who began work on the 28th.

KENT

*(NJK)*

## F.66 KENT (1960—1968) Tanker

Official Number: 302543
Tonnages: 31,763 gross, 19,219 net, 48,873 deadweight. Dimensions: 726.8 (759.2 overall) x 97.7 x 52.0 feet. Draft: 39.8 feet.
High and low pressure turbines, double reduction geared to a single shaft, by the shipbuilders, 18,000 shp, 16.5 knots.

*20.9.1960:* Launched by John Brown & Co. (Clydebank) Ltd, Clydebank, (Yard No. 708), and delivered to Federal 15.12.1960 at cost of £4 million. *28.1.1966:* Transferred to Federal Tankers Ltd, London, (Trident Tankers Ltd, managers). *10.1968:* Sold to Commercial Tankers Inc., Monrovia, (Cosmopolitan Shipping Company Inc., managers), and renamed LESLIE CONWAY. *2.1971:* Sold to the Oswego Merchant Corp., Monrovia, (Marine Transport Lines Inc., managers), and renamed OSWEGO MERCHANT. *15.7.1974:* Collided with the motor tanker GREAT LOYALTY (15,410g, 1966) in Singapore Straits, bound Inchon to Bahrain in ballast. The GREAT LOYALTY caught fire and ran aground. *23.1.1976:* Arrived at Kaohsiung and delivered on the 30th to Chou's Iron & Steel Company Ltd who began work on 6.6.1976.

WESTMORLAND at Sydney

*(JYF)*

## F.68 WESTMORLAND (1966—1973)

Official Number: 308035
Tonnages: 11,011 gross, 6,133 net, 11,300 deadweight. Dimensions: 490.0 (527.6 overall) x 71.2 x 44.5 feet. Draft: 29.4 feet.
8 cyl. 2 S.C.S.A. Sulzer diesel by Sulzer Bros Ltd, Winterthur, 17,600 bhp, 20 knots.
Refrigerated space: 479,700 cu.ft.

*9.9.1965:* Launched by Lithgows Ltd, Port Glasgow, (Yard No. 1158), and delivered to Federal 7.2.1966. *1.10.1971:* Management transferred to P&O General Cargo Division. *19.4.1973:* Transferred to The Peninsular and Oriental S. N. Co. *18.9.1978:* Transferred to Strick Line Ltd., London. *10.6.1980:* Sold to Oceanic Shipping S.A.R.L., Beirut, (Rachid Fares Enterprises of Australia Pty Ltd, managers), and renamed FARES REEFER. *11.8.1981:* Sold to the Dunston Shipping Company Ltd, Hong Kong, (Blue Star Ship Management Ltd, managers) and renamed BEACON HILL. *5.7.1984—14.2.1985:* Laid up at Jebel Ali. *1985:* Sold to China National Metals & Minerals Import & Export Corporation. *6.3.1985:* Arrived at Huangpu for breaking up.

On 28.12.1966 the following 17 NZS vessels were transferred into the formal ownership of Federal, NZS remaining as managers:

**F.50 HAURAKI (1966—1973) See NORFOLK (F.50)**
**F.69 HORORATA (1966—1967) See No. 81**
**F.70 PAPAROA (1966—1970) See No. 83**
**F.71 PIPIRIKI (1966—1971) See No. 84**
**F.72 RAKAIA (1966—1971) See No. 85**

HAPARANGI at Wellington with Federal funnel and mainmast removed                                    *(I.G.B. Lovie/NZA)*

**F.73 HAPARANGI (1966—1971) See No. 86**
**F.74 HURUNUI (1966—1971) See No. 87**
**F.75 HINAKURA (1966—1971) See No. 88**
**F.76 RANGITOTO (1966—1969) See No. 89**
**F.77 RANGITANE (1966—1968) See No. 90**
**F.78 RUAHINE (1966—1968) See No. 91**
**F.79 OTAKI (1966—1971) See No. 92**
**F.80 WHARANUI (1966—1969) See No. 96**
**F.81 OTAIO (1966—1971) See No. 97**
**F.82 TURAKINA (1966—1971) See No. 98**
**F.83 ARAMAC (1966—1968) See REMUERA (No. 99)**
**F.84 PIAKO (1966—1971) See No. 100**

---

**F.85 MANAPOURI/WILD MARLIN (1968—1982) See No. 105**

WILD MARLIN at Auckland                                                                              *(DNB)*

In 6.1969 the following 3 NZS ships were transferred into the formal ownership of Federal, NZS remaining as managers:

**F.86 TAUPO (1969—1971) See No. 101**
**F.87 TEKOA (1969—1971) See No. 102**
**F.88 TONGARIRO (1969—1971) See No. 103**

WILD AUK at Auckland

*(DNB)*

## F.89 WILD AUK (1971—1980)
Official Number: 343017
Tonnages: 7,290/9,601 gross, 3,256/5,317 net, 9,561/10,790 deadweight. Dimensions: 471.3 (510.9 overall) x 70.1 x 41.7 feet.
Draft: 27.5/30.1 feet.
9 cyl. 2 S.C.S.A. B & W diesel by Akers Nylands Verk. A/S, Oslo, 17,400 bhp, 21 knots.
Refrigerated space: 481,500 cu. ft.

Ordered 1970 by F. M. Caribic Frigomaris Kuhlschiffreederei G.m.b.H. & Co., Hamburg, but sold to Federal shortly after construction began. *22.7.1971:* Launched by A/S Bergens M.V., Bergen, (Yard No. 651), and delivered to Federal 18.12.1971. P&O General Cargo Division had become managers from 1.10.1971. *2.6.1980:* Sold to the Astrid Shipping Corp., Piraeus, (Comninos Bros Shipping Company S.A., managers), and renamed

OLYMPIAN REEFER. *1984:* Transferred to the National Preparation Cia Nav., Piraeus. *1989:* Transferred to the Elbow Shipping Company Ltd, Limassol, (Comninos Enterprises S.A., managers), and renamed BUENOS AIRES. *1992:* Transferred to National Ability S.A., Panama, (Comninos Enterprises S.A., managers). *1995:* Renamed AMAZON REEFER; same owners. Still in service

WILD AVOCET at Auckland

*(DNB)*

## F.90 WILD AVOCET (1972 -1980)
Official Number: 358482
Tonnages: 7,291/9,710 gross, 3,242/5,416 net, 9,561/10,790 deadweight. Dimensions: 471.3 (511.2 overall) x 70.1 x 41.7 feet.
Draft: 28.1/30.1 feet.
9 cyl. 2 S.C.S.A. B & W diesel by Akers Nylands Verk. A/S, Oslo, 17,400 bhp, 21 knots.
Refrigerated space: 481,500 cu.ft.

Ordered 1970 by F. M. Caribic Frigomaris Kuhlschiffreederei G.m.b.H. & Co., Hamburg, but sold to Federal shortly after construction began. *16.3.1972:* Launched by A/S Bergens M.V., Bergen, (Yard No. 653), and delivered to Federal 12.7.1972, (P&O General Cargo Division, managers). *26.8.1980:* Sold to the Citragon Shipping Corp., Piraeus, (Comninos Bros Shipping Company S.A., managers), and renamed DELPHIC REEFER.

*1982:* Transferred to the National Preponderance Cia Nav. S.A., Piraeus. *1991:* Transferred to the Warmship Marine Company Ltd, Limassol, (Comninos Enterprises S.A., managers), and registered at Panama as AEGEAN REEFER. *1992:* Transferred to Sea Condor S.A., Panama, (Comninos Enterprises S.A., managers). *1996:* Renamed ALPINA I. Still in service.

WILD CORMORANT at Lyttelton (NJK)

## F.91 WILD CORMORANT (1973—1981)

Official Number: 358827

Tonnages: 7,594 gross, 3,382 net, 9,168 deadweight. Dimensions: 472.4 (506.8 overall) x 70.8 x 43.0 feet. Draft: 28.6 feet. 9 cyl. 2 S.C.S.A. M.A.N. diesel by the Maschinenfabrik Augsburg-Nurnberg, A.G., Augsburg, 17,100 bhp, 22.5 knots. Refrigerated space: 456,500 cu.ft.

*12.10.1972:* Launched by the Lubecker Flenderwerke A.G., Lubeck, (Yard No. 602), and delivered 26.2.1973 to Federal, (P&O General Cargo Division, managers). *15.10.1981:* Sold to the Leslie Shipping Corp., Piraeus, (Comninos Bros Shipping Company S.A., managers), and renamed ATTICA REEFER. *1984:* Transferred to the National Precedence Cia Nav., Limassol. *12.1985:* Transferred to the Embira Navigation Company Ltd, Limassol, and renamed SILVER REEFER. *2.1988:* Renamed BASSRO NORDIC while under charter to Bassro A/S, Oslo. *1988:* Transferred to the Norton Shipping Company Ltd, Limassol, (International Reefer Services, managers), and renamed FLAMINGO REEFER. *1988:* Transferred to the Number Shipping Company Ltd, Limassol, and 21.12.1988 renamed HORNCLIFF for charter to the Horn Linie, Hamburg. *5.1990:* Reverted to FLAMINGO REEFER on completion of charter. *21.1.1991:* Renamed TUSCAN STAR for charter to Blue Star Line Ltd, London. *23.6.1992:* Again renamed FLAMINGO REEFER on completion of charter, and transfer to Ocean Shield S.A., Panama. *1996:* Renamed MARATHON BREEZE. Still in service.

WILD CURLEW at Lyttelton (NJK)

## F.92 WILD CURLEW (1973—1981)

Official Number: 360655
Tonnages: 7,594 gross, 3,382 net, 9,168 deadweight. Dimensions: 472.4 (506.8 overall) x 70.8 x 43.0 feet. Draft: 28.6 feet.
9 cyl. 2 S.C.S.A. M.A.N. diesel by Maschinenfabrik Augsburg-Nurnberg A.G., Augsburg, 17,100 bhp, 22.5 knots.
Refrigerated space: 456,400 cu. ft.

*22.2.1973:* Launched by the Lubecker Flenderwerke A.G., Lubeck, (Yard No. 603), and delivered to Federal 30.6.1973, (P&O General Cargo Division, managers). *2.10.1981:* Sold to Initial Shipping Services Corp., Piraeus, (Comninos Bros Shipping Company S.A., managers), and renamed ATHENIAN REEFER. *1984:* Transferred to the National Predominance Cia Nav., Piraeus, same managers. *12.1984:* Transferred to the Habilitas Shipping Company Ltd, Limassol, same managers, and renamed GOLDEN REEFER. *1.1988:* Renamed BASSRO ARCTIC for charter to Bassro A/S, Oslo. *7.1988:* Renamed CARIOCAS REEFER on completion of charter; same owners and managers.

*1988:* Sold to the Bremen Shipping Company Ltd, Limassol, (Comninos Bros Shipping Company S.A., managers), and renamed HORNSEA in 1.1989, for charter to Horn Linie, Hamburg. *5.1990:* Renamed CARIOCAS REEFER. *29.12.1990:* Renamed CAP CORRIENTES for charter to Hamburg Sud Amerikanische D.G., Hamburg, (International Reefer Services S.A., managers). *16.8.1992:* Reverted to CARIOCAS REEFER following completion of charter. *13.11.1993:* Laid up at Jebel Ali. *17.5.1995:* Arrived at Bombay for demolition. *25.5.1995:* Rishi Shipbreaking Ltd. commenced work.

WILD FLAMINGO

*(VHY/NZA)*

## F.93 WILD FLAMINGO (1973—1983)

Official Number: 360873
Tonnages: 5,014/6,925 gross, 2,700/3,834 net, 8,061/9,750 deadweight. Dimensions: 442.1 (473.8 overall) x 59.2 x 38.1 feet.
Draft: 27.1/29.6 feet.
8 cyl. 2 S.C.S.A. Sulzer diesel by Sulzer Bros Ltd, Winterthur, 13,200 bhp, 23 knots.
Refrigerated space: 381,500 cu.ft.

*21.6.1973:* Launched by Drammen Slip & Verk., Drammen, (Yard No. 76), and delivered 25.10.1973 to Federal, (P&O General Cargo Division, managers). *23.5.1983:* Sold to Sembawang Reefer Lines (Ciku) Pte Ltd, Singapore, (Sembawang Johnson Shipmanagement (Pte) Ltd, managers), and renamed REEFER CIKU. *1987:* Transferred to Sembawang Reefer Lines (Duku) Bahamas Ltd, Nassau, (Sembawang Shipping Company (Pte) Ltd, managers). *11.1987:* Sold to the Bulkserve Shipping Company Ltd, Limassol, (Enias Shipping Company S.A., managers), and renamed FRIO CHILE. *1990:* Transferred to the Pineforest Shipping Company Ltd, Limassol, (Lomar Shipping Ltd, managers). *1993:* Transferred to the Pacific-Sea Maritime Corp., Panama, and renamed LAS PALMAS. *1994:* Transferred to the Pineforest Shipping Company Ltd, Limassol, and renamed FRIO CHILE. *4.1.1995:* Abandoned off Honshu in 38°22'N-150°58'E after taking in water, bound Callao to Hachinohe. She sank on 8.1.1995.

WILD FULMAR at Auckland                                                                                                (DNB)

## F.94 WILD FULMAR (1974—1983)

Official Number: 363183
Tonnages: 5,014/6,925 gross, 2,700/3,840 net, 8,061/9,750 deadweight. Dimensions: 442.1 (473.8 overall) x 59.2 x 38.1 feet. Draft: 27.1/29.6 feet.
8 cyl. 2 S.C.S.A. Sulzer diesel by Sulzer Bros Ltd, Winterthur, 13,200 bhp, 23 knots.
Refrigerated space: 381,500 cu.ft.

*27.11.1973:* Launched by Drammen Slip & Verk., Drammen, (Yard No. 77), and delivered 7.3.1974 to Federal, (P&O General Cargo Division, managers). *3.5.1983:* Sold to Sembawang Reefer Lines (Duku) Pte Ltd, Singapore, (Sembawang Johnson Shipmanagement (Pte) Ltd, managers), and renamed REEFER DUKU. *1987:* Transferred to Sembawang Reefer Lines (Duku) Bahamas Ltd, Nassau, (Sembawang Shipping Company Pte Ltd, managers). *1.1988:* Sold to the Manifest Shipping Company Ltd, Limassol, (Kappa Maritime, managers), and renamed STARSEA. *29.5.1990:* Suffered an engineroom explosion and fire, and

abandoned by her crew 35 miles north-west of Punta Mala, Panama, bound Corinto to Zeebrugge. Arrived Balboa in tow on 1.6.1990 and laid up. *1990:* Sold at Balboa to Paul Cheng & Sons Investments Ltd, Hong Kong, (Trans Globe Marine Ltd, managers), registered at Kingstown, St Vincent, and renamed MIDWAY. *28.7.1991:* Left Balboa in tow of the motor tug ATLANTIC RESCUER (662g, 1969) and arrived at Alang 22.2.1992, via Nauru and Kavieng, for demolition by Esoofbhai, Khanbhai who began work 13.3.1992.

WILD GANNET at Auckland                                                                                                (DNB)

## F.95 WILD GANNET (1977—1983)

Official Number: 377183
Tonnages: 5,017/6,933 gross, 2,639/3,796 net, 8,034/9,592 deadweight. Dimensions: 442.1 (474.9 overall) x 59.2 x 38.0 feet. Draft: 27.0/29.7 feet.
8 cyl. 2 S.C.S.A. Sulzer diesel by Sulzer Bros Ltd, Winterthur, 13,200 bhp, 23 knots.
Refrigerated space: 382,000 cu.ft.

*18.10.1976:* Launched by Drammen Slip & Verk., Drammen, (Yard No. 84), and delivered 4.2.1977 to Midland Gillett Leasing (South) Ltd, London. Leased to Federal, (P&O General Cargo Division, managers). *30.3.1983:* Sold to Sembawang Reefer Lines (Manggis) Pte Ltd, Singapore, (Sembawang Johnson Shipmanagement (Pte) Ltd, managers), and renamed REEFER

MANGGIS. *1986:* Transferred to Sembawang Reefer Lines (Bahamas) Ltd, Nassau; same managers. *1990:* Sold to Marine Liberation. S.A., Piraeus, (International Reefer Services S.A., managers), and renamed IONIC REEFER. Still in service.

WILD MALLARD at Auckland with Lauritzen funnel, AUCKLANDER alongside

*(DNB)*

## F.96 MATAURA/WILD MALLARD (1977—1981) See No. 104

WILD GREBE at Auckland

*(DNB)*

## F.97 WILD GREBE (1978—1983)

Official Number: 377491
Tonnages: 5,017/6,933 gross, 2,641/3,835 net, 8,033/9,592 deadweight. Dimensions: 442.1 (474.9 overall) x 59.2 x 38.0 feet. Draft: 27.0/29.7 feet.
8 cyl. 2 S.C.S.A. Sulzer diesel by Sulzer Bros Ltd, Winterthur, 13,200 bhp, 23 knots.
Refrigerated space: 382,000 cu.ft.

*15.10.1977:* Launched by Drammen Slip & Verk., Drammen, (Yard No. 85), and delivered 31.1.1978 to Federal, (P&O General Cargo Division, managers). *29.4.1983:* Sold to Sembawang Reefer Lines (Nangka) Pte Ltd, Singapore, (Sembawang Johnson Shipmanagement Pte Ltd, managers), and renamed REEFER NANGKA. *1986:* Transferred to Sembawang Reefer Lines (Bahamas) Ltd, Nassau; same managers. *1990:* Sold to Golden Liberation S.A., Piraeus, (International Reefer Services S.A., managers), and renamed AEOLIC REEFER. Still in service.

# VESSELS MANAGED FOR H.M. GOVERNMENT
# FIRST WORLD WAR

POLSHANNON at Wellington in Shell colours    *(IJF)*

## FM.1 TANDEM/POLSHANNON (1914—1919)

Official Number: 139103
Tonnages: 5,639 gross, 3,546 net. 1922: 6,121 gross, 3,944 net. Dimensions: 421.0 (436.6 overall) x 55.1 x 28.7 feet.
Draft: 25.1 feet.
Q.4 cyl. by the shipbuilders, 2,300 ihp, 11 knots. 1922: Boilers converted to oil fuel.

*7.6.1910:* Launched by J.C. Tecklenborg A.G., Geestemunde, (Yard No. 236), and completed 7.1910 for the Deutsche D.G. Hansa, Bremen, as BIRKENFELS. *20.8.1914:* Seized at Cape Town and management allocated to Federal by the British Government; renamed TANDEM. *1915:* Renamed POLSHANNON and served as a Royal Fleet Auxiliary until 7.1921. *1919:* Management transferred to the Anglo-Saxon Petroleum Company Ltd. *4.7.1921:* Sold to the Anglo-Saxon Petroleum Company Ltd,

London. *6.1922:* Rebuilt at Hong Kong as a bulk oil carrier and renamed PINNA. *1942:* Requisitioned for service with the Royal Fleet Auxiliary. *3.2.1942:* Attacked by aircraft in Berhala Strait (00°52'S-104°19'E) bound Pladjoe to Singapore in ballast. Again attacked on the 4th and run ashore as a total loss. 20 lives lost and the remaining 23 crew and passengers taken prisoner.

HAMM as AGHIOS MARCOS    *(IJF)*

## FM.2 HAMM (1915—1921)

Official Number: 142640
Tonnages: 4,598 gross, 2,870 net, 7,650 deadweight. Dimensions: 399.8 x 53.9 x 25.1 feet.
T.3 cyl. by the Reiherstieg Maschinenfabrik, Hamburg, 3,000 ihp, 12 knots.

*8.4.1910:* Launched by the Reiherstieg Schiffswerft, Hamburg, (Yard No. 428), and completed 4.6.1910 for the Deutsch-Australische D.G., Hamburg. *22.12.1913:* Grounded at Port Said. *10.8.1914:* Taken as a prize on entering Cape Town and management allocated to Federal 7.4.1915 by the British Government. *1918:* Registered at London to The Shipping

Controller, (Federal, managers). *12.1921:* Sold to P. Margaronis & Sons, Piraeus, handed over 27.2.1922 and renamed AGHIOS MARCOS. *1930:* Transferred to A., I., and G.D. Margaronis, Piraeus. *1931:* Sold to G. Trilivas, Ithaca. *23.5.1932:* Laid up at Piraeus. *1933:* Reverted to Margaronis. *11.11.1933:* Arrived at Savona for demolition.

APOLDA in German colours at Cape Town in 1914
*(IJF)*

## FM.3 APOLDA (1915—1919)

Official Number: 146704
Tonnages: 4,939 gross, 2,831 net, 7,180 deadweight. Dimensions: 391.0 x 47.8 x 21.6 feet.
Q.4 cyl. by the shipbuilders, 3,400 ihp, 13 knots.

*4.9.1901:* Launched by the Flensburger S.G., Flensburg, (Yard No. 207), and delivered 22.10.1901 to the Deutsch-Australische D.G., Hamburg. *8.8.1914:* Taken as a prize on entering Cape Town and management allocated to Federal on 11.4.1915 by the British Government. Registered at Cape Town. *28.7.1919:* Handed over to the Government of the Union of South Africa, (South African Railways & Harbours Administration, managers). *1923:* Taken over by the Board of Trade, London. *1926:* Sold to Ditta Luigi Pittaluga Vapori, Genoa, and renamed VERBANIA. *24.1.1930:* Laid up at Genoa. *12.1932:* Broken up in Italy.

CALULU at Sydney
*(IJF)*

## FM.4 CALULU (1918—1918)

Official Number: 139019
Tonnages: 4,240 gross, 2,639 net, 7,000 deadweight. Dimensions: 387.8 x 51.0 x 25.2 feet.
T.3 cyl. by the shipbuilders, 2,200 ihp, 11 knots.

*21.8.1907:* Launched by the Flensburger S.G., (Yard No. 274), and delivered 21.9.1907 to the Deutsch-Australische D.G., Hamburg, as OSNABRUCK. *8.1914:* Taken as a prize of war at Sydney by the Australian Government, first commissioned as the transport C 9, then renamed CALULU in 1915. Registered at London. *24.3.1918—5.6.1918:* Requisitioned by the British Government (Federal S.N. Co., managers), for a voyage with wheat. *1923:* Transferred to the Australian Commonwealth Line, still registered at London. *9.1924:* Laid up at Sydney. *1925:* Sold to B.B. Wiltshire, Sydney. *1926:* Transferred to the Austral-China Navigation Company Ltd, Hong Kong. *12.1926:* Suffered a fire in her bunkers, bound Keelung to Manila. The fire was extinguished on arrival at Manila. *1.1930:* Suffered a fire in her cargo while at Hong Kong. No. 5 hold was flooded to extinguish it. *3.1930:* Laid up at Sydney. *1931:* Sold to the Peng Fah Wing Steamship Company, Hong Kong. *1931:* Sold to the Anglo-Danish Shipping Company, Copenhagen, (M.L. Justesen, manager). *1933:* H.J. Christian Snr became manager. *1933:* Sold to the Ming Sing Steamship Company Ltd, Shanghai, and renamed SUNG PENG. *7.1937:* Broken up at Shanghai.

## FM.5 TASMAN (1918—1918)

Official Number: 142607
Tonnages: 5,023 gross, 3,334 net, 3,833 deadweight. Dimensions: 392.0 x 49.0 x 26.0 feet.
T.3 cyl. by the shipbuilders, 470 nhp, 12 knots.
Passengers: 98 cabin, 979 on deck.
Refrigerated space: 6,100 cu.ft.

*9.10.1912:* Launched by Earle's Shipbuilding & Engineering Co. Ltd, Hull, (Yard No. 589), and delivered 3.1913 to the Koninklijke Paketvaart Maats., Batavia. *26.3.1918:* Requisitioned at Brisbane by the British Government, (Federal S.N. Co., managers), for service under the Liner Requisition Scheme. *16.9.1918:* Torpedoed and sunk by U 46 220 miles north by west of Cape Villano, (46°36'N-12°00'W), bound London to Calcutta with general cargo.

WAR QUAIL as TREVEAN          *(A. Duncan)*

## FM.6 WAR QUAIL (1918—1919)

Official Number: 142624
Tonnages: 5,225 gross, 3,217 net. Dimensions: 400.2 x 52.3 x 28.5 feet.
T.3 cyl. by the North Eastern Marine Engineering Co. Ltd, Newcastle, 3,000 ihp, 11 knots.

*27.5.1918:* Launched by the Northumberland Shipbuilding Co. Ltd, Newcastle, (Yard No. 249), and delivered 8.1918 to The Shipping Controller, London, (Federal S.N. Co., managers) *1.7.1919:* Suffered a fire in a storeroom. *21.9.1919:* Sold to the Hain Steamship Company Ltd, St Ives, (E. Hain & Son, managers), and renamed TREVEAN. *1925:* Managers became Foster, Hain & Read Ltd. *7.1.1926:* Arrived at Port Pirie with fire in the bunkers. *21.8.1926:* Collided with the steamer CLAN MACFADYEN (6,224g, 1923) at Antwerp. *24.9.1928:* Collided with the steamer INES (3,106g, 1899) on entering Santos from Barry. *29.6.1929:* Arrived at Rio de Janeiro from Immingham with fire in the bunkers. *21.1.1930:* Collided with the steamer KOLSDAL (1,269g, 1920), bound Liverpool to Cardiff. *25.2.1931:* Went aground 8 miles east of Anatolia Lighthouse, bound Nikolaiev to Boston with ore. *23.5.1931:* Refloated and towed to Trieste 8.1931 for breaking up.

## FM.7 WAR COOT (1918—1918)

Official Number: 142633
Tonnages: 5,175 gross, 3,220 net. Dimensions: 399.5 x 52.4 x 28.5 feet.
T.3 cyl. by Cammell, Laird & Co. Ltd, Birkenhead, 3,000 ihp, 11 knots.

*26.6.1918:* Launched by the Sunderland Shipbuilding Co. Ltd, Sunderland, (Yard No. 318), and completed 31.8.1918 for The Shipping Controller, London, (Federal S.N. Co., managers to 19.12.1918). *10.2.1919:* Sold to the Soc. Transoceanique de Transports, Antwerp, (R. van Hemelryck & Company, managers) and renamed SIERRA ROJA. *6.1923:* Sold to the Societe Belge de Credit Maritime, Antwerp. *1.1925:* Sold to the S.A. per l'Industria ed il Com. Marit. "Nova Genuensis", Genoa, and renamed SERENITAS. *5.7.1940:* Bombed by British aircraft at Tobruk and beached to avoid sinking. *12.12.1950:* Forepart salved and towed to Savona where it arrived 15.8.1951 for demolition.

## FM.8 WAR ARGUS (1918—1919)

Official Number: 142741
Tonnages: 7,912 gross, 4,888 net. Dimensions: 450.0 (465.0 overall) x 58.5 x 29.1 feet. Draft: 29.3 feet.
Twin screw, two T.3 cyl. by the shipbuilders, 5,500 ihp, 13 knots.
Refrigerated space: 392,600 cu.ft.

*1918:* Launched by Workman, Clark & Co. Ltd, Belfast, (Yard No. 436), and ran trials 12.12.1918 for The Shipping Controller, London, (Federal S.N. Co., managers), as the G class standard ship WAR ARGUS. *12.12.1918—17.3.1919:* Taken up under the Liner Requisition Scheme. *17.7.1919:* Managers became the Oceanic Steam Navigation Company Ltd, (White Star Line). *28.7.1919:* Sold to the managers, registered at Liverpool and renamed GALLIC in 8.1919. *1933:* Sold for £53,000 to The Clan Line Steamers Ltd, Glasgow, (Cayzer, Irvine & Company Ltd, managers), and renamed CLAN COLQUHOUN. *12.8.1940—18.4.1946:* Requisitioned for the Liner Division, but served from 20.2.1941—18.6.1941 as a military store ship. *1947:* Sold to the Zarati Steamship Company Ltd, Panama, (J. Livanos & Sons Ltd, managers), and renamed IOANNIS LIVANOS. *1949:* Transferred to Dos Oceanos Comp. de Nav. S.A., Panama, and renamed JENNY. *1949:* Transferred back to the Zarati Steamship

WAR ARGUS as GALLIC at Sydney                                                                                                                 (IJF)

Company Ltd. *1951:* Sold to the Djakarta Lloyd N.V., Djakarta, and renamed IMAM BONDJOL. *1952:* Renamed DJATINEGARA; same owners. *22.10.1955:* Delivered at Djakarta to the Hong Kong Towage & Salvage Company Ltd, but on 1.12.1955 put

ashore in a leaking condition at Lingayen near Manila while under tow to Osaka by the motor tug GOLDEN CAPE (525g, 1942). Refloated 21.2.1956 and arrived on 19.3.1956 at Hong Kong where demolition began in 6.1956.

WAR PICOTEE as TREMEADOW                                                                                                                       (IJF)

# FM.9 WAR PICOTEE (1918—1919)

Official Number: 142565
Tonnages: 5,302g, 3,231 net. Dimensions: 400.4 x 52.2 x 28.4 feet.
T.3 cyl. by the shipbuilders, 3,000 ihp, 11 knots.

*19.12.1918:* Launched by D. & W. Henderson & Co. Ltd, Glasgow, (Yard No. 516), for The Shipping Controller, London, (Federal S.N. Co., managers). She had been allocated provisionally to the Lyle Shipping Company Ltd, Glasgow, for management while still on the stocks. *5.3.1919:* Ran trials and delivered to the Hain Steamship Company Ltd, St Ives, (E. Hain & Son, managers), to whom she had been sold while fitting out, as TREMEADOW.

*1925:* Managers became Foster, Hain & Read. *8.1938:* Sold for £31,400 to Biagio Borriello, Torre del Greco, (Lauro & Montella, managers) and renamed SAGITTA. *9.11.1941:* Sunk by gunfire from HMSs AURORA (5,220 tons, 1937), PENELOPE (5,270 tons, 1936), LANCE (1,920 tons, 1941) and LIVELY (1,920 tons, 1941) 145 miles east of Syracuse, (37°08'N-18°09'E), bound Naples to Tripoli in convoy ''Duisburg''.

# SECOND WORLD WAR

EMPIRE CASTLE 19.11.1943

*(Mariners Museum/NZA)*

## FM.10 EMPIRE CASTLE (1943—1944)

Official Number: 168520
Tonnages: 7,356 gross, 5,126 net, 9,290 deadweight. Dimensions: 431.4 (448.0 overall) x 57.3 x 33.6 feet.
6 cyl. 4 S.C.S.A. B & W diesel by Harland & Wolff Ltd., Glasgow, 2,650 bhp, 12 knots.
Refrigerated space: 396,600 cu.ft.

*25.8.1942:* Launched by Harland & Wolff Ltd, Belfast, (Yard No. 1125), and delivered 31.1.1943 to the Ministry of War Transport, London, (Federal S. N. Co., managers). Registered at Belfast. *31.3.1943—30.5.1946:* Requisitioned for the Liner Division. *3.8.1944:* Management transferred to the Blue Star Line Ltd, London. *25.5.1946:* Sold to the managers and renamed GOTHIC STAR. *23.4.1947:* Renamed NELSON STAR; same owners. *5.9.1958:* Renamed PATAGONIA STAR; same owners. *19.5.1961:* Sold to Gregory Maritime Ltd, London, and renamed EIRINI.

*7.1970:* Sold to the Angila Shipping Company Ltd, provisionally registered at Famagusta, (G.A. Theodorou & Sons (Shipping) Ltd, managers), and renamed BYZANTIUM. *29.9.1970:* Arrived at Gibraltar with engine trouble and laid up. *21.1.1971:* Provisional Cypriot registry expired. *8.7.1971:* Arrived at Malaga in tow of the motor tug NISOS ZAKYNTHOS (1,136g, 1944). *7.1971:* Sold to Felipe Fuster and left Malaga 31.7.1971 for Puerto de Santa Maria where demolition by Desguaces y Recuperaciones del Sur S.L. began on 17.8.1971.

EMPIRE MANOR 17.10.1943

*(Mariners Museum/NZA)*

## FM.11 EMPIRE MANOR (1943—1944)

Official Number: 169118
Tonnages: 7,036 gross, 4,750 net. Dimensions: 431.0 (446.5 overall) x 56.3 x 35.2 feet.
T.3 cyl. by the North Eastern Marine Engineering Co. (1938) Ltd, Wallsend, 2,800 ihp, 11 knots.
Refrigerated space: 400,000 cu.ft.

*26.5.1943:* Launched by Short Bros Ltd, Sunderland, (Yard No. 476), and completed 15.6.1943 for the Ministry of War Transport, London, (Federal S.N. Co., managers). Registered at Sunderland. *15.7.1943:* Requisitioned for the Liner Division. *27.1.1944:* Collided with the steamer EDWARD KAVANAGH (7,176g, 1944) south of Cape Race, bound New York to the Mersey. She caught fire and was abandoned the following day

in 44°05'N-52°35'W, subsequently breaking in two. The after part sank and the forepart was sunk by gunfire and depth charges from HMCS KENOGAMI (925 tons, 1940). In 1974 £1 million in gold was salved from the fore part by the salvage steamer DROXFORD (1,302g, 1958) of Risdon Beazley Marine Ltd.

Funnel and bridge of DURHAM (F.41)

(VHY/NZA)

# LIVERY

**HOUSEFLAG:** A red St George's cross on a white ground with a blue rectangle over the cross in the centre. (Acquired from the liquidators of Money, Wigram & Sons Ltd, which had first adopted it in 1824.)

**HULL:** Black hull with red boot-topping, separated from 1912 by a white line. Vessels built after 1965: Pale eau de nil hull with dark green boot-topping.

**UPPERWORKS:** White.

**MASTS:** Dark brown.

**DERRICK POSTS & DERRICKS:** Dark brown to 1939; white from 1945.

**FUNNEL:** Dark red with black top and houseflag on the red.

**LIFEBOATS:** Varnished until 1900, then white.

The livery of the 3 tankers was a grey hull with dark green boot-topping, white upperworks and masts and the Federal funnel. On the formation of Federal Tankers Ltd in 1966 the letters F T in white on the blue rectangle were added to the funnel and houseflag.

# CADET SHIPS

Apprentices had been carried from the earliest days of NZS, but it was not until just after the First World War that the decision was made to concentrate on a more structured training in designated ships of the fleet where the cadets, as they were now called, would largely replace the normal deck crew.

In 1920 two ships each from the NZS and Federal fleets were allocated the first cadets under the new system, and over the rest of that decade three further Federal ships replaced the original vessels as they were sold. The CORNWALL was added in 1931. A major change came in 1933 when it was decided to confine the training to two ships, and one of the new Federal vessels which had just been ordered in Belfast was chosen to be fitted out for cadet training, the first in the combined fleets to be designed for that purpose. This was the DURHAM, the best remembered and longest serving of all the cadet ships which put over 20 years into this role. It is no coincidence that the society of past cadets is known as the Durham Association. The cadets were accommodated aft, and took responsibility for all deck duties. Senior cadets were involved in navigation while all stood watches at sea, supervised cargo working in port and attended 3 hours of instruction in theory and seamanship each day. Her consort was the HORORATA, and in both ships a classroom was provided and an officer allocated known as ''the schoolmaster'' whose special task was the supervision and instruction of the cadets.

With the outbreak of the Second World War the scheme was suspended for safety reasons, and the DURHAM's cadets were dispersed around the fleet, the HORORATA having been sold a few months previously. Cadet training resumed in a refitted DURHAM in 1946. She was replaced by the RAKAIA in 1950, the cadets taking over the former war standard passenger accommodation. The DURHAM resumed as a cadet ship in 1955.

The last cadet ship, OTAIO (97), at Lyttelton with Federal funnel                                                    (NJK)

The scheme was extended further in 1958 with the commissioning of the OTAIO which trained not only deck but also engineering cadets. Her long centrecastle included classroom, recreation room and an engineering workshop while cadets were accommodated in 3 berth cabins rather than the previous dormitories. Her capacity was for 40 deck and 30 engineering cadets. On the final retirement of the DURHAM the OTAIO continued the sole training role for the joint companies. The scheme was wound up with her sale in 1975 following the absorption of NZS/Federal into P&O General Cargo Division in 1971.

**The Cadet Ships**

| | |
|---|---|
| ORARI | 1920—1927 |
| WHAKATANE | 1920—1924 |
| SOMERSET | 1920—1927 |
| ESSEX | 1920—1927 |
| NORTHUMBERLAND | 1924—1934 |
| DEVON | 1927—1933 |
| WESTMORELAND | 1927—1934 |
| CORNWALL | 1931—1934 |
| HORORATA | 1934—1939 |
| DURHAM | 1934—1939 |
| | 1946—1950 |
| | 1955—1962 |
| RAKAIA | 1950—1968 |
| OTAIO | 1958—1975 |

# AVENUE SHIPPING COMPANY LTD

In 1954 the NZS board decided to separate its smaller non-fully refrigerated ships into a new company which could provide back-up not only to the NZS Group itself but also to the wider P&O Group. Action was triggered by the pending delivery of the 3 new WH- class ships for the North American trade which would free the 5 KAI- class ships, most of which still had some years of useful life ahead of them.

In chosing a name for the new concern, NZS went back into Group history by reviving the name of the old Avenue Shipping Company Ltd which had been the shipowning vehicle for Birt, Potter & Hughes from its formation in 1924 with the ENTON until the loss of its second and last ship, the WINTON, in 1934. In turn, its name came from the

The first ENTON of 1925 at Auckland

(Auckland Museum/WAL)

address of Birt, Potter & Hughes' London office at 2 Fenchurch Avenue. The names selected for the ships were also a throw-back with the return of the Irish county names first used by NZS for the ships purchased from Houlders in 1911/1912.

The new Avenue Shipping Company Ltd was registered on 4 September 1954 with a nominal capital of £1,500,000 which was issued for the purchase of the 5 KAI- class ships KAIMATA, KAIKOURA, KAIPARA, KAITUNA and KAIPAKI from NZS and the much more modern second ENTON from Birt, Potter & Hughes Ltd. The ships were taken over as they completed current voyages over 1954/1955 and the Federal red funnel with black top was adopted, but having the white Avenue flag with blue cross and a blue A on a white diamond in the centre instead of the Federal flag.

W.C. How, the NZS/Federal deputy chairman, was elected Chairman at the first board meeting on 16 September 1954, being succeeded by C.A.W. Dawes on 1 December 1961 and by S.G. Fowler on 1 October 1966. As had been the case with the KAI- ships, Trinder, Anderson & Company Ltd assumed the management of Avenue, and their black swan houseflag was always flown from the foremast of Avenue ships.

The new company's building programme began in 1957 with the DONEGAL which was a slightly updated version of the LIMERICK ex ENTON, followed by the GALWAY in 1959 and the ANTRIM in 1962. All bore strong family characteristics of NZS/Federal, and the last 2 were launched with the eau de nil hull which had first appeared on the ARMAGH in 1958. The older ships were disposed of between 1957 and 1963, and the GALWAY was lengthened in 1967 to increase her capacity.

GALWAY after lengthening

(WAL)

The 4 post-war Avenue ships proved a successful adjunct to the NZS Group, and in March 1958 the then new DONEGAL was the first ship in the extension of the Federal Line's Australian service to New Guinea. During the 1960's the Avenue fleet was increasingly chartered to other P&O Group companies and then later to other liner companies as the decade wore on. The LIMERICK was transferred to the British India Steam Navigation Company Ltd in 1969. With the looming advent of containerisation and the pending P&O Group re-organisation, there was no longer a place for an independent concern with conventional ships, and from 1 October 1971 the 3 ships built for Avenue passed to the management of P&O General Cargo Division. The Avenue colours were replaced by the new Group livery, and the process was completed in March 1972 with formal ownership being taken over by its parent The Peninsular and Oriental Steam Navigation Company. In October 1976 Avenue was renamed P&O Overseas Holdings Ltd and is still in existence.

ARMAGH at Auckland with the new green hull colours                    (RCP)

## A.1 ARMAGH (1954—1961) See KAITUNA (No. 79)

## A.2 ANTRIM (1954—1957) See KAIMATA (No. 75)

ANTRIM at Wellington                    (VHY/NZA)

TYRONE at Auckland *(RCP)*

## A.3 TYRONE (1954—1963) See KAIKOURA (No. 76)

LIMERICK at Sydney *(JYF)*

## A.4 LIMERICK (1955—1969)
Official Number: 184627
Tonnages: 6,211 gross, 3,526 net, 10,177 deadweight. Dimensions: 432.9 (460.3 overall) x 59.0 x 39.5 feet. Draft: 27.7 feet.
5 cyl. 2 S.C.S.A. Doxford diesel by Barclay, Curle & Co. Ltd, Glasgow, 5,500 bhp, 14 knots.

*20.1.1952:* Launched by A. Stephen & Sons Ltd, Glasgow, (Yard No. 633), and delivered 5.1952 to Birt, Potter & Hughes Ltd, London, (Trinder, Anderson & Company Ltd, managers) as ENTON. *27.5.1955:* Sold for £360,000 to Avenue, (same managers), and renamed LIMERICK on 31.5.1955, after having been announced originally as LEITRIM. *3.9.1969:* Sold for £74,000 to the British India Steam Navigation Company Ltd,

London, and renamed HOWRA. *1.10.1971:* Management transferred to P&O General Cargo Division. *8.6.1972:* Sold to Guan Guan Shipping (Pte) Ltd, Singapore, and renamed GOLDEN HAVEN. *19.10.1982:* Arrived at Karachi and demolition by the Amica Construction Works began at Gadani Beach on 30.11.1982.

WESTMEATH at Adelaide *(JYF)*

## A.5 WESTMEATH (1955—1962) See KAIPAKI (No. 80)

ROSCOMMON at Adelaide *(JYF)*

## A.6 ROSCOMMON (1955—1962) See KAIPARA (No. 77)

DONEGAL at Auckland *(DNB)*

## A.7 DONEGAL (1957—1972)

Official Number: 187545
Tonnages: 6,327 gross, 3,509 net, 9,890 deadweight. Dimensions: 432.0 (460.3 overall) x 59.0 x 39.5 feet. Draft: 27.2 feet.
5 cyl. 2 S.C.S.A. Doxford diesel by the shipbuilders, 5,500 bhp, 14 knots.

*19.12.1956:* Launched by A. Stephen & Sons Ltd, Glasgow, (Yard No. 656), and delivered 14.3.1957 to Avenue, (Trinder, Anderson & Company Ltd, managers), at a cost of £1,027,000. *1.10.1971:* Management transferred to P&O General Cargo Division. *29.3.1972:* Transferred to The Peninsular and Oriental S. N. Co.

*13.6.1975:* Renamed STRATHIRVINE. *25.6.1977:* Sold to the Triton Nav. Corp., Panama, (Zenith Management Corp., managers), and renamed ATHINA. *25.5.1980:* Delivered to the Nan Feng Steel Enterprise Company Ltd who began demolition at Kaohsiung on 10.6.1980.

## A.8 GALWAY (1959—1972)

Official Number: 300830
Tonnages: 6,409 gross, 3,541 net, 9,800 deadweight. 1967: 7,167/9,539 gross, 4,141/5,689 net, 11,561/12,781 deadweight.
Dimensions: 432.0 (469.3 overall) x 60.5 x 38.8 feet. Draft: 26.7 feet. 1967: 496.7 (525.3 overall) x 60.5 x 38.8 feet. Draft: 26.4/28.1 feet.
5 cyl. 2 S.C.S.A. Doxford diesel by Hawthorn, Leslie (Engineers) Ltd, Newcastle, 5,500 bhp, 14 knots.

*16.9.1958:* Launched by Smith's Dock Co. Ltd, Middlesbrough, (Yard No. 1253), and delivered 5.2.1959 to Avenue, (Trinder, Anderson & Company Ltd, managers), at a cost of £1,055,000. *22.12.1962:* Collided with the motor tanker CLYDE EXPLORER (8,644g, 1950) off Cardiff. *16.3.1967:* Arrived at North Shields for lengthening by 60 feet by Smith's Dock Company Ltd. The work was completed in a month at a cost of £137,000. *1.10.1971:* Management transferred to P&O General Cargo Division.

*29.3.1972:* Transferred to The Peninsular and Oriental S. N. Co. *19.6.1975:* Renamed STRATHINVER. *10.4.1976:* Sold for $1,850,000 to Guan Guan Shipping (Pte) Ltd, Singapore, and renamed GOLDEN FORTUNE. *9.9.1983:* Driven ashore at Kau Yi Chau, Hong Kong, in typhoon ''Ellen'' and sold while still aground to the Yau Wing Shipbreaking Company Ltd for demolition at Hong Kong. *20.10.1983:* Demolition began.

GALWAY as built, at Auckland

*(DNB)*

## A.9 ANTRIM (1962—1972)

Official Number: 302971
Tonnages: 6,330 gross, 3,510 net, 9,980 deadweight. Dimensions: 432.0 (460.3 overall) x 59.1 x 39.5 feet. Draft: 27.2 feet.
5 cyl. 2 S.C.S.A. Doxford diesel by the shipbuilders, 5,500 bhp, 14 knots.

*19.1.1962:* Launched by A. Stephen & Sons Ltd, Glasgow, (Yard No. 673), and delivered 27.4.1962 to Avenue, (Trinder, Anderson & Company Ltd, managers). *1.10.1971:* Management transferred to P&O General Cargo Division. *29.3.1972:* Transferred to The Peninsular and Oriental S.N. Co. *2.5.1975:* Renamed STRATHINCH. *17.11.1977:* Sold for $1,100,000 through Navigation & Coal Trade Ltd, London, to the Highwater Navigation Company Ltd, Chittagong, (Nerva Maritime Inc., managers), and renamed ISLAMI TAAJ. *7.1979:* Grounded, bound Chalna to Karachi. *5.1980:* Sold to the Jaguar Shipping Corp. Ltd, Panama, (Sam U. Shipping Company Ltd, managers), and renamed SINGAPORE 2. *1981:* Transferred to the Cia Nav. Keelung S.A., Panama, same managers. *16.7.1982:* Stranded on the west coast of Korea, bound Ho Chi Min City to Inchon and arrived at Inchon in tow of the tug KOYO MARU (2,061g, 1967) on the 22nd. *6.8.1982:* Delivered at Inchon for demolition by the Han Sung Salvage Company Ltd.

ANTRIM at Auckland

*(MP)*

## TIME CHARTERED VESSEL

KILDARE at Auckland                                                                                    *(DNB)*

### A.10 KILDARE (1957—1960)

Official Number: 181160
Tonnages: 5,635 gross, 3,071 net, 10,196 deadweight. Dimensions: 420.0 (449.8 overall) x 59.5 x 38.2 feet. Draft: 26.0 feet.
4 cyl. 2 S.C.S.A. Doxford diesel by Wm Doxford & Sons Ltd, Sunderland, 4,400 bhp, 13 knots.

*6.5.1955:* Launched by John Crown & Sons Ltd, Sunderland,
(Yard No. 238), and delivered 9.1955 to the Albyn Line Ltd,
Sunderland, (Allan, Black & Company Ltd, managers), as
THISTLEDHU at a cost of £680,000. *1.8.1957—7.9.1960:*
Chartered to Avenue and renamed KILDARE. *7.9.1960:* Reverted
to THISTLEDHU on completion of charter. *31.1.1966:* Sold for
£390,000 to the Somerston Shipping Company Ltd, Hamilton,
Bermuda, (Chapman & Willan Ltd, managers), and renamed
MERTON. Still registered at Sunderland. *26.2.1968:* Sold to the
Anesis Shipping Company S.A., Panama, (M.C. Fred
Hunter, manager), and registered at Piraeus as RIO DORO. *1974:*
Glysca Cia Nav. S.A. became managers. *5.11.1977:* Grounded
on Hatter Rev, near Samso Island (55°53'N-10°50'E) after a
steering failure, bound Fredericia to Karachi with
superphosphate. She was refloated on the 10th and returned
to Fredericia where she was found to be beyond economic
repair. *16.1.1978:* Arrived at Bilbao in tow of the motor tug
GARANT (298g, 1972). Demolition by Revalorizacion de
Materiales S.A. began the next day.

# THE BLACK BALL COMPANIES

As the Union Steam Ship Company of New Zealand Ltd obtained an ever tighter grip over the ownership of the West Coast coal mines in the South Island of New Zealand and the colliers which served them during the second half of the 1880's, an increasing concern arose among other shipowners in the New Zealand trade. Bunkering in New Zealand was inescapable given the range of contemporary steamers in the direct United Kingdom service, and their owners were reluctant to see themselves beholden to a monopoly supplier.

One of the few remaining independent mine owners was the Black Ball Creek Coal Mining Company Ltd which had been formed in 1886 to take up a 21 year lease from the Crown of a total of 1,914 acres of land on the Grey River some 17 miles north-east of Greymouth. Its Christchurch based promoters were closely linked with the Midland Railway Company, formed to build the line from Christchurch to the West Coast through the Southern Alps. The vicissitudes of that venture plus the general trade depression in New Zealand combined to exhaust the Black Ball Creek Company's capital, and it seldom achieved the projected annual output of 100,000 tons of coal which was to have yielded a profit of £20,000.

The crisis in the Black Ball Creek Company's affairs provided the opportunity for the overseas shipowners. Secret negotiations were conducted with the mine's owners by the ubiquitous Leonard Harper (see P.39) on behalf of the shipowners, and in July 1891 he was empowered to conclude matters for them. The result was the registration in London in April 1892 of the Black Ball Coal Mining Company of New Zealand Ltd which entered into an agreement to purchase the whole of the lands, leases and equipment of the Black Ball Creek Company for the sum of £21,000, only £1,000 of which was in cash, the balance being met by the issue of 2,000 fully paid £10 shares which were promptly re-financed among some 70 largely English investors. It is often stated that the 1892 Black Ball Coal Company was an NZS subsidiary from the start, but this was not so. Although NZS did have the largest single shareholding, it was of only 250 shares. The Company's true nature as a joint venture to serve the needs of shipping companies in the New Zealand trade was clear from its other shareholders who included Walter Savill and James Park of the Shaw Savill & Albion Company Ltd, J.B. Westray of NZS and the Ducal Line and Edward Martin of Turnbull, Martin & Company (the Scottish Shire Line). In a recall of the events on the founding of NZS 20 years earlier, the Christchurch management of the new company was in the hands of C.W. Turner who had been sent to London in 1873 to purchase the first ships for the NZS fleet. The Turner family connection with Black Ball was to remain strong throughout all its remaining years with C.W.'s elder son, C. Harcourt Turner, acting as agent in Wellington. Another son, Clarence F. Turner, after a period as engineer in Blackball ships, in turn became the long serving Wellington manager of the business.

Initially the new company confined its operations to mining coal and then shipping it in other companies' ships, but the operations under the new control proved little more rewarding financially than previously, and in 1894 further capital totalling £20,000 was raised by the issue of preference shares, most of which were subscribed for in Christchurch and Greymouth. This move enjoyed no greater success, and in 1896 NZS finally moved to take control. The 1892 English company was placed in liquidation in March 1897, and a new English company, the Blackball (one word instead of two) Coal Company Ltd, was registered in 1st January 1898 to take over the operation.

The adopting agreement revealed the true nature of the enterprise by referring to the new purchasing company as "the Syndicate", and the place of NZS as the controlling and guiding entity was seen in the NZS London manager, O.R. Strickland, becoming the guarantor for the debenture holders. These investors in the old company were issued with second priority debentures in the new concern subordinated to fresh first debenture capital of £20,000, while shareholders received a pro rata 1 for 3 distribution of ordinary shares. Even at this stage NZS did not dominate the shareholding, though it was the largest single shareholder with 837 shares, and Walter Savill remained a major shareholder. The continuing partnership aspect of the new company was reflected in the directorate with D.M. Dawes representing the NZS interest and Maures Horner the independent investors. A local board was established in Christchurch where the managing office of the previous company was maintained.

By now the overall operations had been placed on a firmer footing with ships as well as a mine, though until a more secure financial base was established the ships remained registered in the name of NZS. The funnel colours adopted during this transition period from the second to the third Blackball company was NZS yellow with a black top and a black ball at two-thirds height. The PAREORA was purchased in September 1896 and arrived on the New Zealand coast at the end of that year to join the HESKETH which had been on charter since December 1894 but was purchased in November 1896. Following the loss of the HESKETH on the Grey River bar in October 1899, she was replaced by the purchase from the Union Company of her sister, the DINGADEE. Both vessels had the unusual machinery arrangement of being twin screw with only one engine, each cylinder of an athwartships

DINGADEE (B.3) in Union Company colours    *(WAL)*

placed compound engine driving its own screw. The DINGADEE was the first of the steamers to be actually registered in Blackball ownership, and as part of the arrangements for her acquisition an agreement was entered into with the Union Company limiting the Blackball ships to the carriage of coal and timber only on the New Zealand coast, but not general cargo, in exchange for an annual subvention payment from the Union Company—the sort of contract that would these days be completely illegal as non-competitive.

The fleet was further strengthened by the newly built PETONE in 1900, and by 1903 the Blackball operation was sufficiently firmly established for the coal mine to be formally leased from E.S. Dawes to the company and for the two U.K. registered steamers to be transferred to it. At the same time the DINGADEE went through the reverse process, being transferred to the English subsidiary, the Dingadee Steam Ship Company Ltd. The growing confidence in Blackball can be partly explained by NZS having acquired over half the ordinary shares by 1903, but prudence still ruled with J.B. Westray & Company retaining a charge over the two steamers in support of the balance owing on their purchase price. C.J. Cowan, then an NZS General Manager, replaced Dawes on the Blackball board in 1905 and was joined by G.T. Haycraft, also of the NZS London office, the following year. Despite the now complete dominance of Blackball affairs by NZS, it was not until the period of the First World War that the Shaw Savill interest was finally taken over with only a few minor private shareholders still remaining.

The resident hulk at Wellington, the JEAN PIERRE, had been in Blackball ownership since 1894, but in 1907 she was replaced by the ELINOR VERNON, acquired at Dunedin that year. The WAI-ITI was purchased for service at Lyttelton, while in 1908 the larger BLACKWALL was also taken over at that port from NZS. Three further hulks, the ENTERPRISE, PRINCE OF WALES and MAYFLOWER were subsequently acquired at Wellington, and to service the bunkering operations there, in 1911 the launch KERERU was built in Auckland. The chain of bunkering hulks at main ports was extended to Auckland when the ELINOR VERNON was towed there from Wellington in 1916, a move reflecting the increased importance of that port as a final departure point for north bound ships following the adoption of the Panama Canal route.

Despite a dispute at the mine at the beginning of 1908 that soon escalated into one of the major union/management confrontations in New Zealand industrial history, the Blackball Company was now enjoying real prosperity for the first time. Over a 5 year period the entire existing collier fleet was replaced with the purpose designed NGA ships. They began with the 1,091 ton NGAHERE in 1908 and rose progressively in size through the 1,138 ton NGATORO in 1910 to the 1,774 ton NGAKUTA in 1913. All three were distinguished by a set of flying derricks rigged high on each mast to enable the direct transfer of bunkers to larger overseas ships, and their advent marked the dropping of the black top to the funnels with the black ball moving up to three-quarters height.

NGAHERE (B.5) bunkering ROTORUA (51) at Wellington                                                                                                                      (IJF)

The NGA class proved very successful in service, but by the end of the First World War the background to the Blackball operation had changed completely. Both NZS and the Union Steam Ship Company of New Zealand were now part of the overall P&O Group, so the previous fears about control of bunkers no longer existed. The reason for Blackball as a separate NZS controlled subsidiary had in fact ceased, so from 1st April 1922 the mine and hulks were taken over by the Union Company and the three colliers taken on charter by that concern which combined their operations with its own fleet. The NGATORO had actually been taken over the previous January and sent to Sydney for the Tasmanian trade under a joint charter to the Union Company and Huddart Parker.

In 1923 formal ownership of the three NGA ships was transferred to Mann, George & Company Ltd of London, a concern within the Cory Bros Group which was then part of the P&O combine and responsible for all the Group bunkering operations. In October 1926 yet another Blackball concern, this time called Blackball Coal Mines Pty Ltd was formed in Wellington to assume ownership of the mine and the two remaining NGA ships, the NGAHERE having been lost on the Grey River bar in May 1924. The shares in the new company remained wholly in the ownership of Mann, George & Company Ltd as trustee for the Union Steam Ship Company which continued as charterers and managers of the ships.

These paper transactions did not affect the running of the NGATORO and NGAKUTA which retained their yellow funnel with black ball. Realities were finally recognised during the Second World War following the sale of the Blackball mine to the New Zealand Government in July 1941. In January 1942 the Union Company acquired formal ownership of the two ships, the 1926 company was struck off the register in February 1943 and Black Ball/Blackball disappeared as a separate operation.

# BLACKBALL COAL COMPANY LTD

HESKETH ashore at Greymouth  *(IJF)*

## B.1 HESKETH (Chartered 1894—1896) (1896—1899) See No. 32

## B.2 PAREORA (Chartered 1896—1903) (1903—1908) See No. 30

## B.3 DINGADEE (1900—1903) (Chartered 1903—1905)

Official Number: 83783
Tonnages: 640 gross, 393 net. Dimensions: 180.4 x 28.1 x 13.6 feet.
Twin screw, One C.2 cyl. by Kincaid & Co., Greenock, each cylinder driving its own shaft, 500 ihp, 10 knots.
Passengers: 20 1st and 32 2nd class.

*3.1883:* Launched by the Queenstown & Passage West Docks Co., Cork, (Yard No. 1), and completed 1883 for the Australasian Steam Navigation Company, Sydney. *24.1.1887:* Transferred to James Munro and then from 23.2.1887 to Duncan Mackinnon & G.S. Mackenzie, all on behalf of the British India & Queensland Agency Company Ltd, Brisbane, but remained registered at Sydney. *27.4.1887:* Transferred to the Australasian United Steam Navigation Company Ltd, Brisbane, but remained registered at Sydney. *3.1888:* Collided with the brig AMY (220g, 1872) in Sydney harbour. *4.1888:* Collided with the steamer WOONONA (643g, 1875) in Sydney harbour. *7.1889:* Chartered to the Union Steam Ship Company of New Zealand Ltd, Dunedin. *19.1.1890:* Struck rocks off Stripe Point, 3 miles north of Milford Sound, bound Westport to Dunedin. Stripped several propeller blades, but returned to Westport under her own steam for repairs. *4.1890:* Sold to the Union Steam Ship Company of New Zealand Ltd, Dunedin. *28.3.1891:* Collided with the ship PLEIADES (1,020g, 1869) while berthing at Wellington from Westport. *6.4.1893:* Broke her starboard propeller shaft, bound Lyttelton to Westport and put into Wellington for repairs on the 7th. *14.2.1896:* Broke the shaft of the main circulating pump off Palliser Bay, bound Napier to Wellington, but came on to Wellington after temporary repairs. *31.3.1896:* Lost her starboard propeller off Cape Runaway, and continued the voyage from Auckland to Napier on the other screw. She left Napier for Wellington in tow of the steamer WAIHORA (2,003g, 1883) to have a new propeller fitted and arrived there on 1.4.1896. The tow rope parted going through Wellington Heads and she nearly went ashore before the WAIHORA picked up the tow again. *15.11.1899:* Rammed by the steamer KENNEDY (193g, 1865) between Kahurangi and Rocks Point bound Lyttelton to Westport. *5.10.1900:* Sold to Blackball, having been on charter since 20.5.1900. She remained registered at Dunedin. *6.4.1902:* Grounded in French Pass, bound Greymouth to Lyttelton. *17.12.1903:* Transferred to the Dingadee Steam Ship Company Ltd, London, a Blackball subsidiary, but remained on charter to Blackball. *1905:* Sold to C. Tanaka, Tokyo, and renamed CHOKYU MARU No. 3. *1919:* Transferred to the Tanaka Kosan K.K., Uraga. *1922:* Sold to Taiwan Sotofuku, Shinagawa. *1924:* Sold to Hayashi Kozo, Shinagawa. *1925:* Broken up in Japan.

DINGADEE loading coal at Greymouth  *(WAL)*

PETONE at Wellington                                                                                                    *(ATL/WAL)*

## B.4 PETONE (Chartered 1900−1903) (1903−1910) See No. 39

NGAHERE off the South Island west coast                                                                                *(IJF)*

## B.5 NGAHERE (1908−1923)

Official Number: 102580
Tonnages: 1,090 gross, 556 net. Dimensions: 225.0 x 33.1 x 15.7 feet.
T.3 cyl. by the shipbuilders, 700 ihp, 9.5 knots.

*29.7.1908:* Launched by A. Rodger & Co., Port Glasgow, (Yard No. 407), and delivered 8.1908 to Blackball. *29.12.1917:* Grounded in thick fog off Sinclair Head bound Greymouth to Wellington. Refloated undamaged. *25.7.1918:* Ran onto a sandbank at the entrance to the river when leaving Gisborne for Greymouth. She was carried by the wind broadside on to the river, but hauled off and returned to her berth for inspection. No damage found. *1.4.1922:* Chartered to the Union Steam Ship Company of New Zealand Ltd, Wellington. *1923:* Sold to Mann, George & Company Ltd, London, on behalf of the Union Company. *12.5.1924:* Ran aground on North Tip Head, Greymouth, as she crossed the bar, outward bound for Wellington, and became a total loss.

## B.6 NGATORO (1910−1923) (1927−1942)

Official Number: 128651
Tonnages: 1,140 gross, 586 net. Dimensions: 225.0 x 33.1 x 15.5 feet.
T.3 cyl. by the shipbuilders, 700 ihp, 9.5 knots.

*5.5.1910:* Launched by A. Rodger & Co., Port Glasgow, (Yard No. 413), and delivered 6.1910 to Blackball. *29.10.1912:* In collision with SURREY (No. F.7) at Wellington. *19.3.1918:* Suffered machinery damage off Westport. *1.4.1922:* Chartered

NGATORO at Adelaide                                                                                              (IJF)

to the Union Steam Ship Company of New Zealand Ltd, Wellington. *1923:* Sold to Mann, George & Company Ltd, London, on behalf of the Union Company. *1926:* Registered at Melbourne; same owners. *1927:* Transferred to Blackball Coal Mines Pty Ltd, Wellington, remaining under Union charter throughout. The registry was not moved to Wellington until

3.9.1929. *4.10.1929:* Stranded at Napier on berthing from the West Coast. Refloated undamaged on the 5th. *31.1.1942:* Transferred to the Union Company. *5.1949:* Sold to the Madrigal Shipping Company Inc., Manila, and renamed AEOLUS. *7.1973:* Broken up at Hong Kong by the Leung Yau Shipbreaking Company Ltd.

NGAKUTA at Adelaide                                                                                              (IJF)

## B.7 NGAKUTA (1913—1923) (1927—1942)

Official Number: 128829
Tonnages: 1,774 gross, 944 net. Dimensions: 275.0 x 39.0 x 17.6 feet.
T.3 cyl. by Richardsons, Westgarth & Co. Ltd, Middlesbrough, 1,200 ihp, 10.5 knots.

*17.6.1913:* Launched by Smith's Dock Co. Ltd, Middlesbrough, (Yard No. 549), and delivered 8.1913 to Blackball. *9.1914:* Shots were fired across her bows from the battery at Fort Dorset, Wellington, for allegedly not showing the proper recognition lights. *1.4.1922:* Chartered to the Union Steam Ship Company of New Zealand Ltd, Wellington. *9.9.1922:* Stranded on the Cobden (north) side of the Grey River when leaving for Wellington and refloated undamaged on the rising tide. *7.5.1923:* Suffered heavy weather damage in Cook Strait. *1923:* Sold to Mann, George & Company Ltd, London, on behalf of

the Union Company. *31.5.1925:* Suffered machinery damage off the south-east coast of the North Island, bound Picton to Auckland. *1927:* Transferred to Blackball Coal Mines Pty Ltd, Wellington, having been on charter to the Union Company throughout, and re-registered at Wellington on 24.5.1927. *31.1.1942:* Sold to the Union Company. *10.7.1952:* Sold to J.S. Costello, Sydney, on behalf of shipbreakers, and registry transferred to Suva. *23.7.1952:* Left Sydney in tow of the landing ship WAN YIU (2,474g, 1944). *30.11.1952:* Arrived at Tokyo and broken up. Demolition was completed in 6.1953

# HULKS

## BH.1 JEAN PIERRE (1894—1908) Wood

Official Number: 89411
Tonnages: 635 gross, 614 net. Dimensions: 161.9 x 33.1 x 17.1 feet.

*1865:* Completed as a barque at Quebec, for A. Cabrol the younger, Bordeaux. *1876:* Sold to Paul Ballande et Fils, (French Company of the New Hebrides), Noumea. *1884:* Sold to John Bickers, Adelaide. *20.2.1894:* Sold to Blackball for use as a hulk at Wellington where she arrived 24.3.1894. *27.11.1908:* Towed out to sea and scuttled 5 miles south-east of Wellington Heads.

## BH.2 ELINOR VERNON (1907—1922) Wood

Official Number: 101474
Tonnages: 570 gross, 545 net. Dimensions: 150.0 x 32.4 x 17.0 feet.

*1877:* Completed as a barquentine by J.B. Nutt, Pembroke, Maine, for J. Boynton's Son, New York. *1887:* Sold to Arnold, Hines & Co., New York. *1894:* Sold to John Mill, Port Chalmers, and converted to a hulk there. *1907:* Sold to Blackball for service at Wellington. *5.9.1916:* Left Wellington in tow of the NGAHERE (No. B.5) and arrived at Auckland on the 8th for service as a hulk there. *1.4.1922:* Sold to the Union Steam Ship Company of New Zealand Ltd. *21.6.1928:* Run ashore and burnt on Rangitoto Island, Auckland.

WAI-ITI as the Norwegian SIGNE in Otago harbour                    *(IJF)*

## BH.3 WAI-ITI (1907—1922)

Official Number: 123141
Tonnages: 733 gross, 689 net. Dimensions: 172.0 x 32.6 x 16.4 feet.

*1891:* Completed as a barque by Fevigs Jernsk., Fevig, near Arendal, (Yard No. 3), for Acties Signe, Christiania, (C. Moller, manager), as SIGNE. *1906:* Sold to the Colonial Sailing Ship Company Ltd, Christchurch; registered at Timaru and renamed WAI-ITI. *28.1.1907:* Capsized against the river bank at Mangawhare, Kaipara harbour. Righted and refloated on 4.4.1907, but condemned as uneconomical to repair. *6.1907:* Sold to Blackball and left Kaipara in tow of the steamer WAINUI (640g, 1886), on 1.7.1907. They arrived at Lyttelton on 4.7.1907 and she was converted to a hulk there. *7.10.1913:* Suffered a fire at Lyttelton. *1.4.1922:* Sold to the Union Steam Ship Company of New Zealand Ltd. *13.8.1935:* Sold to Capt. Duncan McDonald, Lyttelton, for demolition. *30.10.1935:* Scuttled in Starvation Bay, south of Port Levy.

## BH.4 BLACKWALL (1908—1922) See No. H.2

## BH.5 PRINCE OF WALES (19 —1922) Wood barque
Official Number: 484
Tonnages: 507 gross. 1889: 535 gross, 486 net. Dimensions: 135.0 x 28.5 x 18.0 feet.
1889: Twin screw, two C.2 cyl. by J.B. Oake, London, 30 nhp.

*1850:* Built by Money Wigram & Co., Northam, Southampton, for the Hudson's Bay Company, London. *1886:* Sold to Nelson Bros Ltd, London, and converted to an auxiliary steamer for service as a freezing hulk in New Zealand. *26.10.1889:* Arrived at Gisborne. *1.1891:* Transferred to Picton. *1899:* Returned to Gisborne to serve as a storeship. *7.1901:* Transferred to Port Chalmers. *1905:* Registry transferred from London to Napier. *1906:* Sold to E.G. Pilcher, Wellington on behalf of the Union Steam Ship Company of New Zealand Ltd and arrived at Wellington on 13.12.1906. She was converted to a coal hulk in 1907. *19?:* Sold to Blackball. *1.4.1922:* Reverted to the Union Steam Ship Company. *23.7.1941:* Left Wellington in tow of the motorship KARU (1,044g, 1935) and beached at Matiere Point, East Bay, Queen Charlotte Sound, on the 24th for dismantling.

## BH.6 ENTERPRISE (19 —1922) Wood
Official Number: 52393
Tonnage: 84 gross. Dimensions: 84.7 x 20.7 x 7.4 feet.

*1866:* Completed by Rock Davis, Brisbane Water, N.S.W., for W. & J.H. Short, Sydney. *1871:* Sold to W.H. Levin & Co., Wellington. *1877:* Sold to John Hay, Auckland. *1878:* Sold to M.N. Baillie, R. Burrett & J.S. Cherrett, Wellington. *1880:* Sold to W.R. Williams, Wellington. *1880:* Sold to T.T. Brownell, Christchurch. *1881:* Sold to William Hay, Port Molyneux; re-registered at Dunedin in 1884. *17.10.1892:* Sold to Keith Ramsay (32 shares) and George Findlay & J. Murdoch (32 shares jointly), all of Dunedin. *13.2.1893:* Keith Ramsay purchased the remaining shares. *21.6.1902:* Sold to William Henderson, Dunedin. *2.7.1902:* Transferred to the Macquarie Island Fishing Co. Ltd, Dunedin. *23.7.1903:* Sold to James Mill, Dunedin (and hulked). *191?:* Sold to Blackball. (An in house transaction which was never registered.) *1926:* Register closed, still in Mill's name.

## BH.7 MAYFLOWER (1914—1922) Wood
Tonnage: 124 gross.

*1868* or *1873 (accounts vary):* Built at St Johns, Newfoundland. *1914:* Registered as a hulk at Wellington for Blackball (may have been acquired earlier). *1.4.1922:* Sold to the Union Steam Ship Company of New Zealand Ltd. *1923:* Sold to the Anchor Shipping & Foundry Company Ltd, Nelson, and towed there in July 1923. No further information.

# HULK LAUNCH

## BH.8 KERERU (1911—1922) Wood
Official Number: Not registered.
Tonnage: 5 gross. Dimensions: 35.0 x 9.5 x 3.2 feet.
3 cyl. semi-diesel by Andersons Ltd, Christchurch, 25 bhp, 10 knots.

*1911:* Built by C. Bailey, Auckland, for Blackball, for service at Wellington. *1.4.1922:* Sold to the Union Steam Ship Company of New Zealand Ltd, Wellington. *1922:* Resold for private pleasure use to Wm Cable Jnr & F.A. Kiernan, Wellington. No further information.

# DERIVATIONS OF NAMES

(All Maori names are in New Zealand. All other names, except those Australian and Indian names so indicated, are in the British Isles)

| | |
|---|---|
| ANTRIM | County in Northern Ireland. |
| AORANGI | The Maori name for New Zealand's highest mountain, situated in the Southern Alps, and also known as Mount Cook. It is now more usually rendered as Aoraki. |
| ARGYLLSHIRE | Shire in western Scotland. |
| ARMAGH | County in Northern Ireland. |
| CAMBRIDGE | County in eastern England. |
| CORNWALL | County in south-western England. |
| CUMBERLAND | County in north-western England. |
| DERBY | County in the midlands of England. |
| DEVON | County in south-western England. |
| DINGADEE | Railway station near Taree, New South Wales, Australia. |
| DONEGAL | County in northern Eire. |
| DORSET | County on the south coast of England. |
| DURHAM | County in north-eastern England. |
| ESSEX | County in south-eastern England. |
| GALWAY | County in western Eire. |
| GLOUCESTER | County in western England. |
| HAPARANGI | Mountain south of Rotorua, North Island. |
| HAURAKI | Gulf at the approaches to Auckland. |
| HERTFORD | County north of London. |
| HESKETH | Derivation not now known. |
| HINAKURA | Township 29 miles south-east of Featherston, North Island. |
| HORORATA | River and town south-west of Christchurch. |
| HUNTINGDON | County in the eastern midlands of England. |
| HURUNUI | River and town in northern Canterbury. |
| KAIKOURA | Mountain range in eastern Marlborough. |
| KAIMATA | Localities near Inglewood, Taranaki, North Island, and near Greymouth, South Island. |
| KAIPAKI | Locality 6 miles west of Cambridge, North Island. |
| KAIPARA | Harbour north-west of Auckland. |
| KAITUNA | River in western Bay of Plenty, North Island. |
| KENT | County in south-eastern England. |
| KILDARE | County in eastern Eire. |
| KIRITONA | Literally a pimple, i.e. a small vessel. |
| KOHINUR | Mountain of light in Persian, i.e. best of its class. |
| KOUTUNUI | Northern headland of Tokomaru Bay, East Coast, North Island. |
| LEICESTER | County in the midlands of England. |
| LINCOLN | County in eastern England. |
| MANAPOURI | Lake in the south-west of the South Island. |
| MATAURA | River and town in southern Southland. |
| MIDDLESEX | County north and west of London. |
| MIOWERA | Homestead west of Katoomba, New South Wales, Australia. |
| NGAHERE | Township 15 miles north-east of Greymouth at the junction to the Blackball mine, South Island. |
| NGAKUTA | The native New Zealand rush, or swamp plant. |
| NGATORO | The scout. |
| NORFOLK | County in eastern England. |
| NOTTINGHAM | County in the midlands of England. |
| NORTHUMBERLAND | County in north-eastern England. |
| NURJEHAN | Wife of Jehangir, the Mogul Emperor (1605—1627). |
| OPAWA | Suburb of Christchurch. |
| ORARI | River in South Canterbury. |
| OTAIO | River near Timaru in South Canterbury. |
| OTAKI | River and town north-west of Wellington. |
| OTARAMA | Settlement on the Waimakariri River, North Canterbury. |
| PAKIPAKI | Township south-west of Hastings, North Island. |
| PAPANUI | Suburb of Christchurch. |
| PAPAROA | Mountain range in Westland, South Island. |
| PAREORA | River in South Canterbury. |

| | |
|---|---|
| PETONE | Town on the northern shore of Wellington harbour. |
| PIAKO | River flowing into the Firth of Thames, North Island. |
| PIPIRIKI | Settlement 50 miles north of Wanganui, North Island. |
| PURIRI | Settlement 10 miles south of Thames, North Island. |
| QUILOA | Malabar coast town in Kerala, India. |
| RAKAIA | River in Canterbury. |
| RANGITANE | Settlement 10 miles south-west of Palmerston North, North Island. |
| RANGITATA | River in Canterbury. |
| RANGITIKI | An amended spelling of either the Rangitikei river flowing into the South Taranaki Bight or the Rangitaiki river flowing into the Bay of Plenty, both in the North Island. |
| RANGITOTO | The island volcano at the entrance to the Waitemata harbour, Auckland. |
| REMUERA | Suburb of Auckland. (The bay is on the southern shore of the Waitemata harbour) |
| RIMUTAKA | Mountain range north-east of Wellington. |
| ROSCOMMON | County in central Eire. |
| ROTORUA | Lake and town in the Bay of Plenty, North Island. |
| RUAHINE | Mountain range north-east of Palmerston North, North Island. |
| RUAPEHU | Volcano in the centre of the North Island. |
| SHROPSHIRE | County in western England. |
| SOMERSET | County in south-western England. |
| STAFFORD | County in the midlands of England. |
| SUFFOLK | County in eastern England. |
| SURREY | County south of London. |
| SUSSEX | County in south-eastern England. |
| TASMANIA | Island state of Australia. |
| TAUPO | Lake in the centre of the North Island. |
| TEKOA | Sheep station in Canterbury, South Island. |
| TONGARIRO | Volcano in the centre of the North Island. |
| TRENEGLOS | Parish near Camelford, Cornwall, England. |
| TURAKINA | River flowing into the South Taranaki Bight, North Island. |
| TYRONE | County of Northern Ireland. |
| WAIKATO | New Zealand's longest river flowing into the Tasman Sea 30 miles south of Auckland. |
| WAIMATE | Town in South Canterbury. |
| WAIMEA | Tributary of the Mataura river in Southland, and plains south of Nelson, South Island. |
| WAIPA | Tributary of the Waikato river, North Island. |
| WAIROA | River and town in northern Hawkes Bay. |
| WAITANGI | River flowing into the Bay of Islands, Northland. Also the site of the signing of the Treaty of Waitangi in 1840. |
| WAITARA | River and town in northern Taranaki, North Island. |
| WAKANUI | Township 5 miles south-east of Ashburton, Canterbury, South Island. |
| WANGANUI | River and city on the south-west coast, North Island. |
| WARRIMOO | Township west of Katoomba, New South Wales, Australia. |
| WESTMEATH | County in central Eire. |
| WESTMORLAND | County in north-western England. |
| WHAKATANE | River and town in the western Bay of Plenty, North Island. |
| WHANGAROA | Township and harbour on the north-eastern coast of Northland. |
| WHARANUI | Township 38 miles south-east of Blenheim, South Island. |
| WILD AUK | Diving sea bird. |
| WILD AVOCET | Long legged wading bird. |
| WILD CORMORANT | Sea bird. |
| WILD CURLEW | Wading bird. |
| WILD FLAMINGO | Pink coloured tropical wading bird. |
| WILD FULMAR | Ocean going sea bird of the petrel family. |
| WILD GANNET | Large sea bird. |
| WILD GREBE | Diving water bird. |
| WILD MALLARD | Duck. |
| WILD MARLIN | Swordfish. |
| WILTSHIRE | County in south-western England. |

Note: In the case of many of the Maori names, there is more than one location or natural feature of the name. Only the most prominent or those with the closest connection with NZS have been listed.

# BIBLIOGRAPHY

**Primary Sources:**
Lloyd's Register of Shipping Information Section, London:
  Lloyd's Registers
  Wreck Books
Lloyd's War Losses, First World War

Guildhall Library, London:
Lloyd's Lists: St 458 Lloyd's War Losses, Second World War
            St 459/460 Lloyd's Confidential Indexes
            St 475/476 Weekly Casualty Reports
            St 457 Lloyd's Confidential Sheets, 1939—1945
            LB 303/304 Ships in the Service of H.M. Government, Second World War
Ministry of Defence, London:
  Ships in the Service of H.M. Government, First World War

National Maritime Museum, London:
NZS/1/1 & 3-20 London Board Minutes, 1874—1880
NZS/1/28—1/19 Rough Minutes, 1875—1880
NZS/1/22—27 New Zealand Minutes, 1890—1908
NZS/47/2—6 Federal Board Minutes, 1892—1964
NZS & Federal Movement Books.
NZS/48/1 & 6 NZ & African S.S. Co. minutes and historical summary
NZS/51/1 Avenue Board Minutes
NZS/51/2 Avenue Annual Reports
NZS/53/4 Bethell Gwyn historical notes
NZS/54/5 Birt, Potter & Hughes and Birt, Potter & Westray historical notes.

Public Record Office, Kew:
BT/108—111 Ship registers

Maritime Safety Authority:
New Zealand Ship Registers

New Zealand National Archives (Auckland, Christchurch & Dunedin)

Lyttelton Harbour Board Records

JANAC (Joint Army-Navy Assessment Committee), Washington:
Japanese Naval & Merchant Shipping Losses, (1947)

Mercantile Navy Lists

**Journals:**

The Times, (London)
The New Zealand Herald, (Auckland)
The Weekly News, (Auckland)
The Dominion, (Wellington)
The Lyttelton Times, (Lyttelton)
The Press, (Christchurch)
The Weekly Press, (Christchurch)
The Otago Daily Times, (Dunedin)
The Sydney Morning Herald, (Sydney)
The Brisbane Courier, (Brisbane)

The Maori Club News, (1952- 1964)
Crossed Flags, (1965—1971)
Sea Breezes, (1919— )
Marine News, (1947— )

**Secondary Sources:**

Bott, A., The Sailing Ships of the New Zealand Shipping Company, 1873—1900, (Batsford, 1972)
Brett, Henry, White Wings, (Brett Printing Co., Volume 1, 1924; Volume 2, 1928)
Fagg, A., Westrays, A Record of J.B. Westray & Co., (Westray, 1957)
Farquhar, I.J., Union Fleet, 1875 -1975, (2nd edition, New Zealand Ship & Marine Society, 1976)
Gibbs, C.R. Vernon, British Passenger Liners of the Five Oceans, (Putnam, 1963)
Hook, F.A., Merchant Adventurers, 1914 -1918, (A. & C. Black, 1920)
Holman, G., In the Wake of Endeavour, (Charles Knight & Co., 1973)
Lyon, D.J., The Denny List, (National Maritime Museum, 1976)
Maber, J.M., North Star to Southern Cross, (T. Stephenson & Sons, 1967)
Rabson, S. & O'Donoghue, K., P & O, A Fleet History, (World Ship Society, 1989)
Rohwer, J., Axis Submarine Successes, (U.S. Naval Institute Press, 1983)
Spindler, Rear Adm., Der Krieg zur See: Der Handelskrieg mit U-booten, Volumes 1 to 5, Mittler & Sons, 1932—1966)
Waters, S.D., Clipper Ship to Motor Liner, (NZS, 1939)
            Ordeal by Sea, (NZS, 1949)

*Part 1:* The names of ships owned or managed by NZS, Federal, Avenue and Blackball are printed in capital letters, followed in **bold type** by the chronological number in the relevant fleet list, the dates of entering and leaving the fleet (in brackets), preceded by the year of construction if not newly built. *Part 2:* Names borne by these ships before they entered or after they left Company service, and all other ships mentioned in the text, which are printed in upper and lower case type.

## Part 1

*Part 2*

The New Zealand Team. Left to Right: Bill Laxon, Nigel Kirby and Ian Farquhar at work on the book in Nigel's house overlooking the NZS original home port of Lyttelton, November 1994

## LIST OF MASTS & SPARS

FOREMAST HEEL TO HOUNDS _ _ _ _ _ _ _ _ _ _ 65-6, 36, 31¾, 25
    HOUNDS TO HEAD _ _ _ _ _ _ _ _ _ _ 30-6, 23, 5
MAINMAST HEEL TO HOUNDS _ _ _ _ _ _ _ _ 70-0, 24, 23¾, 20
    HOUNDS TO HEAD _ _ _ _ _ _ _ _ 30-6, 20, 5

2 SIDE DERRICKS (STEEL) ON DERRICK POSTS OVER N°1 HATCH   LENGTH   55-9
4    "    "    "    "    N°2    "    56-3 & 35-6
4    "    "    "    "    N°3    "    55-3 & 48-0
1 CENTRE    "    FORE MAST    "    N°4    "    61-6
4 SIDE    "    DERRICK POST    "    N°4    "    55-0 & 54-0
4    "    "    "    "    N°5    "    56-6 & 58-9
2    "    "    "    "    N°6    "    49-8

SIGNAL YARD ON FORE MAST (STEEL TUBE) _ _ 25-0, 5
GAFF ON MAIN MAST   (   ) _ _ _ 25-0, 5
JACK STAFF (STEEL TUBE) _ _ _ _ _ _ 15-6, 2½
ENSIGN STAFF (PITCH PINE) _ _ _ _ _ _ 20-0, 4
SOUNDING BOOMS (GI TUBES) _ _ _ _ 20-0, 2½
2 STORE DERRICKS (STEEL) _ _ _ _ _ _ 10-0, 5½

## TONNAGES.

OFFICIAL NUMBER _ _ _ _ _ _ _ _ _ _ 183041
CODE LETTERS _ _ _ _ _ _ _ _ _ _ GDVS
PORT OF REGISTRY _ _ _ _ _ _ _ _ LONDON
GROSS TONNAGE _ _ _ _ _ _ _ _ 11272 40 TONS
NETT TONNAGE _ _ _ _ _ _ _ _ 6648 40 TONS
SUEZ CANAL TONNAGE GROSS _ _ _ 14241 33 TONS
    "     "     NETT _ _ _ 10123 85 TONS.
PANAMA   "   "    GROSS _ _ _ 14144 30 TONS
    "     "     NETT _ _ _ 9744 77 TONS.

## ENGINES

TWO SETS 5 CYLINDER DOXFORD ENGINES
CYLINDERS 725 MM DIA 2250 MM STROKE
BHP 6625 EACH AT 120 REVS. PER MIN.
BUILT BY JOHN BROWN & C° LT° CLYDEBANK

## ELECTRICAL INSTALLATION.

FOUR SETS DIESEL ENGINE ELECTRIC PLANT
CAPACITY EACH 380 K.W.     220 V.
1 SET DIESEL ENG. EMERGENCY PLANT.
CAPACITY 31 K.W.

## WIRELESS INSTALLATION.

MARCONI SYSTEM _ _ _ _ _ _ _ ½ K W. I.C.W SET
AUTO-ALARM & DIRECTION FINDING APPARATUS FITTED
CALL SIGNAL _ _ _ _ _ _ _ _ G.D.V.S.
SENDING RANGE _ _ _ _ _ _ _ 800, 2500 MILES
RECEIVING RANGE _ _ _ _ _ _ UP TO 12,000 MILES

## REFRIGERATION.

REFRIGERATING MACHINERY BY J. & E. HALL LT°
CORK INSULATION BY MERSEY INSULATION C° LT°

# T.S.M.V. "HINAKURA"
# CAPACITY PLAN.

**BUILDERS: JOHN BROWN & CO. LTD. CLYDEBANK**

JUNE 1949.

## PRINCIPAL DIMENSIONS.

LENGTH OVERALL _ _ _ _ _ _ _ _ _ _ 560'
LENGTH BETWEEN PERPENDICULARS _ _ _ _ 530'
BREADTH MOULDED _ _ _ _ _ _ _ _ 70'
DEPTH MOULDED TO UPPER DECK _ _ _ _ _ 47'

EXEMPTED SPACE – BRITISH TONNAGE ONLY
UPPER TWEEN DECKS FROM AFT TO FRAME 132.

### LOADING SCALE

| DRAFT | DEADWEIGHT | TONS PER 1" |
|-------|-----------|-------------|
| 33 | 15,000 | 72 60 |
| 32 | 14,000 | 72 20 |
| 31 | 13,000 | 71 79 |
| 30 | | 71 35 |
| 29 | 12,000 | 70 85 |
| 28 | 11,000 | 70 34 |
| 27 | 10,000 | 69 85 |
| 26 | 9,000 | 69 35 |
| 25 | | 68 80 |
| 24 | 8,000 | 68 25 |
| 23 | 7,000 | 67 70 |
| 22 | 6,000 | 67 09 |
| 21 | 5,000 | 66 57 |
| 20 | 4,000 | 66 03 |
| 19 | | 65 47 |
| 18 | 3,000 | 64 91 |
| 17 | 2,000 | 64 35 |
| 16 | 1,000 | 63 79 |
| 15 | 0 | 63 13 |
| 14 | | 62 58 |

LOAD DRAFT 32-5"
DEADWEIGHT 14680 TONS

LIGHT DRAFT 14-7½" { DRAFT FORD 11-5½" }
LIGHT SHIP 5655 TONS { DRAFT AFT 17-8½" }

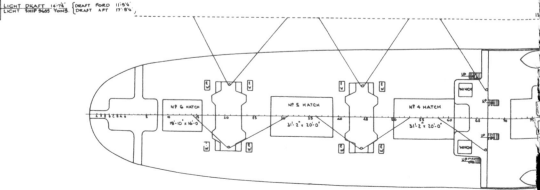